The Hollywood History of the World

The Hollywood History of the World

George MacDonald Fraser

FILM STILLS FROM THE KOBAL COLLECTION

THE HARVILL PRESS

LONDON

ALSO BY GEORGE MACDONALD FRASER

The Flashman Papers:
Flashman
Royal Flash
Flash for Freedom!
Flashman at the Charge
Flashman in the Great Game
Flashman's Lady
Flashman and the Redskins
Flashman and the Dragon
Flashman and the Mountain Light
Flashman and the Angel of the Lord

The McAuslan Stories:
The General Danced at Dawn
McAuslan in the Rough
The Sheikh and the Dustbin

Mr American
The Pyrates
The Candlemass Road

History:
The Steel Bonnets: the story of the
   Anglo-Scottish Border Reivers

Autobiography: Quartered Safe out Here

First published by Michael Joseph 1988

This revised updated edition first published in 1996
by The Harvill Press · 84 Thornhill Road · London N1 1RD

1 3 5 7 9 10 8 6 4 2

© George MacDonald Fraser 1988, 1996

George MacDonald Fraser asserts the moral right to be identified as the author of this work

A CIP catalogue record for this book is available from the British Library

ISBN 1 86046 201 4

Designed and typeset in Galliard at Libanus Press Ltd · Marlborough · Wiltshire

Printed and bound in Great Britain by Butler & Tanner Ltd · Frome

Half title page: Sergei Bondarchuk's brilliant recreation of the French cavalry attack on the British squares in *Waterloo*.
Title pages: "A picture more vivid than Tacitus or Gibbon" . . . the chariot race from *Ben Hur*.
Overleaf: Possibly just as expensive and certainly more glossy and hygienic than the original: a Versailles ballroom in *Marie Antoinette*.

Contents

FOR MY GRANDDAUGHTERS
JULIE, SOPHIE, GENEVIEVE AND EMILY
WITH LOVE

Introduction

More than nine thousand extras were used in a single **scene** of *Land of the Pharaohs*. The figure being carried in state by some of them is Jack Hawkins. Previous page:The fortifications of the Danube frontier in *Fall of the Roman Empire*.

Introduction

Sixty years or so ago, when Ronald Colman and Clark Gable were giving new meaning to the moustache, and half the civilised world yearned for Greta Garbo or Jean Harlow while the other half gazed enraptured on Gary Cooper and Robert Taylor, when David Niven was an unknown extra being ejected from a Barbary Coast saloon, Buck Jones was still wearing that enormous hat, Fred Astaire was dancing the spirit of Wodehouse across the screen, and no one thought twice if John Wayne turned up as an ice-hockey player, or Humphrey Bogart as a Mexican bandit complete with accent – in those happy days, when the talkies were just a few years old, an interesting paradox was to be observed in the cinema.

Despite the coming of sound, and a generation of actors and actresses who, unlike many of their successors, could speak clear and articulate English, it was still not enough for cinemagoers to be able merely to see, hear, and understand: they had to be able to read, too.

Of course this had also been vital in the silent days, when captions like "And so her dark suspicions grew . . ." and "All night long he wrestled with his Beast" and "Harness my zebras, gift of the Nubian king!" were essential complements to the visual drama, but when motion pictures began to talk there were those who supposed that the day of the written word was over, and not only in the cinema. My history teacher – and he was one who regarded motion pictures as the greatest disaster for education since the burning of Alexandria – saw the talking film as the final nail in the coffin of literacy. Why, he asked in despair, should his charges bother with reading, when that infernal silver screen talked to them?

He need not have worried. That flawed glory of the cinema, the costume picture, was going to demand a far higher standard of literacy from its viewers than ever the silent films had done. Hardly a historical epic of the 1930s but started off with a written prologue which might have taxed the comprehension of some of today's filmgoers. It often began, portentously, with the words "In the Year of Our Lord . . .", and then there would follow a concise summary of the War of the Spanish Succession, or the condition of the English peasantry in the twelfth century, or the progress of Christianity under Nero. And, by and large, they were not inaccurate. They and the films they introduced paid the audience the compliment of supposing them to have at least an elementary knowledge of, and interest in, times past, and with all their faults (and they were many) they took history seriously.

In view of some of the monstrosities that have been put on the screen in the past sixty years, that may seem a bold claim. There is a popular belief that where history is concerned, Hollywood[1] always gets it wrong – and sometimes it does. What is overlooked is the astonishing amount of history Hollywood has got right, and the immense unacknowledged debt which we owe to the commercial cinema as an illuminator of the story of mankind. This although films have sometimes blundered and distorted and falsified, have botched great themes and belittled great men and women, have trivialised and caricatured and cheapened, have piled anachronism on solecism on downright lie – still, at their best, they have given a picture of the ages more vivid and memorable than anything in Tacitus or Gibbon or Macaulay, and to an infinitely wider audience. Nor have they necessarily

1 Here and throughout, "Hollywood" is used as a convenient term for the film industries of the English-speaking world.

been less scrupulous. At least they have shown history, more faithfully than they are usually given credit for, as it was never seen before. For better or worse, nothing has been more influential in shaping our visions of the past than the commercial cinema.

For example: take a walk through the huge excavation of ruined ancient Rome, and consider that a tourist of two centuries ago could envisage the reality of the city of the Caesars only dimly, by reference to written accounts and a few highly imaginative paintings. But today all the world knows what it looked like, thanks to William Horning and Edward Carfagno and John de Cuir among others (and who outside the industry could identify them as cinema art directors?). Again, all the eyewitness accounts and historians' descriptions of Waterloo have less impact than Sergei Bondarchuk's breathtaking vista of the ragged British squares with Napoleon's cavalry streaming past them. When Dr Johnson wrote "Rasselas" he had no clear conception of what Abyssinia or old Egypt looked like – Cecil DeMille could have shown him, down to Cleopatra's hairpins, and

Rome rebuilt, as only the cinema could do it: the huge Forum set in Samuel Bronston's *Fall of the Roman Empire*.

parted the Red Sea for an encore. As James Thurber is alleged to have said of *The Ten Commandments*: "It makes you realise what God could have done if He'd had the money."

Of course we know that no physical recreation of the past can be wholly accurate; television reminds us of this regularly with its dramatised attempts to show us what we looked like (and did, and said, and even *thought* without apparently realising it, God help us) in the 1930s and '40s. And that is just the recent, visible past. This came home forcibly to me on a film location when I and a member of the cast, a former paratroop sergeant, laboured in vain to make a modern actor look right in war-time battledress. He was a splendid actor, too, of international reputation, but while we could crease his trousers with soap and put lead weights above his anklets and rest his hands just so on his pouches, we could not make him look or move like a soldier of 1944; he would have had to spend five years in the Second World War, we concluded.

Still, we got him reasonably right, and the director and the man's own acting talent did the rest; the result might not have satisfied Montgomery, but it served. Similarly, the recreators of ancient Babylon and Shakespeare's London and colonial Virginia do their best, and it too serves.

More or less, anyway. You cannot please everyone, not in the twentieth century. Where our ancestors gaped in awe at the magic lantern and the bioscope, we take a more critical view. We accept as a matter of course the technical miracle of the *Ben Hur* chariot race, or Sabu flying on the Genie's back, or John Ford's aftermath of the battle of Shiloh, or the huge spectacle of Cleopatra's arrival in Rome – and are moved to mirth when she says to Caesar: "We've gotten off to a bad start, haven't we? I've done nothing but rub you the wrong way." Of course we are; we are only human, even scriptwriters.

This is only one of the pitfalls in the path of the historical film-maker; more than ordinary films, they are liable to strike a false note. Those who make them know that while millions

Marlon Brando as Napoleon.

of dollars' worth of planning and building, and painstaking research beyond the dreams of many academics, and sheer technical brilliance, can pass without much notice, one bad line (and it doesn't even have to be a bad line, it just has to sound amiss), or one visual anachronism, or piece of unhappy casting, or directorial slip, will have the customers falling about. There have been enough of these – as well as more culpable commissions of bad taste, wilful philistinism, and sheer ignorance – to give costume movies, if not a bad

Anna Neagle as the young Queen Victoria.

Charles Laughton as Captain Kidd.

name, at least a patronised and faintly derided status. My history teacher was reluctant to see *The Sign of the Cross* because he feared he might be offended by the sight of gladiators who chewed gum and talked like gangsters.

Without being unduly defensive on their behalf, one has to say that those who make historical films face hazards unknown to workers in other artistic fields. Take the novelist, pampered creature, in his one-dimensional world; he can state simply that Sir Francis Drake rolled in and bowed to the Queen, or that Marie Antoinette flung herself,

sobbing wildly, on the bed, and that's it; the reader visualises the scene. The film-maker has to create it entire, from the coat-of-arms above the throne to the last diamond in the Queen's ruff, and while cinema audiences contain mercifully few authorities on Elizabethan costume, they are well able to spot a wristwatch worn by a cutlass-waving pirate, a microphone boom reflected in a Roman breastplate, a zip fastener on a kilt, an uplift bra on a Byzantine bosom, or a Greyhound bus in the far background of a Western – all of which have happened, and no doubt there is worse to come.

Getting it visually right is one thing; it must also sound right, and historical films abound with instances when it didn't. This is a delicate area, since the writer is usually committing an enforced anachronism by writing in English, when his characters should by rights be talking Norman French or Latin. But it must be English, and acceptable in both North Shields and Wichita, Kansas, at that; so given the task of constructing a conversation between King John and the Abbot of Canterbury he must simply use his mother wit and sense of period, avoid anachronisms not only of fact but of usage, respect the author (if he happens to be adapting a historical novel), and hope that the producers will cast George C. Scott or Charlton Heston or Oliver Reed, who will give it that indefinable thing called style. He must also bear in mind that while there are mistakes which don't matter much (only a few experts are going to frown at the anachronism of the word "sabotage" in the mouth of Captain Bligh), there are times when strict accuracy can be fatal – let the script refer, quite properly, to an English public school junior as a "fag", and no one in Wichita is going to hear the next line.

Which brings us to the subject which scriptwriters hate and movie buffs delight in – those famous lines which seemed all right when written in good faith and cold blood, but were not. There is no insurance against them and no defence. Let the Lionheart's Queen exclaim: "War, war! That's all you think about, Dick Plantagenet!", and the audience will erupt, and it is not a blind bit of use pointing out that Berengaria of Navarre probably said something very like that to Richard I, more than once. As who knows better than I, who coined the deathless protest: "But I don't want to marry the Queen of Scots! She's only six years old!" It may well have been a true reflection of the feelings of his youthful majesty Edward VI, but that didn't save it. The list is endless: "Take a letter. Mark Antony, the Senate, Rome . . ."; "This Tartar woman is for me, and my blood says, 'Take her!' "; "Delilah, what a dimpled dragon you can be"; and so on. We can console ourselves that the greatest screenwriter of all had clocks striking in Ancient Rome, and caused his Latin working men

to talk like Elizabethan Londoners (and who knows that Burbage did not throw Hamlet's soliloquy back at him, swearing that he would sooner retire than repeat *that* in public. And how, exactly, would Burbage have phrased his rebuke to the unhappy playwright? There's an interesting exercise in dialogue-writing.)

Such matters are the small change of historical film-making. Honest mistakes and follies happen, but what does one say to those more solemn critics who charge Hollywood with trivialising and distorting history, as well as with vulgarity, ignorance, bad taste, and all those other faults which my history teacher recited as, against his better judgement and with grave misgivings, he conducted us to the local cinema to see *The Sign of the Cross*?

Well, Hollywood is not a school for teaching history; its business is making money out of entertainment, and history needs considerable editing and adaptation (which can, in some cases, justifiably be called distortion and falsification) before it is submitted to the paying public. This is something from which writers, directors and producers have seldom flinched. In this they are not necessarily more culpable than many serious historians who, if they seldom deliberately falsify, are often inclined to arrange, shape, select, emphasise, and omit in order to prove a case, or confound a rival, or make propaganda, or simply present what they wish to believe is the truth. This, it seems to me, is a rather greater offence than that of the screenwriter who knows perfectly well that Gordon and the Mahdi never met, but who still makes them meet in the script. He is not writing history, but fashioning drama, and like Shakespeare before him he supplements fact with fiction as seems best to him. For me, provided he does not break faith with the spirit of history by wilful misrepresentation or hatchet job, he may take liberties with the letter – but he should take as few as possible.

My own impression, from a lifelong addiction to costume pictures and the history on which they are based (so far as I know it), is that Hollywood's liberties have been fairly venial,

John Ford gets it right: Generals Sherman and Ulysses S. Grant given authentic images by John Wayne and Henry Morgan in *How the West Was Won* . . .

. . . and wrong: Mary Queen of Scots and James Hepburn, Earl of Bothwell, romanticised beyond recognition by Katharine Hepburn and Fredric March in *Mary of Scotland*.

and that its virtues far outweigh its faults. There have been glaring cases of distortion (the first two Bounty mutiny films come to mind), more often of trivialisation, and most frequently of all, of harmless embroidery. Under the last heading one may place the case of Josef von Sternberg and the Vestal Virgins, which is typical of good box-office (if not of good historical) thinking, and is a common failing of costume pictures.

In the documentary, *The Epic That Never Was*, which dealt with Alexander Korda's aborted production of *I, Claudius*, the costume designer John Armstrong described how he obtained from a Neapolitan statue authentic details of the dresses for Vestal Virgins, of whom there were to be six, the proper number, fully clothed. This was not good enough for the director, von Sternberg. "I want sixty, and I want them naked," he told Armstrong, who obediently came up with costumes resembling bikinis under gauzy drapery. "It looked lovely," Armstrong conceded, "but it had nothing to do with the Roman religion." How far that kind of departure from truth matters, is debatable; my history master might well have condemned it – but recalling his reaction to Claudette Colbert in *The Sign of the Cross*, I doubt it.

On a different plane there was the experience of the late Alan Badel in a biblical epic. Going through the script, it seemed to him that unjustifiable liberties had been taken with Holy Writ; the words of Christ, in fact, had been rewritten. Badel complained to the director, high words ensued, minions ran to and fro, the head of the studio (one of the celebrated Hollywood moguls) was summoned, and finally the scriptwriter was asked to explain himself. And according to Badel, the poor soul leafed nervously through the script, compared it with a Bible, coughed, shuffled, and finally said: "Well, you see, Alan, we thought Jesus sounded just a bit cocky in there."

Plainly, it takes all kinds to make historical films; some have the passion of DeMille for accuracy, and some have not. I am no Egyptologist, but I am told that the research done

Christopher Columbus, and below, as impersonated by Fredric March.

Claudette Colbert as the Empress Poppaea bathing in asses' milk in *The Sign of the Cross*.

for *The Ten Commandments* was so exhaustive that it eventually extended scholarship on the subject, and it probably did. Longships built to scale with meticulous exactness for *The Vikings* were so successful that they astonished their builders by cutting through waves without pitching or rolling, and were eventually sailed across the Atlantic. In both cases, the producers could have compromised, and probably no one would have been any the wiser; it is not strictly necessary to hunt out the details of Nelson's uniform from his naval tailors, or study the technique of stonemasonry in the twelfth century BC, or scour medieval records for everything from recipes to hairstyles, but the fact that these things have been done as a matter of course should weigh for something with those who, misled by some of the film industry's wilder flights at history, mistakenly conclude that Hollywood could never care less so long as the money comes in at the box office.

It is worth remembering that the often-despised film moguls were the greatest patrons of the arts since time began; Hollywood employed more scholars and experts and diverse talents than any philanthropic or learned institution – and, incidentally, paid them better. They gave, and got, their money's worth, and in the process they built us old Baghdad, new and shiny, and the Pyramids, and the Colosseum; they refought Trafalgar and Thermopylae for our benefit, and sent Columbus to the sands of Watling Island, Marco Polo to the courts of Cathay, Major Rogers to St Francis, Rowan to Garcia, Drake around the world, and Stanley in search of Livingstone (to the tune of "Onward, Christian Soldiers", which hadn't been written then, but sounded wonderful); they brought Clive and Zola, Lincoln and Saladin, Buffalo Bill and Catherine the Great, Wellington and Dick Turpin, Florence Nightingale and Calamity Jane, to life again; they showed us Argonauts and Mountain Men, Vikings and Jane Austen's ladies, gladiators and Roundheads, Chinese warlords and Pilgrim Fathers, Regency bucks and Zulu impis. Really, it was the greatest show on earth.

Some of it was historical nonsense; most of it was not. If some of the images were blemished, they were better than no images at all. Samuel Pepys has given the most brilliant and finely detailed memorial of Restoration London that could be imagined – but imagined is the word; we must form our mental pictures from what he tells us, and from artists like Lely and Kneller; is it sacrilege to suggest that *Forever Amber, Frenchman's Creek,* and *Hudson's Bay* add something worthwhile, if it is only a visual impression? All the world knows that when the Light Brigade charged in the San Fernando Valley, it was as the climax to a film that had no more to do with Raglan, Cardigan, and Balaclava than with *Little Women* – but even Lord Tennyson might have had his imagination enlarged by the most spectacular recreation ever seen of cavalry going neck or nothing into cannon fire. Bette Davis or Flora Robson could play only an imaginative personation of the great Elizabeth, but they gave us something that the historian cannot. Personally, I always doubted that an army could be stopped by flashing polished shields until I watched it on the screen; I envisaged the Gordian knot as a vague tangle of rope until Richard Burton was confronted with something that looked like a spherical doormat. What the beginning of the Exodus was like, no one will ever know – DeMille brought it to life. The sight of old Vladimir Sokolov perishing in the snow while Charles Boyer made sympathetic noises, conveyed some sense of what the Retreat from Moscow was like; the scene in which Jack Palance pulls on his glove while Elisha Cook stands wary and angry in the mud is art of a high order; it is also as true an impression of a Western gunfight as we are ever likely to get.

There is something else that the costume picture has done. I have lived long enough in the world of historical fiction to know how strongly it can work in turning readers to historical fact; Hollywood, by providing splendid entertainment, has sent people to the history shelves in their millions.

Which brings me to the purpose of this book. It is an odd fact that as films have declined in popularity, books about them have proliferated – film histories, appraisals, evaluations, tributes, compilations of this director's or that star's pictures, ranging from the popular to the scholarly, the adulatory to the lurid exposé. Many of them have dealt with costume films in one way or another, but I have yet to discover one which compared history, as depicted in films, with the real thing (whatever that is). Plainly it is an impossible task; to do it properly would require a huge panel of the most erudite historians, and they would have to sit through every Hollywood epic ever made, and serve them right. But without pretending to authority, it may at least be possible to take a selective look at history as Hollywood has presented it, starting with the Creation and ending in the twentieth century – a sort of illustrated tour of the Biblicals, medievals, Westerns, swashbucklers, biopics, gangster, war, romantic, and semi-documentary films which, taken together, form an eccentric and astonishing catalogue of history – or at least, to paraphrase *1066 And All That,* all the history I can remember.

It is not anything like comprehensive. Even a confirmed

Perhaps the most famous depiction in the cinema of trench warfare: the young German (Lew Ayres) takes cover beside a dead *poilu* in *All Quiet on the Western Front*.

cinema and history soak can see, read, and absorb only so much; the survey has to consist of films which I have found interesting or instructive from a historical point of view, either because they enhanced understanding, or educated, or helped to illuminate, or distorted, or disfigured, or carried a conviction of truth, or (perhaps just for a split second) gave a specially vivid image of the past. They are not all "good" films, by any means; some of them have been excoriated both by critics and minors' matinees (and the latter are the

ones to worry about); some are virtually unknown, and some will seem odd choices indeed. My purpose is to look at them in the light of history as I understand it – with their relative merits *as films* I am not particularly concerned. I had enough of that when I was a film critic (a much-sought-after employment in my early newspaper days, and invariably given to the junior reporters, on the apparent assumption that while only responsible journalists could review books, plays, concerts and art, any idiot would do for the cinema. I suppose it was a form of artistic snobbery, or perhaps it was born of the knowledge that while authors, playwrights, musicians, and artists have been known to write furious letters and call on editors with horsewhips, the film industry usually sails on with a bland indifference to criticism. One reason why it does, of course, is that the film-worker – actor, writer, director, designer, or technician – has devoted all his energies to satisfying the exacting standards of his colleagues and the producer, and if they are satisfied, all that matters thereafter is whether the public turn up or stay away, which they will do without reference to critical opinion. I learned that much as a film-reviewer).

With one or two exceptions, the films touched on in this book have been drawn from the English-speaking cinema: that is, from the Los Angeles and British studios, and from that international film industry which operates worldwide making pictures primarily in the English language. And I have dealt only with sound films for theatrical presentation, not with television, which has produced much historical drama in the past few years; that would have been to widen the field too far, and I have not watched enough of it.

My approach is that of an enthusiastic viewer, for while I have worked occasionally in films – an exhilarating experience akin to being whirled into a multi-coloured maelstrom from which one emerges, damp and dazed, clutching a cheque – my viewpoint remains somewhere halfway back in the stalls of a cinema of yesterday, when the screen was sharp and clear, and colour (before it became fuzzy, chemical and universal) was a joy to behold, when players were audible, either because sound engineering was better or the actors had been properly trained, when time was not wasted in interminable long shots of cars arriving and departing (or being mindlessly wrecked after chases quite as exciting as a dandruff commercial), when players' faces had some character, and did not resemble Barbie dolls or male models or silver-haired plastic robots dressed in Rodeo Drive chic, when it was not thought necessary to assail the audience with blood-spattered death agonies, or filthy language, or "explicit" sex – these last usually being the untalented amateur's substitute for the professional skill and imagination that the cinema used to take for granted. Fortunately there are still some film-makers as gifted as any of their predecessors; some of their work appears in this book; they are the moderns – producers, directors, actors, and the rest – whose talents and love for their medium are proof against an increasingly debased public taste and declining artistic standards.

Lastly, since this is a compilation of *views* of history, it is well to remember that these change. People of each generation tend to think that they alone see clearly, with a vision unclouded by what they regard as the prejudices and misconceptions of the past; it seldom occurs to them that their own views may seem prejudiced and misconceived to future generations. The 1990s are probably no more convinced of their superior wisdom and morality than their forebears were; certainly values and standards were just as fixed in my childhood as they are now, although they were very different. Whether they were sounder than today's or not is by the way; the point is that it is futile, and indeed harmful, to apply modern ethics to the past, or to the past's *view* of the even more remote past. The film-makers of the thirties and forties lived in a different world from our own; they accepted different premises and applied different standards, which were not necessarily wrong because they now seem dated and reactionary. This would seem obvious, yet there are some modern writers on film who become positively peevish because the film-maker of sixty years ago, poor unenlightened soul, did not see things as they see them. This, with respect, is no way to look at old movies; they were products of their time, and of the thinking of their time. And if the modern viewer looks at them again today, tolerantly and fairly, he may be astonished, like Mark Twain, to discover just how much the old boys have learned in the past sixty years.

THE FIRST AGE
The Ancient World

Eyeless in Gaza: blind Samson (Victor Mature) with Delilah (Hedy Lamarr) in DeMille's *Samson and Delilah*, and previous page, the spectacular parting of the Red Sea in *The Ten Commandments*.

a barren volcanic world, where he encountered dinosaurs left over from a previous era, before being rescued from a giant turtle by Miss Welch and a bevy of Cavebirds. This tribe, a fair race practising primitive agriculture and cave-painting, adopted the stranger, love and jealousy bloomed, more dinosaurs attacked, and Raquel was carried off by a pterodactyl which fortunately dropped her in the sea before she could be fed to its chicks. Rescued, she fell into the clutches of Percy Herbert, at which point the inter-tribal politics became confused, and civil war was interrupted by a volcanic eruption and earthquake from which only the better elements escaped.

One Million Years BC was the kind of film that is commonly greeted with derision. It happened to be good in every respect, and did little to shake my faith in the Children's Encyclopedia version of life in the Stone Age. The sets were excellent, Ray Harryhausen's dinosaurs were unusually realistic reproductions of Triceratops, T rex, and others, the players behaved like savage children with discernible characters, and the final eruption was first-rate. Michael Carreras had the enviable task of writing a screenplay whose dialogue consisted entirely of grunts and cries in Cave-talk – and thereby hangs one of those tales so typical of the film industry: it is said on good authority that Miss Welch's voice lacked the true prehistoric timbre, and her shrieks and exclamations had to be dubbed by a specialist who is now, of all things, a barrister.

Which brings us to a point that should be touched on briefly before we move into Hollywood's First and grandest Age proper, when Mankind had become articulate, and Pharaohs, Caesars, empresses, handmaidens, prophets, and even the *barbari* had to be able to speak English. The question being: what kind of English?

Accent has always been a minor problem in period films, at least to audiences. Britons are used to sniggering at Bronx gladiators, or Priestesses of Isis who talk like Miss Adelaide; no doubt a cockney centurion sounds just as grotesque to the Middle West. Their scorn is not always justified; the

British reviewer who scoffed at US accents in Nelson's navy was evidently unaware that American seamen were common in the British service at that time – the *Bounty* carried at least one, and there was a sizeable American contingent on the *Victory* at Trafalgar. Similarly, a US critic showed a sad ignorance of his country's pioneer development when he took exception to Sean Connery's Scots accent in the Western *Shalako*. Yet both complaints made a genuine point: authenticity is fine, but it is a question of what audiences *expect* to hear and find acceptable in certain roles, and some interesting unwritten conventions are to be found in costume pictures.

Generally, the voice of authority and aristocracy, be it Classical, medieval, or bewigged, has tended to be British, especially if the part is an unsympathetic one; on the other hand, the sturdy commonalty, including peasants, slaves, guards, soldiers, gladiators, and (most important) worthy or heroic figures of humble or yeoman origin and their followers, have more commonly been played by Americans.

Now this is a sweeping generalisation, riddled with exceptions: more than half the screen Julius Caesars have been American, and so have a number of English monarchs. But in the main the rule holds good, that the man on the throne, or riding in pride with attendant lackeys, or smiling cruelly on the protesting mob, has spoken with the voice of the West End stage, while the fearless spokesman of the oppressed, the self-made hero or rebel, the people's choice, is good old American. When Sanders confronts Mature, or Olivier locks glances with Kirk Douglas, or Henry Daniell turns his cold eye on Cornel Wilde, their accents not only tell us who, socially, is who; they also tell us whose side we are meant to be on.

This business of accent-association reflects the basic themes of sectarian, class, national, and racial conflict which run through most period films, and probably has subconscious links with the events of 1776. It is quite simple: for sixty years American audiences have equated the British accent with

The upper crust, from top left clockwise: Basil Rathbone in *A Tale of Two Cities*, George Sanders in *Lloyd's of London*, Laurence Olivier in *The Devil's Disciple*, and Cedric Hardwicke in *The Hunchback of Notre Dame*.

audiences like to see happening to authority.

To the British film patricians must be added those Americans and Canadians whose voices sounded "anglified" to US ears – Price, Calhern, Massey, Macready, Plummer, Cregar, Dumbrille and Jay Robinson have always been perfectly acceptable tyrants and historical heavies. So have the suave Continentals of the sibilant-sinister school, like Veidt, Slezak, Brynner, Lom and Schildkraut, although their roles have just as frequently been sympathetic, possibly because they are

The sturdy democrats, from top left clockwise: Henry Fonda in *Drums Along the Mohawk*, Victor Mature in *Captain Caution*, Robert Stack in *John Paul Jones*, and finally, British arrogance (Henry Wilcoxon, left) casts a suspicious eye on colonial independence (Randolph Scott) in *The Last of the Mohicans*.

gentility, or "class" – the golden voices of Colman, Karloff, Rains, Rathbone, Marshall, Sanders, Sutton, Hardwicke, Daniell, Wilcoxon, Hunter, Atwill, Zucco, Love and Coulouris saw to that in the Thirties – and a pretty bunch of upper-crust villains they were on film, with one or two exceptions. (To be sure there were plenty of British-accented heroes, but they were usually gentlemanly heroes, and the British heavies outnumbered them, especially when middle age set in.) The progression is natural: British accent equals gentility equals authority – and we know what American

Continental sophistication: Conrad Veidt in *Jew Suss*.

less austere than the British, radiate charm and sophistication, and on occasion make excellent martyrs.

About actresses one cannot generalise, except to say that Continental beauties have done well in the depraved-empress-seductress-villainess stakes. The British have brought a ladylike touch to countless queens, duchesses, slave-girls, heroines, harlots, priestesses, nurses, and kindly noblewomen; in a way they have carried on the tradition of the Raj's *memsahibs*, their mere presence implying that afternoon tea is about to be served in Roman villa, Egyptian palace, or gladiatorial kitchen. (Kindly Oxford-accented noblemen have also been a prominent historical species, but usually as the hero's father, or cultured and rather helpless onlookers – Felix Aylmer, Leo Genn, Torin Thatcher, Herbert Marshall, Norman Wooland, et al.)

One or two actors defy vocal classification. Heston, for example, is simply international, and acceptable as hero, tyrant, patriarch, statesman, king, or commoner; probably only Olivier matches him for historical variety. And there is one very special voice which ought by rights to be a hopeless anachronism in the Ancient World, but is the classic example of acceptability, so much so that he practically presided over the pictures in which he appeared as a mere supporting player. Dear old Finlay Currie was a presence rather than a performer, with that massive white-robed bulk, the abundant silver hair, heroic profile, flashing eye, and gentle broad Scottish voice that always seemed to be on the point of saying "Finally, brethren . . . " It says something (I am not sure what) about the Protestant ethic that, whether addressing Roman Senate or Early Christians, he radiated a majestic reassurance that matched the spectacle; when the orgies had rioted to a conclusion, the last martyr had gone to the lions, the galleys were all sunk, the chariots wrecked, and Rome itself had gone up in flames, one could imagine the great head being shaken with a resigned compassionate sigh of "Aye, weel".

If Heston was the embodiment, Currie was the patron saint of Hollywood's First Age, which might be called the DeMille Epoch, after its greatest exponent, but more

English roses for all climes: Jean Simmons in Ancient Rome, Binnie Barnes on the throne of Russia, and Gladys Cooper in the drawing-room.

Hollywood's patron saint of the Ancient World, Finlay Currie as St Peter in *Quo Vadis?*

"Come and get us": Leonidas's spearmen at Thermopylae in *The 300 Spartans*.

properly the Egypto-Biblo-Classic era, since threads from all three were often intertwined in its productions. This was the great period in which Edmund Purdom invented brain surgery, the walls of Troy were besieged more than once for love of Hedy Lamarr and Rossana Podesta, Richard Egan's Spartans held the pass (with support from Ralph Richardson), Gregory Peck remembered the slaying of Goliath, Kirk Douglas voyaged home past giant-haunted caves to Ithaca, Darius and Xerxes brought hordes of extras out of the east, Howard Hawks and James Robertson Justice built pyramids, Claudette Colbert luxuriated in asses' milk, and Rita Hayworth undulated before a lip-smacking Charles Laughton and was rewarded with the head of Alan Badel on a plate.

And these were only minor glories of the days when art directors and set designers could really spread themselves with enormous reconstructions of the Forum, the walls of Acre, the treasure cities of Egypt, the Circus Maximus, Solomon's Temple, the Avenue of Sphinxes, the Temple of

Dagon, Cleopatra's pleasure barge and the fortifications of the Danube frontier; directors could stage great battles by land and sea, huge processions, chariot races, and gladiatorial combats; baying hordes of extras turned down their thumbs, fled screaming from the wrath of the Lord, or were entombed under toppling temples; bevies of dancing girls who would have gladdened von Sternberg's heart frolicked before Caesar and Pharaoh, and the Legions marched with nodding crests and SPQR standards to the boom of drums and the bray of horns which may well have sounded exactly like *bucinae*.

Those were the days before the money ran out: the Golden Age in more ways than one, and until some film laboratory genius comes up with a new process for recreating the battle of Actium and the Last Days of Pompeii by computer, we shall not look upon their like again.

Spectacle on a vast scale was their mainstay, and the excitement of seeing age-old stories and immortal characters come to life; they also relied not only on the conventional attractions of love, cruelty, destruction, and disaster, but on the knowledge that there are few things an audience likes better than a good persecution. The Children of Israel oppressed by the Philistines or bound in Egypt; the Early Christians martyred by the Caesars; the tyranny of Rome and pagan despots; the struggle for physical and spiritual liberty – these were common if not universal themes, and they were preached in ringing tones. Freedom is a simple, straightforward message, as every politician, demagogue, and film-maker knows who has employed its rousing phrases without examining too closely what freedom means. It is not simple at all, but historical films acknowledge that fact only rarely, as in the thrown-away line in *The Ten Commandments* when Edward G. Robinson, the renegade slave-master, is himself subjected to march discipline during the Exodus, and observes wryly: "So now, my brother, we have new task-masters."

Spectacle, liberty – and the other great staple of the First Age is grand romantic passion. It seldom works well as a primary theme, as witness the Cleopatra films, or those about the more susceptible Israelite kings: mere mortals and their selfish emotions are dwarfed by palaces and pyramids. But blend the love affair with the grand heroic theme

and, with a sure hand at the helm, box office is the result, especially if it is a Bible story.

There are two of special interest, both released to thunderous publicity, well hammered by the critics, and admired by the public. I am with the public and for, I suspect, the same reason: whatever shortcomings the professional critics may find in *Samson and Delilah* and *The Ten Commandments*, they were splendid visual entertainment, did justice to their subjects, and were historically illuminating.

Samson showed the worst of DeMille's faults. It was wordy, and they were not good words; that mine of great dialogue, the Authorized Version, got a poor showing, although the plotline was adhered to and embellished only slightly by making Delilah the younger sister of Samson's wife (Angela Lansbury), who was conveniently disposed of during a brawl. It often looked and sounded vulgar; the Philistines celebrated at the wedding like cowhands on pay day, and the great seduction scene took forever without raising the temperatures even, apparently, of the participants.

On the other hand, to those simpletons like myself who think of those three chapters of the Book of Judges as a series of immortal action sequences, DeMille gave of his best. Victor Mature was a Samson fit for fundamentalists and

The image of the image: Moses by Michelangelo, and Charlton Heston in *The Ten Commandments*.

Covenanters; he could have carried away the gates of Gaza in his sleep; the lion never stood a chance. When he put forth his hand and took the ass's jawbone, it was a revelation – that, we realised, was what the jawbone of an ass looked like, and he smote the Philistines, heaps upon heaps. He did not, admittedly, catch three hundred foxes and attach torches to their tails to burn the standing corn, for obvious reasons, but in every other respect his anger was kindled, with gratifying results.

Delilah was less of a success. There is no warrant for it in the Bible, but we expect her, the arch-betrayer, to be a snaky seductress, all lovely venom, and that Hedy Lamarr was not. George Sanders, who had a knack of wearing biblical armour as though it were made of well-cut tweed, was an urbane leader of Philistines, raising his glass with rueful approval as the temple collapsed about him.

That, of course, was one of Hollywood's great moments – two minutes twenty seconds, to be exact, from the time the first tiny crack came at the foot of the pillar, with Mature heaving to wake the dead, and then the eerie silence, another crack, and the whole colossal structure coming down in awful ponderous ruin. We had visualised, from childhood, a sort of roofed cathedral; DeMille, with authority, gave us a huge open temple, the great god Dagon with a fire in his belly toppling on the Philistine mob. It was sublime, and worth whatever it cost – which was a fraction of what it took as the No. 1 box office success of its year. It may not have been great art, but we had seen Samson and Delilah.

We have also seen the Children of Israel coming out of Egypt, a progress which in terms of spectacle and visual grandeur was above anything that has ever been put on the screen, *Ben Hur* and Eisenstein included. *The Ten Commandments* was DeMille's masterpiece; like every masterpiece it contained the faults as well as the virtues of its maker, but the faults here were lost in spectacle which for once was not confined to a few set-pieces but pervaded the whole film. If nothing else, *The Ten Commandments* was

Yul Brynner hardening his heart as Pharaoh.

huge, and the best of it was not in such highly publicised effects as the Red Sea parting, which looked like an artificial Niagara in reverse (although how else do you show it?), or in the rather jet-propelled inscription of the Commandments. Far more impressive were the Egyptian sets, the swarming brick-pits and endless construction works where the Israelites (and the film crew) were obviously serving with rigour, the enormous blocks of dressed stone moving ponderously into place, the massive pylon being erected before Pharaoh's city – it looked as though it was really happening, and with DeMille in charge it probably was. Loyal Griggs photographed it all superbly: one remembers best a breath-taking Egyptian dawn, and the beginning of the Exodus, with the great confused rabble, twelve thousand strong, setting off into the desert, carts and children and old folk

The Queen of Sheba as seen by Hollywood, exotic and passionate: Gina Lollobrigida in the driving seat in *Solomon and Sheba*.

and farm animals ploughing up the dust, the screen teeming with detail, and Heston striding majestically away towards the Promised Land. This is what historical films should be for, to set the legend in the mind's eye.

As usual, DeMille took a critical hiding, but there was an almost card-index quality about the strictures, as though reviewers had rummaged under the heading "DeMille" and come up with the obligatory complaints of vulgarity, tediousness, sex, cruelty, wordy script, etc. (all of which have probably been levelled at the Old Testament, too). One sometimes wonders what critics are looking for in a film of this kind, how they think it should have been made, and if their real objection is not simply that it was made at all. In the absence of constructive comment on *The Ten Commandments* one can only conclude that its scale put it

beyond normal critical reach; in a way, it is rather like criticizing an elephant or, more appositely, the Great Pyramid: one can only admire the sheer size of the thing, and let it go at that, with an acknowledgement to the quality of the cast. Heston was an impressive Moses, and Yul Brynner a properly stiff-necked Pharaoh; when given the language of the Bible they spoke it with authority. Anne Baxter was a distinct success as Queen Nefretiri, and the supporting cast included such luminaries as Edward G. Robinson, Vincent Price, Henry Wilcoxon (who was also associate producer), and Cedric Hardwicke. But the stars were the huge sets, the special effects, the teeming crowds of extras, the Plagues, the Golden Calf, and what are called the production values; together, they made a monument to a film-maker who, whatever his shortcomings, did it with his might.

That, with a passion for detail, was probably his secret: all or nothing. It was not a quality much in evidence in those chronologically later Biblicals, *David and Bathsheba* and *Solomon and Sheba*, both of which were short on spectacle by DeMille standards, and concentrated on the love affairs of their principals, with very different results.

David and Bathsheba is rightly regarded as one of the best film translations from Scripture: it succeeds by its very restraint. The temptation must surely have been there to make a full-blooded epic out of King David, whose career was nothing if not colourful; instead, the story is confined to those two chapters of 2nd Samuel in which David (Gregory Peck) sees Bathsheba (Susan Hayward) bathing, falls in love, and removes her inconvenient husband, Uriah the Hittite (Kieron Moore) by placing him in the forefront of the battle and abandoning him – as dirty a trick as is to be found even in the Old Testament. The film takes just a touch of the guilt off David by hinting that Bathsheba was the willing victim of his majesty's passion, and presenting Uriah as a true mutton-head of a career soldier who actually invited his own death; otherwise it is faithful to the story, which at times has some of the flavour of a woman's magazine serial in biblical costume; it is good old-fashioned love-and-guilt, and works well, despite the amount of reminiscence and prayer which induced the kind of stupor I used to feel during sermons. Peck is a commanding David and Susan Hayward a creditable Bathsheba, and Raymond Massey is in fine voice as the prophet Nathan; the colours are muted, the costumes are straight from an illustrated Bible, and if the interiors are more luxurious than I imagined old Jerusalem to be, they are in perfect taste, like the whole film. If it seemed all too steady and sober, the fault probably lay in me – I was only there for Goliath, who made a grand appearance in flash-back, all six cubits and a span of him, roaring defiance before being smitten in the forehead and falling, not upon his face as described in Samuel, but on his back. A niggling detail, like Pharaoh surviving the inundation in *The Ten Commandments*; one just wonders why.

David and Bathsheba was slow and stately, but it seemed to gallop along by comparison with *Solomon and Sheba*, which must have been a frustrating subject to its makers. This monarch is best known for having seven hundred wives, princesses, and three hundred concubines; unfortunately, the only woman with whom his relations appear to have been entirely circumspect was the Queen of Sheba. According to 1 Kings 10, and Josephus, she merely paid him a state visit, marvelled at his wisdom, gave him gifts of gold and spices, and went home to Saudi Arabia. Not the stuff of epics, so a fine steamy fiction had to be concocted to enable Gina Lollobrigida to smoulder and heave in a series of plunging gowns, drive a chariot with abandon, dance in a curious balletic orgy, and seduce Solomon (Yul Brynner) for political purposes. Into this was woven a highly embroidered version of the rivalry between Solomon and his brother Adonijah (George Sanders), which here began at the deathbed of King David (Finlay Currie) and ended in a laboured sword duel. There was much pretentious talk, passionate breathing, and bad acting, the incident of the disputed infant was dragged in, the Temple was destroyed,

and the overthrow of an Egyptian army, dazzled by flashing shields, only proved that one brief, striking visual effect in almost two and a half hours of tedium is not enough.

In distorting its source material and building a false melodrama around semi-historical characters, *Solomon and Sheba* was an exception among Early Biblicals, most of which tried to stick to the received stories. How far, or by what standard, they succeeded, is a matter of opinion; they have been well derided by the press, and the public have flocked to them in droves, but neither of these things is the concern of this eccentric work. To treat them as pictures of history is to raise the immediate question: how far is the Old Testament to be regarded as history, by a Gentile at least? To this Gentile, they gave the pleasure of seeing Sunday School stories brought vividly to life, and created an imaginative but not necessarily inaccurate vision of their distant time; that is something. They may be charged with glamourising and sensationalising, to which DeMille's answer was that those who accused him of exploiting sex and violence had evidently not studied the Old Testament very closely.

Even at their best, they have not attracted the kind of study devoted to other areas of the cinema. The glib rejoinder is that they aren't worth it, but I have sometimes wondered if behind the indifference and occasional distaste there does not lie a subconscious reluctance even to think about, let alone examine, subjects which, even in film form, touch the root of sacred belief. Behind the box-office popularity and the intellectual disdain there is a hint of uneasiness about Old Testament movies; perhaps it is a sense that they are not quite suitable material for the cinema, for a variety of reasons. It is strange that (although DeMille was at pains to enlist clerical support for *The Ten Commandments*) the Church has kept fairly quiet about Biblicals, possibly feeling that to approve would be as risky as to condemn.

It may be as good a yardstick as any by which to judge these flawed and fascinating entertainments – I wonder what John Knox and Francis Xavier would have made of them, or

Medallion of Alexander the
Great, and right, Richard Burton
as Alexander and Fredric March
as Philip of Macedon in
Alexander the Great.

Thomas Aquinas and Duns Scotus (assuming they could have been got into the same row of the stalls). No doubt things would have been thrown at the screen from time to time, but on the whole I believe they would have approved. Knox, at any rate, would surely have got a sermon out of *Samson and Delilah*.

At this point in the First Age I am confronted by a problem which exercised the Persians, the Romans, and especially King Priam of Troy, namely: what to do about the Greeks? Hollywood, for its part, has done very little, and nothing to compare to the lavish spectacles it has devoted to the Holy Land, Egypt, and Rome, which seems shabby treatment for the cradle of Western civilization. True, Richard Burton has conquered the world in the name of Alexander, Thermopylae has been defended to the last, Jason has twice

sought the Golden Fleece in Colchis (once in the company of Steve Reeves as Hercules), and Laurence Olivier, Maggie Smith and Ursula Andress have bickered in Olympus over the fate of Perseus,[1] but without causing any great excitement among the film-going public. Still, Greece cannot be ignored altogether, so I turn to the two most famous of its historic legends, *Helen of Troy* and *Ulysses*.

As I remember, it was the supernatural agency of Venus that caused Helen to run away with Paris, but here it is simply love at first sight between handsome Jacques Sernas and statuesque Rossana Podesta, with Helen's maid (Brigitte Bardot) observing brightly: "A man, my lady? How interesting." The lovers flee to Troy, and the outraged husband Menelaus (Niall McGinnis), Achilles (Stanley Baker), Agamemnon (Robert Douglas), and Ulysses (Torin Thatcher)

1 In *Alexander the Great, The 300 Spartans, Jason and the Argonauts, Hercules, Clash of the Titans* respectively.

The wooden horse dragged home in triumph by the unsuspecting Trojans in *Helen of Troy*.

are only too glad of a chance to loot the city. The siege follows Homer fairly closely, with Agamemnon and Achilles quarrelling over a girl, and the latter sulking until the time comes to duel with Hector (Harry Andrews), who is duly dispatched and dragged behind the victor's chariot. Paris shoots Achilles in the heel, and the city finally succumbs to Ulysses' ruse of the wooden horse, with Paris being killed and Helen reclaimed.

None of which is terribly exciting on screen, despite huge crowds of extras advancing on the walls of Troy, with siege engines, catapults, and impressive-looking crested helmets. The wooden horse is on the large scale, although I remain unconvinced that Priam (Cedric Hardwicke) and his people would have been fool enough to bring it indoors and then revel themselves into a stupor; it struck me as implausible in the schoolroom, and is no more credible in the cinema. The only other feature of interest is that the doors in the Greek palaces are so enormous that the players have to strain visibly to move them; this may well be an authentic period detail.

Ulysses is a handsome, condensed, and rather stilted version of the Odyssey, which makes interesting use of the flashback technique which was Homer's gift to Hollywood. Thus the film opens with Penelope (Silvana Mangano) waiting in despair on Ithaca for Ulysses (Kirk Douglas) to come home from Troy, and resisting the advances of her suitors (of whom Homer had 308, but the film makes do with about twenty). Meanwhile Ulysses, doomed to wander the Mediterranean for offending the Gods, is suffering a selection of the hardships described in the Odyssey – we see him shipwrecked and discovered by Nausicaa (Rossana Podesta again); bound to his mast, listening to the Sirens' song while his ear-plugged crew man the oars; trapped in the cave of the Cyclops Polyphemus and escaping after blinding the giant with his own staff; bewitched by Circe (also played by Miss Mangano, an imaginative touch), while his crew are transformed into swine; and communing with the shades of the dead. After all that, one can excuse, though not without regret, the omission of Scylla and Charybdis, the Lotus Eaters, the cannibal Laestrygones, and the sea-nymph Calypso.

Finally, disguised as a beggar, Ulysses returns to Ithaca, is recognized by his dog Argus, confounds the suitors by bending the bow which has defied their efforts, shoots an arrow through the twelve axe-heads, and slaughters the suitors in true Homeric style, starting with Anthony Quinn. All told, it is a faithful rendering of the great epic so far as space permits, and if the dubbing from Italian into English is a nuisance, Polyphemus alone is worth the price of admission.

Ancient Egypt has meant two things to Hollywood, Cleopatra and walking mummies. There have been three notable Queens of the Nile, Claudette Colbert, Vivien Leigh, and Elizabeth Taylor, but the mummies were arguably greater artistic and financial successes, and their films have some claim to historical attention: mere spine-chillers though they were, they helped to fix in the public mind the idea of old Egypt as a cult-ridden, curse-stricken land of mystery given over to embalming, necrolatry, interbreeding, and the worship of gods with animal heads. In this way they were cashing in on Rider Haggard, Conan Doyle, and the sensational rumours current about the Tutankhamen excavations of the 1920s, and the rediscovery that "horror" had great audience appeal.

There were two memorable films in this class, the first being, simply, *The Mummy*, with Boris Karloff looking dreadful and sounding melodious in the role of Imhotep who, as every 1932 schoolboy knew, stole the Scroll of Thoth containing instructions on how to revive his dead beloved Princess (Zita Johann). For this sacrilege he was entombed alive, only to be reanimated by Bramwell Fletcher on an archaeological dig; having shed his wrappings, Imhotep was soon on the trail of a modern heroine (the Princess reincarnated), and since he had the mysterious power of inducing coronaries, the screen was soon awash with corpses, including a dog killed, predictably, by the White Cat Goddess, Bast. Fortunately, before he could sacrifice the heroine, Karloff was turned back into a mummy by the Goddess Isis, and broke up, literally.

Tom Tyler assumed the sarcophagus with distinction in *The Mummy's Hand* a few years later, stealing the sacred tana leaves for the traditional Princess-revival, being entombed (the thrifty producers lifting the sequence from the Karloff film), and breaking loose in the twentieth century before returning to the dust of ages in another memorable death scene.[2] Both films were notable for the effect they achieved

---

2 Tyler specialised in these, as witness his demise in *Stagecoach*, when after his shoot-out with John Wayne he returned to the saloon apparently none the worse, before collapsing unexpectedly at the bar. He played a variation on this exit in *San Antonio*.

by the use of shadow and sinister settings, without recourse to the ketchup and grisly detail which mar modern thrillers; tripe, no doubt, but not uninfluential in their modest way, if only in making museum visitors keep their distance.

It would be fanciful to suggest that some ancient curse hangs over "Egyptian" pictures, but it remains that the three best-known Cleopatra films failed to live up to their publicity or to the vast expenditure of cash, effort and talent that was lavished on them. DeMille's film of 1934 was one of his least successful epics; Pascal's 1945 version of Shaw was the most expensive British film ever made, and the 1963 production by Twentieth Century Fox became a byword for extravagance, crisis and disappointment. But as recreations of history two of them are worth looking at, and make for interesting comparisons.

There is enough evidence about Cleopatra VII to have bred some debate among scholars; along with the writings of Plutarch, Suetonius, Josephus, and others there is dramatic literature, including Shakespeare, and the popular impression has grown of a beautiful subtle Oriental sex-symbol who seduced Roman conquerors, luxuriated on gilded barges, poisoned enemies, and committed suicide by snake-bite – most of which appears to be true, the main questions being her motives, and her relationships, romantic and political, with her celebrated lovers Julius Caesar and Mark Antony.

In fact, she was Greek, not Egyptian, intelligent, witty, ambitious, and of magnetic charm;[3] she was also murderous, even with her own family, but possibly not as depraved, cruel and unscrupulous as historians like Josephus suggest. As to her known history, she was in her early twenties and struggling to regain her share of the Egyptian throne when she met Julius Caesar in Egypt, being rolled out of a carpet in his presence. He was captivated, established her on the throne, had a son by her, and when he returned to Rome, she

followed. After Caesar's assassination she turned her charms on Antony, who was enslaved, and they lived together, more or less, for twelve years, and had three children. Octavian, Antony's rival for power in Rome, used the love affair and the popular fear of her influence to turn public opinion against the couple, and war followed: Cleopatra persuaded Antony to fight at sea, he was heavily beaten off Actium, and subsequently committed suicide, dying in Cleopatra's arms. She tried to conciliate the victorious Octavian, without success, and killed herself, leaving history to decide how far her remarkable career was inspired by love, and how far by political ambition. Either of her Roman lovers might, but for chance, have elevated her to supreme power, and it has been said that Rome had more cause to fear her than any foreigner since Hannibal.

As lover or politician, she is not the easiest of film subjects. DeMille tended to romance rather than statecraft, with Cleopatra (Claudette Colbert) and Antony (Henry Wilcoxon) as star-crossed lovers. In the 1963 *Cleopatra* it was difficult to tell, because Elizabeth Taylor and Richard Burton railed, snarled and emoted at such length that their relationship became confused; they even fell to blows at one point, but on the whole Cleopatra-Taylor, while thoroughly enamoured, seemed to have a stronger grip on *realpolitik* than Cleopatra-Colbert; she may have lacked the instant charm of the French actress, but she certainly exhibited that force of character of which Plutarch writes. I imagine she was closer to the real thing.

Both pictures were faithful in the main to history, the DeMille version slightly less so, partly because it condensed the story into 101 minutes, while the 1963 film ran to an interminable four hours. To do it justice, it was the spectacular to end all spectaculars – and just about did. The sets were enormous, the costumes dazzling, the aftermaths of Pharsalia and Philipi masterpieces of detail, Actium a fine welter of flying missiles and burning ships, and Cleopatra's entrance into Rome, enthroned on an enormous Sphinxmobile hauled

---

3 Plutarch says her beauty was not of the incomparable sort, but that she was irresistibly attractive, with a delightful voice which could switch from one language to another with ease.

Five faces of Egypt. Clockwise from top left: Cleopatra VII, Elizabeth Taylor, Claudette Colbert, Amanda Barrie with asp and Antony (Sid James), and Vivien Leigh.

Julius Caesar, followed by Warren William, Claude Rains and Rex Harrison.

by sweating musclemen, was, to coin a phrase, colossal. And yet . . . perhaps DeMille's Cleopatra, borne on a litter through narrow, teeming streets, with the crowds gaping and craning at the lovely shining figure, admiring and passing their comments, was nearer historic reality. Comparison makes one wonder if Cleopatra's Egypt and Caesar's Rome were quite as huge and highly polished as the immaculate coloured images of 1963 suggested.[4] For me, at any rate, DeMille's crowded, constricted sets were more convincing; so were his male leads.

This has something to do with modern star-exposure – the personalities are so well-known, so covered in news columns, TV bulletins, and chat-shows, so thoroughly identified as *themselves*, that screen personation, especially in costume, becomes almost impossible. They are not Antony and Caesar, they are Burton and Harrison; it may be unfair, but it is

true. Yet even without that disadvantage I doubt if the players of 1963, given that they had a script so modern in its approach, would have been as credible as Wilcoxon and Warren William, who had a simple quality that Burton and Harrison lacked – they looked as though they might have commanded armies and shaped the destinies of nations. William, grim, hatchet-faced, snapping brusquely over his maps and models, was a proper Caesar; Wilcoxon, powerful, truculent, given to drink and women, and withal rather simple, was the playboy Antony of Plutarch's account. If the prose they were given was purple,[5] they could deliver it with the unselfconscious force of the old-school film actor; they were just fitter men for the roles, and they were not dwarfed by forty million dollars' worth of production.

Supporting players have little chance to shine in a Cleopatra

4 For all their splendour, they achieved no effect so spectacular as DeMille's dramatic slow pull-back from Cleopatra's couch along the full length of a galley between great banks of beating gilded oars.

5 *Cleopatra* (1934) had its share of script gems, e.g.: Cleopatra: "Together we could conquer the world." Caesar: "Nice of you to include me."

picture, but the 1963 version had a striking Octavian in Roddy McDowall – cold, remorseless, and (in his quieter scenes) compelling; it was easy to believe that he would shortly become the Emperor Augustus.

Gabriel Pascal's *Caesar and Cleopatra* was Britain's lavish contribution in 1945; it carried a fortune in production costs, as well as the formidable writing credit of George Bernard Shaw, who had his own highly personal view of the subject and was less concerned with history than with drama. Unlike Shakespeare's, his plays do not lend themselves to Technicolored screens and gigantic sets (not without music, anyway), but the production had great style and looked superb, as did Vivien Leigh. Claude Rains walked away with the honours as a most Shavian Caesar, Stewart Granger was a dashing Apollodorus, and a distinguished supporting cast gave the master's dialogue full value. But history was its vehicle, not its purpose, and one could say the same of *Carry On, Cleo* which, with its famous mock poster, its ribaldries, its marching legions ("Sinister! Dexter! Sinister! Dexter!"), its frenzied Caesar (Kenneth Williams) crying: "Infamy! Infamy! They've all got it in for me!" and its sprightly Cleopatra (Amanda Barrie) bouncing apples off her biceps and flapping enormous eyelashes, was a delightful sustained send-up, and among the best of the Carry On Films. Lampoons of history are a study in themselves, and not a trivial one.

One other recreation of Ancient Egypt deserves an honourable mention; historically it is perhaps the most interesting of them all. *Land of the Pharaohs* caused no great excitement as a film, although the plot, about a Pharaoh obsessed with the building of his own tomb, had some novelty; its distinction lay in the almost documentary nature of those scenes devoted to the design and construction of a pyramid – and if that sounds unexciting, it was not. Howard Hawks, who is said to have counted the film a failure, built massive sets and photographed them and their swarming workers with a care and attention to detail that convinced me, at least, that I was seeing how a pyramid was really

made. As a piece of research and exposition it was impressive; whether there is historic evidence for the system whereby the whole huge edifice was sealed by falling blocks and streams of sand, I do not know, but it made a spectacular climax. Jack Hawkins was Pharaoh, Joan Collins his slinky Queen, and

Mark Antony, with Richard Burton, below left and Henry Wilcoxon, right.

James Robertson Justice his architect, but the stars were Hawks and his designers.

If the people of the future had to rely solely on historical films for their knowledge of the Ancient World, they might conclude that Rome's importance was confined to a single century, from the ending of the Republic to the death of Nero in 68AD. Many other periods of Roman history offer good cinematic material – the Tarquin-Lucrece episode which culminated with Horatius holding the bridge, for example, or Hannibal's invasion (which admittedly has made a musical[6]) – but Hollywood has concentrated on those first centuries BC and AD for obvious reasons: this is the Rome that we know from our childhood, the Rome of Julius and Cleopatra and Antony and, infinitely more important, of the Early Christians, the centre of the world when Jesus lived, the scene of the great struggle which, for better or worse, was to shape our civilization. It may be called Western man's spiritual beginning – that certainly is how Hollywood has presented it, and it is rich in the elements of which film epics are made: persecution, martyrdom, faith, love, terror, violence, betrayal, redemption, cruelty, great spectacle, and the simple confrontation of "right" and "wrong". Its heroes and villains are obvious, its message plain.

It is also the Rome of the only memorable Emperors (for who knows anything about the later ones except that Hadrian built a Wall and Trajan had a column?), all five of whom have appeared before the cameras. Augustus (Octavian) we have seen played by Ian Keith and Roddy McDowall in the Cleopatra films; Tiberius, that debauched and capable tyrant, has been portrayed as a not unkindly, doddery old stick by Ernest Thesiger and George Relph in *The Robe* and *Ben Hur*; Claudius, appropriately, has had one film and an abandoned half-film, Barry Jones playing

6 *Jupiter's Darling*, with Howard Keel as Hannibal, and Esther Williams.

An immaculate piece of casting: left, Augustus Caesar, and Roddy McDowall in *Cleopatra*.

him in *Demetrius and the Gladiators*, and Laughton in the unfinished *I, Claudius*; both these pictures had their Caligulas (Jay Robinson and Emlyn Williams), and Malcolm McDowall made a third in, simply, *Caligula*. And, of course, there is Nero.

Whether Rome of the cinema could have survived without him is doubtful; it would certainly have been a duller place. Nero has raved and wept and flounced and gloated in at least ten major pictures, invariably stealing the show, and perpetuating that image of depraved and almost ludicrous wickedness which has made him the most recognizable figure in Roman history – the fat monster who fiddled while Rome burned. A monster he was, cruel, debauched, and murderous (his victims included wife and mother), pretending to eminence as a poet, musician, actor, and intellectual, a creature of childish vanity and caprice as much as of viciousness. In his defence, it has never been proved that he was responsible for the great fire; he was not in Rome when it started, and far from revelling in the sufferings of its victims, he organized relief and shelter for them. This according to Tacitus, who was no admirer. No doubt his music and poetry needed all the flattery they could get, but the story that he sang of Troy's destruction while Rome burned rests on rumour – which has never stopped Hollywood from making the most of it. Against that, his most famous crime – using the Christians as scapegoats for the fire, and massacring them in the arena with hideous cruelty – is well vouched for.

As to his portrayers, I had always assumed that that fine actor, Edward Arnold, dicing with Eddie Cantor in *Roman Scandals* (which incidentally contains Busby Berkeley's best choreography), was meant to be Nero; in fact, he was playing a fictitious emperor called Valerius, a name possibly inspired by Galerius and Valerian, but probably not. That by the way. There have been at least eleven screen Neros, including Peter Lorre, Francis L. Sullivan, and Emil Jannings,

but only two are memorable: Laughton in *The Sign of the Cross* and Peter Ustinov in *Quo Vadis?* You take your pick: Laughton, in a false nose, stretching and lolling like an obscene fat cat and smirking of "delicious debauchery", had the time of his life in a fine, over-the-top study in short space; Ustinov, in the beard which films usually omit, played him as a spoiled, petulant, and vicious child, vain, easily swayed, yearning for praise and never quite believing it, for his Nero had a furtive intelligence which kept showing through. It was a splendid performance, consistent with what we know of Nero, and I don't see how it could have been better done.

The films in which these two appear bear a close resemblance to each other in plot, and are based on works from the Victorian era, when religious fiction had a great vogue, especially when it involved faith unto death in the arena. *Quo Vadis?* was an 1895 bestseller by a Polish writer, Henry Sienkiewicz; it was adapted and produced in the theatre by Wilson Barrett, the famous actor-manager, who was also the author of *The Sign of the Cross*. In both cases the story tells of

The Emperor Nero and his two most famous impersonators: Charles Laughton, left, and Peter Ustinov.

a beautiful Christian girl who excites the passion of a hand-some Roman aristocrat; he, arrogant young tyrant that he is, is impatient of her religious scruples, but when she is condemned to die in the arena he rallies to her – with dire consequences in *The Sign of the Cross*, but a happy ending in *Quo Vadis?* You couldn't go wrong with this kind of thing in 1895 – or in 1951, for that matter, when *Quo Vadis?* was MGM's greatest success since *Gone With the Wind*. In 1932 *The Sign of the Cross* had been a more modest, but still significant, success for Paramount and Cecil DeMille.

Comparing the two films is like comparing the two *Cleopatra*s. *Quo Vadis?* is huge, magnificent to look upon, graced by fine acting from Ustinov, Leo Genn (Petronius), Patricia Laffan (Poppaea), and Finlay Currie at his most magisterial as St Peter; the sets are eye-filling, Rome burns on a vast scale, crowds surge in panic, the legions have never marched better (with the correct wild-beast skins on the standard-bearers for once), Christians are martyred – with, it is said, Elizabeth Taylor among them as an extra – and so far as history comes into it, the images are all that could be wished. Nero is given sole credit for the fire, and sings excruciatingly; he strangles Poppaea, when in fact he kicked her to death (and not at the time of the fire, either), and did not commit suicide until four years later. But the persecution of the Christians as scapegoats for the fire is all too truly authentic, and the film does not spare them.

The most interesting martyrdom is that reserved for Deborah Kerr, the heroine, tied to a post where she is to be gored by a wild bull; Buddy Baer, her faithful and gigantic minder, intervenes and disposes of the bull in three falls – unnecessarily, in my view. A few years ago I was invited to do the screenplay for a remake of this film, and the producer and I could not imagine that a bull, however wild, would pose a threat to someone tied to a post. In the book, Sienkiewicz has the victim *placed* on the bull's horns before-hand, which sounds more sensible, although one can see why MGM did it their way. Fortunately the remake never

got beyond the discussion stage; even with its fine track record (there were several silent versions, one with Emil Jannings as Nero), I doubt if *Quo Vadis?* is right for modern audiences; martyrdom does not strike a chord nowadays, at least not among Christians.

Apart from the slight historical liberties mentioned above – and a doubt as to whether chess was played in Rome *c.* AD 64 – my one cavil with *Quo Vadis?* concerns the suggestion that Early Christianity was anti-slavery; Hollywood is always eager to suggest that its heroes, be they Christians, Jews, American colonists, or Elizabethan sea-dogs, were champions of universal liberty, and I am not aware that

Buddy Baer, who in his boxing days once knocked down Joe Louis, prepares to defend Deborah Kerr from a wild bull in *Quo Vadis?*

this is historic truth. Slave-owners and slave-dealers were numerous among all of them.

Quo Vadis? may be one of the cinema's most splendid views of the grandeur that was Rome, but it suffers from being over-long and over-scripted (although having laboured through Sienkiewicz, I sympathise with the adaptors) and from the miscasting of Robert Taylor as the imperious tribune – I suspect that he was as nice a man as he looked, and his arrogance does not ring true. In marked contrast, Fredric March's Marcus Superbus strides through *The Sign of the Cross* glowering with whip in hand, Imperial Rome incarnate, and the contrast with Elissa Landi's innocent Christian maid is one of the pleasures of the film. Another is Claudette Colbert's Poppaea: cast quite out of her normal screen character, she is as wicked an empress as ever tempted hero or disposed of rival, and all the more effective for looking angelic. Miss Laffan's villainy may be more patent, but they are two good historical portraits of a lady who, Tacitus tells us, was beautiful, clever, charming, debauched and cruel.

Partly because of its four leading players, this is perhaps the best of all DeMille's films; *The Ten Commandments* was a masterpiece of spectacle, but *The Sign of the Cross* is even more successful in fulfilling an idea of history, as well as being well acted, directed, and edited, and beautifully photographed – this is one of those films where black-and-white is an advantage. As in his *Cleopatra*, this Rome is credible, as the camera ranges through narrow, well-used streets, into homes noble and simple, from throne-room to prison to orgy to dungeon, and finally to the arena – the goal of every Roman epic, which suggests that gladiatorial games would be sold out today if they were permitted. In the meantime, *The Sign of the Cross* will have to do; one of the least lavish of "gladiator" pictures, it is by far the best, and the most shocking. It is a cruel film, much more so than those which go for sickening coloured close-ups; DeMille was an artist in suggesting horror without showing it, and

this film contains the worst torture scene I remember – it consists of a Roman official, in a shadowy cellar, sitting on a stool and looking down through an open trap-door. That is all you see; nothing more is necessary.

The arena sequence gets its effects by brilliant inter-cutting. Down on the sand, the trampling elephants, the net-and-trident men, wild beasts, barbarian women fighting dwarves, the sudden close-up of a spiked cestus on a fist – and away to the audience making bets, jeering, gloating, guzzling, or just plain bored and even flirting, with a married couple bickering and changing places because the husband hasn't got them better seats. It is a study in decadence and cruelty, and not all the Technicolored epics of gladiators hacking away before roaring crowds, or all the descriptions written, can convey as much as DeMille's one inspired, chilling shot of a young woman spectator's face, sullen and half-interested, dissolving into the snarling mask of a tiger in the arena.

There are other typical touches, like the asses being milked before Poppaea's famous bath scene, with the kitten lapping at the edge of the pool, or the little girl giggling during the Christian's prayer-meeting, and later smiling eagerly at the novel prospect of going into the arena. All told, it carries conviction; my one historical doubt concerns the title, and the repeated symbolic device used not only in this film but in many others. Surely the Cross did not become the emblem of Christianity until six centuries after Nero's time, in Constantinople, when it was authorised by the Quinisexte Council? I have always understood that the fish was the symbol of the earlier Christians, as honouring St Peter, which seems more appropriate than the Roman gallows.

On the face of it, both films are about the triumph of Christian faith; in fact, what drew the customers were the strong central love themes and the promise of lurid spectacle. They are not at all religious films, but worldly entertainments, and any spiritual element they contain is just an added bonus – not that any film publicist in his right mind would put it quite like that. This is not to say their makers were insincere, but they knew the priorities, and that religion needs careful handling if it is not to swamp the ship. This is especially true when the heart of the matter is approached, as it has been several times, and a film is attempted of the life of Jesus.

So far as I know, this has never been done well, at least since the silent days, when DeMille's *King of Kings* was highly acclaimed. It is a daunting subject, fraught with difficulties, one of which is that this is an area where the writer can be allowed no licence, as Alan Badel's colleague discovered. Another is that everyone in the audience, believer or not, will have a definite personal view, and a fixed mental picture along with it, which a film will inevitably disturb, probably disappoint, and possibly outrage. Film-makers have always been sensitive to this, as witness the reluctance even to show Christ as other than a distant or partially-seen figure – a convention which has been used with excellent dramatic effect, notably in *Ben Hur*, where Jesus's face was never seen, and the impact of His presence was shown in the expression of a Roman soldier confronting Him – truculent, then puzzled and uneasy, and finally abashed. I don't know the actor who played the Roman, but he won himself a small place in cinema history.

As with an incident, so with whole films: for dramatic purposes the story of Jesus and His followers is best used as mere background to the fiction. It is a rule that Sienkiewicz and Barrett understood. They used a period a little removed from the Four Gospels, but most of the other successful Early Christian films have been set around the time of the Crucifixion, weaving their plots into the New Testament and taking full advantage of an old and well-tried narrative device: to bring the reader or viewer up short, in the middle of a fiction, with a scene or incident which he recognises, and knows (or at least believes) to be fact.

An excellent example is *The Robe*, a film which has much that is historically satisfying about it, but whose virtues have perhaps been obscured by the fact that it was the first Cinemascope production, and was handled in those highly

H.B. Warner in *King of Kings*.

emotional terms which suggest occasional embarrassment on the part of the makers. To be fair, it is hard to see how it could have been done otherwise. It was based on a bestseller by Lloyd C. Douglas, who had a splendid idea and did not execute it as well as he might have done; the film, to me, is a good deal better than the book.

The robe is the garment worn by Christ on the way to Calvary, where it is won at dice by the young tribune (Richard Burton) in charge of the Crucifixion. It passes into the hands of his slave (Victor Mature), who has already been converted, and the film describes how the tribune, harrowed by guilt, eventually becomes not only a Christian but a martyr.

The Crucifixion in *The Robe*, with Richard Burton among the soldiers dicing at the foot of the Cross and Victor Mature in background.

Dramatically, it is a bold step beyond Sienkiewicz and Barrett, running parallel to the biblical account, which acts as a kind of sub-plot: the betrayal, trial and death of Jesus are incidental, impinging first with Christ's entry to Jerusalem on the ass forming a backcloth to the tribune's own arrival; then at the baths the tribune is seen handing his centurion the money needed to procure the Messiah's betrayal; his slave is too late to prevent it, but has a chance encounter in a dark street with Judas (this is good cinema); the tribune is assigned the task of execution by Pilate (Richard Boone, demonstrating what a good actor can do with very little); finally, the Crucifixion takes place as a matter of routine. Perhaps for that reason, it has never been done better in a film: to the perpetrators, it was no doubt a commonplace.

This, surprisingly since it was a lavish production, is *The Robe*'s chief virtue. It looks and sounds authentic, and takes care with historic details: the interior of the Roman villa looks like a place where people live, and they are seen using it with an easy familiarity that sometimes suggests the documentary style, and this is true for the slave-market, the galley to Palestine, the Jerusalem scenes, the catacombs, Tiberius's villa on Capri, and so on.

For that, one can abide the celestial choir, yearning music, and Hallelujah finale, and admire the stoicism with which Victor Mature endures an impossible role in which he is called on to stare upwards in ruptured nobility for long periods. Given lines, he acts well, and holds his own with Burton, who is a very proper Roman. So too are Jean Simmons and Torin Thatcher, and Michael Rennie is an impressive Peter, although it is hard to imagine him becoming Finlay Currie.

Demetrius and the Gladiators, exploiting *The Robe*'s success, was much better than most sequels, perhaps because it too achieved a marriage between fiction and fact, in this case the history being Roman rather than Christian, and familiar to those who know their Robert Graves. The fiction here is that the Emperor Caligula (Jay Robinson) having martyred Burton in the first film, institutes a search for the robe, because he mistakenly believes that it holds the secret of immortality.[7] Mature, who has it hidden, resists the searchers violently, and is condemned to become a gladiator, in which capacity he catches the famous roving eye of Messalina (Susan Hayward), wife to the Emperor's doddering uncle, Claudius. Being religious, Mature is a reluctant gladiator until a Christian girl is mishandled by his colleagues at an orgy (the restraint of this scene is a rebuke to the excesses of the modern cinema), after which he goes berserk in the arena, slaughtering man and

7 The germ of this story is at least 1500 years old. According to the apocryphal Gospel of Nicodemus, the linen kerchief with which Christ's face was wiped on the way to Calvary, and which bore the imprint of His features thereafter, was sought out by Pilate on the instructions of Tiberius (not Caligula) and brought to Rome, where it healed the Emperor of a skin disease.

Top left, Messalina and Claudius, top right, Caligula. Centre, Messalina (Susan Hayward) with Caligula (Jay Robinson), and below, with Claudius (Barry Jones) in *Demetrius and the Gladiators*.

beast alike, renounces Christianity, and becomes Messalina's plaything before seeing the light again.

Ripe melodrama, but not bad history, either. What we see of Imperial affairs is sound, with Caligula deteriorating into mania, deifying himself, and being assassinated by Cassius Charea and his associates, who name Claudius as his successor (not exactly according to Suetonius, but close). There is a fair impression of Roman attitudes to Christianity, and an informative exposition of the gladiatorial mystique – the professionalism, the training, the favoured status, the possible rewards, etc. – by a veteran trainer (Ernest Borgnine). The only misrepresentation is trivial: Claudius, I believe, had no notion of what a man-eater Messalina was until much later in their marriage, when he had her killed.

Speaking of man-eaters, the arena highlight comes when Mature, in the red trunks, despatches four successive tigers, the stupid beasts having no idea of team-work. The script is well above par for this kind of film, with some wit, and the acting also. Mature is again called on to address heaven, but performs with spirit, Susan Hayward is a calculating seductress, Barry Jones a timid, decent Claudius (although without twitch or stammer), and Robinson stalks and snarls and goes mad with style.

As Demetrius remarks, life for a Christian in Imperial Rome is seldom dull. The same may be said for a patriotic Jew, as we know from *Ben Hur*, arguably the most famous Ancient World epic of them all. If so, it is fitting, for its original author, General Lew Wallace, was the most successful of "Biblical" fiction writers, and *Ben Hur* one of the bestsellers of the nineteenth century. Wallace, a distinguished American soldier, diplomat, and Governor of New Mexico (a post which brought him into contact with Billy the Kid), published *Ben Hur* in 1880; whether he was inspired by earlier writers like Lord Lytton[8] and Dean Farrar, I do not

know, but he was the spiritual father of the Hollywood Roman epic, and revived the popularity of the chariot race as mass entertainment.

All the world knows the 1959 film, which follows the career of a young Jewish noble, Judah Ben Hur (Charlton Heston), who refuses to assist his boyhood friend, the Roman Messala (Stephen Boyd) to suppress Jewish nationalism. Messala imprisons Ben Hur's family and sends him to the galleys, en route to which he is given water by the Carpenter of Nazareth. He escapes from the oar during a sea-battle, and rescues the Roman admiral (Jack Hawkins, who has the best line in the film: "Your God, in His eagerness to save you, has also saved the Roman fleet"). Thereafter Ben Hur defeats Messala in a chariot race and repays Jesus's kindness on the way to Calvary; his mother and sister, released from prison, are miraculously cured of leprosy during the Crucifixion, and Ben Hur marries his steward's daughter.

The film kept close to Wallace's novel, the only major difference that I can recall being that in the book the evil Messala is crippled during the chariot race but not killed. In the film, of course, he was bound to die, gory and unrepentant; this was forcibly brought home to Boyd at a gala showing of the picture when he was attacked by a mob of vengeful children – a disturbing example of the effect the cinema can have on impressionable minds, as well as being a tribute to Boyd himself. He had a strong presence in historical films, and wore Roman armour as though it belonged to him.

Remarkable film though it is, *Ben Hur*'s historical interest is centred on its most famous sequence, the chariot race, for which exhaustive research must have been done. Perhaps it was not entirely typical of such events: four, not six, was the usual number of chariots; no one that I noticed seemed to be wearing the faction colours (red, blue, green, or white); the normal start was from the gates, so that drivers had to jockey for inside position on the *spina;* and in a sport which was as intensely partisan, highly organized, and professionally controlled as any we know today, I wonder if

8 *The Last Days of Pompeii*, which bore little resemblance to Lytton's book, was unsuccessfully filmed in 1935; its main interest was Basil Rathbone's performance as Pontius Pilate.

Messala would have been allowed to use barbed hubs. And, while circuses were built in many parts of the empire, was there such an impressive stadium, bronze dolphins and all, in Palestine? I ask out of genuine curiosity about minor details; for me, Messala could have had a British war chariot with scythes on its wheels.

As a spectacle, it remains unsurpassed, and for sight, sound, and danger is a faithful reconstruction of those astonishing races which were, quite literally, the talk of Rome for six centuries. We could believe that we were seeing the real thing; it was something which Hollywood could stage without the kind of restraint necessary in depictions of gladiatorial combats and arena displays, many of which, as shown to the Roman mob, would have been quite unsuitable for modern family viewing. And the better man won, even if Messala (according to Boyd) had the faster team.

Ben Hur also provides a brief, harrowing insight into galley slavery, and has a rattling good sea-battle; it seems almost ungrateful to say that it contains no other pictures of the past that have not been better done elsewhere. It was well played – whatever famous names were considered in casting, the film was fortunate in Heston and Boyd, and there never was an Arab sheikh to touch Hugh Griffith, or a Pilate with more bored aplomb than Frank Thring.

He is one of a distinguished list who have played the Procurator of Judaea – Rathbone, Gabin, Boone, Steiger, and Arthur Kennedy among them. This last was odd casting of a good actor, but then *Barabbas* was an odd film. Adapted by Christopher Fry, Nigel Balchin, and others from Per Lagerkvist's novel, it had a quality rare in Biblical pictures – I can only call it domesticity. The story is a credible imagination of what happened to Barabbas after his release in place of Christ: as he returns to his old haunts, bewildered and relieved, and resumes his trade of banditry, which leads him to life imprisonment in the sulphur mines, he develops a resentment against his Saviour; this is fuelled by his encounters with Christian slaves, who regard him with a mixture of hatred

Portraits of Pilate: top left, Frank Thring in *Ben Hur*, and right, Richard Boone in *The Robe*; below, Basil Rathbone in *The Last Days of Pompeii*. Opposite, Arthur Kennedy, with Anthony Quinn as *Barabbas*.

and reverence. Finally, he becomes a gladiator – all Roman roads lead to the arena – and subsequently a Christian, suffering crucifixion. I'm not sure I believe the end, but for the rest, whether one cares for it as a film or not, it looks ordinary and everyday and real, which is probably as high a compliment as one can pay to a historical picture, and to Barabbas (Anthony Quinn), Richard Fleischer (director), and Mario Chiari (art director). The mines, the arena, and the catacombs are all well done, and Quinn is a past master at playing vulnerable brutes, but the virtue of *Barabbas* is its worm's-eye view; there is not much Roman grandeur, and a good deal of squalor, but it is a more believable image than many a glossy epic.

The reason for making *Salome* was presumably to give Rita Hayworth the chance to undress to music in the presence of Charles Laughton (Herod), which she does with considerable spirit as the climax to a glossy and expensive fiction based on the fragment of history described in the Gospels. According to Matthew and Mark, Salome asked for the head of John the Baptist at the instigation of her wicked mother, Herodias; the film, however, acquits Miss Hayworth of all blame, laying the guilt squarely on Judith Anderson, and inventing a love affair between Salome and a young Roman officer (Stewart Granger) who is a secret Christian and friend of the Baptist (played with authority by Alan Badel). Dancing and decapitation apart, it is not a memorable film, and ends with the lovers united and attending the Sermon on the Mount; in fact, according to

Rita Hayworth dances before Herod in *Salome*.

Josephus, Salome married not a Roman but two members of her own family, Philip the Tetrarch and Aristobulus.

So much for the Early Christians as seen through the eyes of Hollywood; their monopoly of Roman films is almost complete, but not quite. Two major productions set their sights outside the era, and one was at least a qualified historical success.

A slight mystery about *Spartacus* is why it was not made until 1960. As a story of revolt against tyranny it would seem to be a natural for the cinema, and I can only assume that the political flavour clinging (quite unjustly) to the man himself, led the moguls of old Hollywood – assuming they had ever heard of him – to regard him in the same light as did the Roman Senate in 73 BC: as a dangerous subversive to be buried as quickly as possible.

He was, apparently, an enslaved Thracian bandit who led

a revolt of gladiators at Capua, raised a slave army, and held Rome at defiance for two years, during which he thrashed several armies, captured cities, overran great areas, and even threatened Rome itself. Finally he was defeated and killed, and his followers crucified by the thousands. In modern times he has occasionally been hailed as an early personification of the political Left, a symbol of popular revolt against authority. At least three major novels have been written about him – by J. Leslie Mitchell, Arthur Koestler, and Howard Fast – and depending on one's theory of history, it is possible to interpret him as the first red-banner revolutionary.

This, in fact, is nonsense. He was an illiterate peasant, not a political theorist, or even an opponent of institutional slavery;

his fight for freedom was personal and natural, and far from trying to conquer Rome (which he might, conceivably, have done) his chief aim was to get himself and his followers out of Italy. At one point he made for the Alps; at another, he tried to ship his huge following overseas; a rebel he was, but not a revolutionary. And he was, incidentally, one of the great battlefield generals; that is the real mystery.

The film, obviously, cannot plumb it. Folk like Spartacus are not to be understood. He had a genius which enabled him to organize and hold together and transport a great slave army and its families, and at the same time outgeneral and outfight the greatest power in the world in its own heartland; there has never been anything like him. All a film

can do is try to imagine what he was like, and how he did it, and this Stanley Kubrick and Kirk Douglas achieved as well, probably, as could be. Dalton Trumbo's script, necessarily embroidering history and Fast's novel, shows Spartacus (Douglas) in the gladiatorial school of Batiatus (Peter Ustinov), falling in love with a slave-girl (Jean Simmons), and rebelling after a private games staged for Crassus (Laurence Olivier), the general who did, in the end, put down the revolt. There is an accurate, if condensed account, of the slaves' campaign and their betrayal by the pirates who had agreed to carry them out of Italy. Other strands of plot involve Tony Curtis, as an escaped slave, and Charles Laughton as a Roman politician who arranges the escape of

Secutor versus retiarius in the arena: Spartacus (Kirk Douglas) in action against Draba the Nubian (Woody Strode) in *Spartacus*.

"Ave, Imperator, morituri te salutamus!": gladiators in action in Richard Fleischer's *Barabbas.*

Spartacus's wife and baby after the gladiator's crucifixion.

The film makes the point that Spartacus as an idea was even more dangerous than the man himself, the battle scenes are adequate (though I would think the slave army was a good deal more disciplined than it looks here), Douglas is a credible Spartacus, Laurence Olivier a repellent Crassus, and Ustinov and Laughton together are a delight to watch.

There is little delight in *The Fall of the Roman Empire* apart from two of its sets; the enormous fortifications on the Danube frontier, and the reconstruction of the Forum, said to be the largest film set ever built. It looks it; I would not be surprised if it were bigger than the original. The story behind the film's daunting title bears little relation, so far as I can see, to real events in the last days (*c.* AD 180) of the Emperor Marcus Aurelius and the subsequent reign of his abominable son Commodus, which is a pity, for Commodus had every bit as much star quality as Nero or Caligula. He was said to be the handsomest and strongest man of his day, a debauched and bloodthirsty tyrant who advertised himself as Hercules reincarnated, and was probably the most successful gladiator of all time, with 735 victories to his credit. Rigging has been suggested. But of this nothing is seen in the film, which is factual insofar as it shows Aurelius (Alec Guinness) as wise, good, worried, and dying in an outpost of empire (possibly by poison, as in the film, possibly from natural causes). Thereafter Commodus (Christopher Plummer) shows tyrannical tendencies which alarm the dead Aurelius's protégé Livius (Stephen Boyd) who is in love with Commodus's sister Lucilla (Sophia Loren) whom Commodus marries off to an Eastern monarch (Omar Sharif). Confusion ensues, in my mind at least, as Livius, prompted by a saintly slave (James Mason), promotes the idea of the Roman Empire as a sort of universal brotherhood of peace-lovers; the talk is endless, and there are ambushes, and troop decimations, and high-speed chariot crashes, and massacres of Germans, and battles with Parthians, and the mass burning of more Germans, and a ridiculous spear-duel between Livius and Commodus (in the Forum, of all places), which ends with Commodus dead and Livius nobly refusing the imperial crown. After which the empire presumably starts falling, for several centuries.

Gibbon, in his ignorance, knew little of all this; his famous history does suggest that Commodus's reign marked the beginning of Rome's decline, but, unlike Livius, he understood the dangers of integrating alien subjects into the imperial system. He would have been hard put to it to recognize in the dewy-eyed Miss Loren, yearning chastely for Stephen Boyd, the real Lucilla, a murderous adultress who tried to assassinate her own brother. Nor would he have been impressed by the film's climactic duel: in fact, Commodus was stupefied with poison by his mistress and then strangled by a professional wrestler (I fully expected Anthony Quayle, playing a gladiator, to be assigned this role, but he turned out to be Commodus's real father – which, historically, may be true – and was stabbed for his pains and thrown into a bath.)

One thing the film does achieve: in the sheer size of its sets and its parade of foreign monarchs, it reminds us of what a mighty power Rome was at its height, and what it did for civilisation. It was not all gladiators and persecuted Christians, or mad emperors and their lecherous consorts, as one might be tempted to believe from Hollywood's versions. Still, imperfect as they are, they have been well worth while, and not only in terms of box-office returns.

THE SECOND AGE
Knights & Barbarians

Kirk Douglas and his gangers in *The Vikings*. Previous page, Charlton Heston in *El Cid*.

Knights and Barbarians

Hollywood, like God and His angels, took little notice of the Dark Ages. After the Technicolored lights of Rome went out there was a gap of almost a thousand years which the cameras barely touched, before the next Age of cinema. This is not surprising; the intervening centuries are unfamiliar ground to all but the specialists, with few of those instantly recognizable historic symbols which the cinema requires. But one at least there is which Hollywood has presented with style and authenticity – the dragon-headed longship surging out of the mist to pour its helmeted berserkers into the camera, flourishing their axes as they storm ashore in cross-gartered fury, while tonsured priests, peasants, and livestock scatter and take to the hills.

There have been three films about the Norse sea-rovers, and one of them ought to be shown regularly to British school children as a fine image of the distant past. *The Vikings* is what a historical epic should be: an excellent film in its own right, and a striking evocation of period. It is fiction against a carefully researched historic background, shot wherever possible in the proper locations, and presented with feeling for its subject.

The story concerns the sons of a hairy old ganger chief (Ernest Borgnine). One is his acknowledged heir and lieutenant (Kirk Douglas, who was born to play a Viking); the other (Tony Curtis) is the unsuspected result of the old chief's passing enthusiasm for a Northumbrian queen encountered on a raid. In the natural course of historical fiction Curtis becomes his brother's slave, there is bitter rivalry, a beautiful princess (Janet Leigh), an evil Northumbrian monarch (Frank Thring), and any amount of exciting and sometimes brutal action (Borgnine goes to the dogs, literally) which is so well handled that it is rather less gruesome than many TV news bulletins and medical programmes.

All of which matters nothing beside the film's atmospheric quality: it is the North on film, rough and cold and raw and beautiful to see, the longships gliding in sunlit triumph up magnificent fiords or slipping away into clammy mist, the gangers carousing in the coarse splendour of their hall, the minute detail of costume and weapon and custom, the triskelion shields advancing over dune and promontory, the axes whirling away and thudding into a raised drawbridge to make a ladder into a besieged fortress – among them Fleischer and Jack Cardiff and their artists and researchers have managed to conjure memories of Beowulf and the sagas; there is a fine fury about the action sequences, the playing is robust, and the whole thing looks and sounds as though it might well have happened around Lindisfarne a thousand years ago.

The Vikings might well be the last word on the subject; *The Long Ships*, with Richard Widmark and Sidney Poitier encountering a barbarian queen (Rosanna Schiaffino) who disposes of delinquents by dropping them on an enormous razor-blade, is useful only as a reminder that the Vikings ranged as far as Africa. They also penetrated Russia and the Orient, and were the first to cross to America, which is the theme of *The Norseman*, a film which I almost hesitate to mention.

It is, on the face of it, a run-of-the-mill adventure about a party of Vikings reaching the shores of Vinland in search of comrades who prove to have been captured by Indians and must be rescued. There is an awful, unnecessary commentary, some of the acting is fearful, and the script often invites derision – as when a hairy Norse warrior, landing in North

America *c.* 1006, reports glumly: "No sign of civilisation." It could be dismissed as cheap hokum, except that now and then it catches the attention with a vivid image – the vast, empty coast with the little longship lying off, and the Norsemen slowly wading through the surf to a new shore; or again, the longship cruising warily up a forest river, the rowers listening to the bird cries in the solitude. Perhaps that is exactly how it was when the first Europeans set foot in the New World; just now and then I found myself convinced. The film features Lee Majors, Mel Ferrer and others, including Cornel Wilde, who took history seriously; it has been worse served than by *The Norseman*, with all its faults.

The Vikings have almost had the Dark Ages to themselves, but not quite. Among all those waves of Vandals, Visigoths, Ostrogoths and other barbarians who invaded the Roman Empire there was one Scythian chief whose fame the film industry could not overlook, Attila, King of the Huns, who in the middle of the fifth century conquered Central Europe from the Caspian to the North Sea, with such slaughter and devastation that he became known as the Scourge of God. He invaded France in 451, but was defeated near Troyes in one of the decisive battles of history by the Roman commander Aetius in alliance with the Visigoths. In the following year he stormed into Northern Italy, sacking Milan, Padua and Verona, and demanding marriage with Honoria, sister of the Western Emperor Valentinian, and the surrender of half the imperial provinces, and these are the events dealt with in *Attila the Hun*, an elaborately costumed but not very exciting epic in which Anthony Quinn strides about truculently in leather and hairy boots, looking not at all like Attila, whom Gibbon describes as "scarcely human", with a flat nose, small eyes, and a squat body "of disproportioned form".

In this version Aetius (Henri Vidal) leads an embassy to the Huns' joint kings, Attila and his brother Bleda, who complain of Roman desecration of Hun graves and demand tribute and the release of hostages; Bleda is pacific, but Attila is obviously spoiling for a fight. He gets his chance when

Honoria (Sophia Loren), having failed to seduce Aetius into supplanting her effete brother, Valentinian, offers herself and half the empire to Attila (which Gibbon primly describes as an "indecent advance"). Attila, having disposed of his brother and declared, "Today the Romans, tomorrow the world", descends on Italy, slaughtering legions and crucifying bishops, but his advance is checked by the appearance of Pope Leo at the head of a Christian procession; they meet in midstream on the river Mincio, the pontiff mildly asks him to withdraw, and Attila, for no obvious reason, complies.

Not quite according to Gibbon, but still formidable: Anthony Quinn as *Attila the Hun*.

This would seem unlikely if it were not true; Attila did retreat, and this was hailed as a miracle, although disease among the Huns and famine in Italy may have been as influential as the papal persuasion. Gibbon suggests the invaders had been laid low by Italian cooking. In the film, Honoria meets with a gory death; in fact she perished in prison. Within a year of leaving Italy, Attila died of a burst blood vessel while on honeymoon with the latest of his numerous wives. Indirectly, the arch-destroyer was a great patron of the arts, for refugees from his Italian invasion fled to neighbouring islands, which later became the Republic of Venice.

Attila rides again in *Sign of the Pagan*, noteworthy for an admirable performance by Jack Palance; his Scythian is a thinking savage, philosophical and murderous by turns, and no less convincing for that. The film concentrates on his bullying of the other (Eastern) Roman Empire, ruled by the

Jack Palance in *Sign of the Pagan.*

incompetent Theodosius and his spirited sister Pulcheria – the first woman, Gibbon tells us, to be accepted as a sovereign by the Romans. There is a heroic centurion of humble origins, Marcian (Jeff Chandler), who falls foul of Attila, arouses the interest of the Hun's unruly daughter (Rita Gam), woos and wins Pulcheria (Ludmilla Tcherina), and organises resistance to the barbarian incursion – some of which is historically true, give or take the usual dramatic embroidery. The film has been dismissed as period horse opera, and indeed it is not short of rousing action, but it has fine images of the Huns swaggering and rioting at the Roman court, dialogue which is nicely formal without being stilted, some depth to its characters, is well played by its principals, and gives a believable impression of its period.

There are liberties: Marcian was considerably older than Jeff Chandler, Pulcheria's attachment to him was political rather than romantic, and while, as already noted, Attila expired from the attentions of his wife, Ildico, there is no evidence that she knifed him. The meeting with Pope Leo (Moroni Olsen in good hectoring form) is given an interesting twist with the suggestion that Attila retreated in superstitious awe of the Christian God.

Outside the Dark Ages, in distance if not in time, the Abbasid Dynasty of Persian Caliphs were ruling in Baghdad, and that is all the excuse I need for including, as historical films, all those splendid Arabian Nights fantasies, and especially *The Thief of Bagdad*. If anyone objects, I am prepared to identify the film's young ruler, Ahmed (John Justin), with any one of the four Ahmeds who reigned between 862 and 940, and defy them to prove me wrong.

The 1940 *Thief* is, for me, the most brilliant fairytale ever put on the screen. Despite the fact that the war caused its production to be split between Denham and California, that its romantic leads, Justin and June Duprez, were comparative unknowns,[1] and that the film itself is told partly in bewildering flashback, it succeeded beyond even Korda's dreams. The

1 The original choices were Jon Hall and Vivien Leigh.

Sabu underfoot in *The Thief of Bagdad*.

simple story of how Ahmed is deposed and magically blinded by the wicked Vizier, Jafar (Conrad Veidt), but regains his throne and the Princess with the aid of the little thief, Abu (Sabu, who spends part of the film in the shape of a dog), is the vehicle for a succession of dazzling scenes and special effects – the flying horse; the Genie (Rex Ingram) emerging from his bottle and flying Abu over the roof of the world; the Silver Maid, a many-armed mechanical toy which stabs as it embraces; the Temple of the Goddess of the All-Seeing Eye; the giant spider with which Abu battles on an enormous web; the flying carpet; even the un-magical sets and scenes of Basra harbour, the Princess's garden, the Sultan's toy collection, and the streets and bazaars of Baghdad have been designed with a care and imagination that make the film a visual transportation into the Thousand and One Nights. The script, by Miles Malleson (who plays the Princess's puffing little father) and Lajos Biro, with song lyrics from Sir Robert Vansittart the diplomat, is a piece of poetry, and Miklos Rozsa's music was perhaps the best of his distinguished film career. If there is a scene to remember it is the little thief cowering under the Genie's huge horny foot, but really it is all unforgettable.

There were many successors in the next decade, but none matched the inventive spectacle of *The Thief of Bagdad*, and only *Arabian Nights* rose above the ordinary. It plundered its source material for names, if nothing else, with Jon Hall as Harun al-Raschid feuding with his wicked brother Kamar el-Zaman (Leif Erickson), and Sinbad (Shemp Howard) and Aladdin (John Qualen) lending support; Maria Montez and Sabu were the co-stars, Edgar Barrier was an impassive villain, and a Turkish supporting player, Turhan Bey, emerged briefly as a matinée idol of the forties.

However, all these Vikings, Huns, Caliphs, genies, and dancing girls are only the prologue to Hollywood's Second Age, which begins in earnest around AD 1000, and is a vague period in which history and legend co-exist and frequently mingle; it can be called medieval, because while it contains films of folk myths from an earlier time, they are presented in the costumes and atmosphere of the Middle Ages; a film publicist, if cornered, might define it uneasily as the time when people wore armour, and if he were an American he might quote the title of a book once popular on his side of the Atlantic, *When Knighthood Was In Flower*.

He would quote it without enthusiasm, because while this Age contains one or two magnificent motion pictures, it is not a period in which the film industry has ever really been at home. Like the general public, it probably finds the Middle Ages more remote, in a spiritual sense, than the Classical World of a millennium earlier; thanks to its authors, we seem to be closer to the people of Imperial Rome than to our medieval ancestors; there is enough intimate history of the Caesars and their people for us to be able to see them as not very different from ourselves, and identify with them. It is hard to do this with the twelfth century, when the picture is not so clear, and there is simply less personal information to help us. Perhaps it is because of this, as much as because of the chivalric ideal of the Middle Ages, and the semi-legendary nature of so many of its figures, that we tend to look at them through an almost romantic mist; no one could call the Romans even remotely romantic. They are real, and look real, thanks to their writers and artists (and Hollywood), in a sense that the medieval men and women, with their permanently stiff necks, do not.

To some extent, Hollywood has had to create the Middle Ages in its own image, and has not been helped by the fact that men in armour are difficult to take seriously. They not only look clumsy and overdressed, clanking about and inviting ribaldries about spanners and tin-openers, they seldom sound right either. This is largely the fault of Sir Walter Scott, who imposed his own style of "Look-for-the-knight-of-the-Fetterlock-fair-Rebecca" dialogue on the Age of Chivalry, setting a pattern which survived well into talking pictures; in the 1950s they were still "prithee-my-liege"-ing away because it was the traditional thing to do, and audiences were supposed to expect it. Perhaps they did; it may be that the popular conception of the knightly ideal and its artificial code of manners and standards, required an equally artificial style of speech. Of late the chivalric aspect has been less in evidence, and on their rare appearances medieval characters have spoken in a more modern idiom (sometimes they have been downright chatty, as in *The Lion in Winter*), but old ways die hard, and a feeling persists that a face peering out from beneath a raised visor should talk in a way to match the armour. And that takes careful handling by the writer, and much style in the performer. Indeed, only one writer has really conquered this period for the cinema, and that is Shakespeare.

His films might seem to deserve a category of their own, but there is no point in subdividing an Age whose pictures come from so many sources: European and "barbarian" history, classic novels and plays, folk-lore, and semi-legend. There are even one or two films which do not belong in this Age at all, but are closer to it than to any other in spirit; if there is a common characteristic throughout, it may be called heroic violence – a reflection of the temper of the times.

First, then, to the armourer's, and a suspicion of mine that however faithful the research, costumes, weaponry, and the like, no representation of medieval combat can give us a wholly accurate impression of what it was really like. We may read Froissart, and try to picture it, or watch Charlton Heston and Christopher Rhodes hacking away at each other, and believe it, but I would still like to see two modern armies clad in plate and mail, the cavalry cap-à-pie on shire horses, and equipped with the best our museums could provide, and let them get on with it. I have a notion that within fifteen minutes they would all be prostrate, yet this, presumably, did not happen at Crécy or Bannockburn or Agincourt. We know that only a small proportion of medieval fighters wore full armour, but they are the ones I am concerned with, and I must suppose either that combat took place in slow motion or, more probably, that there was a technique to wearing and moving in armour that has been lost. I also suspect, in the face of scholarly opinion, that our ancestors, whatever their stature, were stronger than we are, and anyone who doubts this will oblige me by going to Glasgow's Kelvingrove Museum and lifting, let alone wielding, one of the two-handed claymores on display there.

But whatever reservations we may have about paladins capering nimbly across our screen in plastic and textile, they look authentic; their appearance probably serves history well enough. And in presenting them on the screen, Hollywood has tried, even in its least serious entertainments, to live up to an ideal. The Age of Chivalry was a savage time of sanctified slaughter when the knightly code of honour and service and devotion was frequently forgotten (we know that even *preux chevaliers* like Bertrand du Guesclin, Robert Bruce, and the Cid could behave barbarously on occasion), but it existed, and was a model for the ages. Film-makers have tried to reflect it, seriously, in pictures like *El Cid*, and it has been duly honoured in those happier pageants in which the Knights of Culver City and Shepperton, with Robert Taylor at their head, rode forth as the paladins of Ava Gardner, Kay Kendall, and Joan Fontaine. Even false knights like George Sanders were touched by it – indeed, the only cinema knight I can think of

A pride of Lionhearts; from left, Richard I, Ian Hunter (in *The Adventures of Robin Hood*), Richard Harris (*Robin and Marian*) and opposite . . .

who could be called truly outlandish was Duncan Lamont, as de la Marck "the Beast of the Ardennes", in *Quentin Durward*, and he merely enabled Taylor to shine more brightly by comparison.

The spirit has been followed, but seldom the letter. In all its excursions into the lists, Hollywood has hardly ever tried to deal with straight history; the concentration has been on folk-tale and legend, and on the semi-historical works of Shakespeare and Scott. This is perhaps as well; one may regret that Chandos and Bayard have never cantered across the screen, that Bruce has never sat his pony waiting for Bohun, or that Hereward has never defied the Normans in the Fens, but the treatment of Richard Lionheart in leading roles suggests that these other heroes may be better left alone. He has done well enough in supporting parts, usually arriving back from the Crusades just in time to put the royal seal of approval on the triumph of Robin Hood or Ivanhoe over the usurping Prince John. These brief appearances in various

costume adventures have correctly established Richard as a brawny, neglectful monarch who won fame as a leader in Palestine (although he never reached Jerusalem), made peace with Saladin, was held prisoner in Austria and ransomed despite his brother's efforts to prevent it, and magnanimously forgave John for his treachery. So far so good; his guest appearances have been in the robust figures of Ian Hunter, Norman Wooland, George Sanders, Anthony Hopkins, Richard Harris, and others including even Frankie Howerd, but the one film fully devoted to him, *The Crusades*, was an artistic and historic disaster.

It is DeMille at his worst, a confused romantic mess of a film ostensibly trying to condense into two hours the essence of a chapter of human history which lasted two centuries and shaped the future of Europe – DeMille called it "telescoping history". In his version, the Saracens invade the Holy Land, desecrating crosses, burning books, and selling Ann Sheridan into slavery; Aubrey Smith, as a Peter the Hermit figure, rouses

... Henry Wilcoxon astonished as Saladin (Ian Keith) cuts a veil in two in *The Crusades* ...

... and George Sanders with a less demonstrative Saladin (Rex Harrison) and Laurence Harvey in *King Richard and the Crusaders.*

the Christian monarchs, including Richard (Henry Wilcoxon), who goes crusading to avoid wedlock but subsequently marries Berengaria of Navarre (Loretta Young). There is much horseplay, hearty chorus work (mostly by Alan Hale as a dreadful Blondel), a tolerable assault on the walls of Acre, and some real comic-strip nonsense in which Saladin falls in love with Berengaria, and Richard, if I was not deceived, becomes a convinced Christian. DeMille hoped the film would give an idea of what the Crusades were about; since it ignores the economic and social causes (to say nothing of the effects) and concentrates on religious emotion, love interest, historical fiction, and Wilcoxon scowling (possibly at the script), it was a misplaced optimism. Mischa Auer plays a monk.

At that, it was marginally better than *King Richard and the Crusaders*, which made free with Scott's *The Talisman* and placed the mantle of Coeur-de-Lion on George Sanders.

Rex Harrison gave Saladin an Oriental charm, Laurence Harvey attempted a Scots accent as a crusading knight, and Virginia Mayo, immaculately gowned and made-up, spoke the immortal line "War! War! That's all you think about, Dick Plantagenet!" After which we can only abandon the Holy Land to the infidel and examine the film treatment of another real and remarkable figure, Joan, Maid of Orléans.

She is an impossible subject, really: fiction would not dare invent an illiterate peasant girl who, instructed by divine voices, prevailed on the rulers and generals of France to let her rally her country's armies and inspire them to a series of astonishing victories. But she did, and all a film can do is try to make her credible. Most reviewers were bored by *Joan of Arc*; perhaps my tolerance was greater because I was content to see the story truly and simply told – of the critic who thought it "childishly oversimplified" I can only say that he must have historical sources denied to me. It is a fair presentation of known facts, well dramatised, beautifully photographed in rather over-luminous colours, and well acted. Ingrid Bergman emerges with credit from the daunting task of playing a character who is simply not to be understood, and Jose Ferrer is a superb Dauphin. The hand-to-hand fighting on the walls of Orléans is bloody and convincing, and the trial, recantation, and martyrdom are faithful to historical accounts of what was, by any standards, as shameful a judicial murder as even the Middle Ages can show – redeemed only by the act of the English soldier who handed her a makeshift cross at the stake, an incident from childhood memory which the films shows. It may not be the most gripping two and a half hours we have spent in a cinema, but it is Joan of Arc.

She has received more scrupulous treatment than another celebrated medieval saint, Thomas à Becket, that accomplished knight, diplomat, courtier and sophisticate who became chancellor and Archbishop of Canterbury, enraged Henry II by championing the Church against the crown, and was murdered, if not by the king's command, at least in accordance

Above, Ingrid Bergman as *Joan of Arc*. Below, left, Henry II, and right, Peter O'Toole as Henry with Richard Burton as *Becket*.

Family Christmas with the Plantagenets in the *Lion in Winter*: Henry II (Peter O'Toole), seated centre, with his queen, Eleanor of Aquitaine (Katharine Hepburn) standing right. Philip of France (Timothy Dalton) stands behind Henry, and Richard, later Lionheart (Anthony Hopkins) is seated left.

and while he was the first native-born "Englishman" since the Conquest to attain supreme office, he did not have to overcome any disadvantage of birth to do it. It is a pity the Saxon myth was introduced; it was not necessary in an otherwise good and literate film whose most memorable moment is a proper image of history, with the defenceless Becket being cut down by Percy Herbert and others.

Becket was almost the least of Henry II's problems; he was also plagued by family difficulties which bear some resemblance to soap opera of the Dallas–Dynasty variety, and this has done his screen image no service. His wife was the spirited and intelligent Eleanor of Aquitaine, a lady of free and easy disposition who had accompanied a previous husband, Louis VII of France, on a Crusade, taking with her an armed female bodyguard; after her divorce from Louis she bore Henry a remarkable family, including Coeur-de-Lion and Prince John, whose quarrels and rebellions against their father at Eleanor's instigation eventually brought his grey hairs in sorrow to the grave. In her defence it may be said that Henry was neither a faithful nor considerate husband; he imprisoned her for sixteen years.

Some of this may be gathered from *The Lion in Winter*, a domestic imagination of a family Christmas with Henry and Eleanor (Katharine Hepburn) in which they and their sons wrangle in twentieth-century language. In its way, it is possibly a fair impression of affairs *chez Plantagenet*, the costumes are excellent, and one realises how extremely cold and uncomfortable castle life must have been. Peter O'Toole again plays Henry, and as in *Becket* comes across as a clever, unprincipled, sorely tried monarch. In neither film does the script allow him to play Henry in full, as the capable and enlightened ruler that he was.

What Shakespeare might have done with Becket is an interesting speculation; we know the hatchet job he performed on Joan of Arc, and there are those who consider it mild compared with his treatment of Richard III – my own view is that someone put those bodies under the stairs, and who stood to

with his majesty's apparent wish. *Becket*, a screen adaptation of Anouilh's play, was a prestigious film, and charted fairly enough the stormy relationship of Henry (Peter O'Toole) and his erstwhile friend and confidant Becket (Richard Burton); unfortunately it plays fast and loose with history by suggesting that a vital factor was Becket's position as a Saxon upstart in a Norman hierarchy (Saxon nationalism always makes for good racial-social confrontation). In fact, Becket was a full-blooded Norman, of parents both born in France, profit thereby? But whatever use he made of history, he coloured his countrymen's view of it as no other writer except Scott has done; if he distorted and maligned on occasion, he also painted in true and imperishable colours, and never better than in that monumental play which Olivier turned into one of the cinema's enduring masterpieces, *Henry V*.

It is a matter of taste. For me, *Henry V* is the best film ever made, and the play, along with the preceding parts of *Henry IV*, the peak of Shakespeare's achievement. It stands alone as a study of men at war, and I believe only a soldier could have written it. Whether Shakespeare was ever in the army we do not know, but if he wasn't then he was an even greater genius than I have always thought him.

The film version of *Henry V* is better history than the play, with its added glimpse of the playhouse and players (an idea which the late Alan Dent, who worked on the screenplay, assured me was Olivier's alone). As to Agincourt, what happened on St Crispin's Day was that about 6000 English, exhausted and half-starved, found their way barred by 24,000 French, well-armed and strong in cavalry, who had forgotten the lessons of Crécy and Poitiers. Their advance was shot to pieces by the English long-bows, and their knights (many of whom fought on foot) were helpless against the more lightly armed archers at close quarters. So outnumbered were the English that Henry had all prisoners killed (something which Shakespeare tactfully omitted), and in half an hour it was over; 10,000 Frenchmen died, and a few hundred English. Cinema can give only an impression of such a battle, but Olivier's film caught the vital fact of Agincourt in one moment: that terrible whistling discharge of the English arrows which everyone remembers, and which is one of the great climaxes of motion pictures.

Praise is superfluous, but apart from Olivier's Henry, I would pick out Max Adrian's obnoxious Dauphin, Leo Genn's sardonic Constable, Robert Newton's magnificent blustering Pistol, and that eve-of-battle sequence which is without its like in literature: the French nobles, confident but subdued, talking curtly, hiding their nerves, fidgeting impatiently and in their boasting betraying the inevitable doubt; and the English trio of common soldiers, fed up and far from home, resigned, derisive, opinionated, their emotions open, waiting, steady – it is true. I've seen them. If there was a little collective award it should go to Genn, Adrian, Francis Lister, and Russell Thorndyke, and to Jimmy Hanley, Arthur Hambling, and Brian Nissen. And a permanent, all-time Oscar to the original scriptwriter.

Forty-five years later Kenneth Branagh, greatly daring, re-made *Henry V* to general critical acclaim. It was a more sombre production altogether than Olivier's, and for my money a worthy second best; Branagh is quoted as saying that he wanted to reclaim the play from jingoism, which I'd have thought an impossibility, given Shakespeare's text, but his film did record one important truth which Olivier's did not: Agincourt was fought not across a sun-kissed meadow, but in a muddy quagmire in which the armoured French were bogged down.

Bosworth Field was a much less satisfactory battle, at least from the point of view of Richard of Gloucester; one third of his army refused to advance, and another third joined the enemy, whereafter the King, in the historian's words, deliberately threw away his life. Olivier made the most of this in *Richard III*, expiring in a welter of ketchup at the end of a splendid screen version of the play, but I don't intend to tempt fate by discussing its claims to historical accuracy, except to say that whether Crookback Dick was a villain or not, Shakespeare's picture of a misshapen, hunch-backed monster with dragging foot is generally thought to be false. Richard's portraits show a normal, strong-featured, dour individual, somewhere between Olivier and Basil Rathbone, who played him in *The Tower of London*, a fine Gothic affair with Boris Karloff as Mord the Hangman. In *Richard III* it was Gielgud who went, in accordance with tradition, into the butt of malmsey; in *Tower of London* it is Vincent Price, and the film has a nice authentic piece of furniture which I have not seen screened elsewhere: a large enclosed pew in the centre of the room, designed for sitting out of those medieval draughts.

Macbeth has been filmed several times too often, with unhappy results; this might seem like an appropriate judgement to the original Macbeth, who was not nearly as black as Shakespeare painted him from Holinshed, who in turn was drawing on Scottish historians to whom Macbeth's intrusion in the royal line was an offence. He may well have killed Duncan, probably in battle, but he seems to have ruled acceptably for seventeen years before being deposed and killed in his turn – quite a normal reign for medieval Scotland. Orson Welles growled and brooded through the best-known film version, and convinced me yet again that (with the exception of the Ian Cuthbertson–Anne Kristen production at Glasgow Citizens' years ago) *Macbeth* is for reading, not watching.

Contemporary with Macbeth was another medieval man of action, almost unknown to the English-speaking world until Samuel Bronston made him the subject of a three-hour epic which has a strong claim to eminence among films of the Middle Ages. Ruy de Bivar, the Spanish champion known as El Cid, is a mixture of truth and legend; Cervantes observed that there was no reason to doubt his existence, but reason to doubt the feats attributed to him. The Cid is supposed to have killed his sweetheart's father for an insult offered to his family, won the city of Calahorra for Castile in a trial by combat against a knight of Aragon, and performed prodigies against the Moors, culminating in his capture of Valencia *c.* 1084. All this, and his service to various monarchs, the film relates in a great leisurely pageant which is unusual among costume films in paying as much heed to human psychology as to action, and in making credible the concept of the stainless knight. Charlton Heston is the personification of honour and duty and steadfastness to his lady Ximena (Sophia Loren); it rings true for the film, and may be just a little kind to the Cid of historic legend, who is said to have been twice married and to have marred his

The ultimate weapon of medieval warfare: English longbowmen at Agincourt in *Henry V.*

conquest of Valencia with ferocious massacre. The film ends with him, mortally wounded, insisting on being strapped into his saddle so that he may ride out and rout the enemy; the received story is that he died of grief and rage, after which the Moors recaptured Valencia.

It remains a worthy, if sombre, attempt to capture a legend and an ideal, and there are spectacular highlights, chiefly the trial by combat in which Heston and Christopher Rhodes seem to be genuinely trying to kill each other, the battles before Valencia in which Herbert Lom commands the Moors with ruthless efficiency, and a crunching broadsword fight

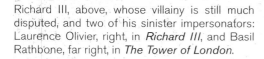

Richard III, above, whose villainy is still much disputed, and two of his sinister impersonators: Laurence Olivier, right, in *Richard III*, and Basil Rathbone, far right, in *The Tower of London*.

involving Andrew Cruickshank, in whom television buffs will recognise the staid and elderly Dr Cameron of *Dr Finlay's Casebook*.

El Cid takes its subject seriously; most knights-in-armour movies approach it with light-hearted energy. They are wise. Arthur of the Britons, the King Who Was and Will Be, is a folk-legend close to the heart of what T. H. White called "the matter of Britain", but his countrymen prefer him clanging about with Excalibur in the garb of the fourteenth century, several hundred years after his real time, supposing he ever existed. Legends are precious things, to be treated with as much reverence as "real" history, of which they are a vital part, which is why I am content that Arthur should appear as he does in *Knights of the Round Table*. It is not adult enter-

tainment, but simple schoolroom stuff, in brilliant colours and fairytale costumes, with gallant knights like Lancelot (Robert Taylor, naturally) and Arthur (Mel Ferrer), and the fairest of ladies, Queen Guinevere (Ava Gardner), Elaine (Maureen Swanson), and the designing Morgan Le Fay (Anne Crawford). Merlin and the sinister Mordred could only be played by Felix Aylmer and Stanley Baker, the Round Table is established, the Green Knight (Niall McGinnis) overcome, the Picts (led by Ralph Truman with a thistle on his surcoat) vanquished, Arthur dies in his last battle, and the script resounds with cries of "Pursue and slay!" "The day is ours!" and "Let him be, you rattlepate!" My only objections are to the poisoning of Merlin (who surely ended up in a tree with a wood-nymph?), the strictly chaste love affair of

Lancelot and Guinevere, and the offhanded way in which Lancelot (not Bedivere) tosses Excalibur into the sea. Not even into a lake, and no supernatural hand, clothed in white samite, mystic, wonderful, to catch it either.

This, and other armoured epics, owed much to Robert Taylor, who was not an obvious costume player. As a clean-cut heart-throb of the late thirties he seemed to belong in slacks and sports jacket, but while he was no Flynn or Power or Fairbanks when it came to swashbuckling, he had something they lacked, an air of stern but good-natured gentlemanliness. It seemed to fit him exactly for the tales of Walter Scott, and it is pleasant to think that he brought something of the great enchanter's work to millions who would never have ploughed through the originals.

Ivanhoe is possibly Scott's most popular book, and the film holds to it, more or less, with Taylor fully stretched to keep the fair Rowena (Joan Fontaine) and the beauteous Rebecca (Elizabeth Taylor) out of the lustful clutches of Malvoisin (Robert Douglas) and Bois-Gilbert (George Sanders). Scott's other characters are given a fair run, notably Isaac of York (Felix Aylmer), Wamba the Jester (Emlyn Williams), and Cedric the Saxon (Finlay Currie), the castle of Torquilstone is energetically besieged, and besides sundry jousts there is a most realistic duel between Ivanhoe and Bois-Gilbert to decide whether Rebecca is burned as a witch. Anyone interested in the technique of the medieval weapon known as the flail (a spiked ball and chain on a short handle) will find this scene illuminating.

Quentin Durward is a Scottish mercenary at the court of Louis XI (Robert Morley), whose intrigues against Charles the Bold of Burgundy (Alec Clunes) are a constant trial to the wealthy heiress Lady Isabelle (Kay Kendall), whom Durward (Taylor) shepherds through ambush, assault, pursuits, and burning churches. There is an original duel between our hero and the renegade de la Marck (Duncan Lamont) in which they swing resoundingly on bell-ropes over a sea of flame, but the main historical interest is in Robert Morley's portrayal of

Robert and Elizabeth Taylor in *Ivanhoe*.

Louis, that cunning little spider of a king whose talent for corruption, treachery, and mischief so enlivened fifteenth-century French politics. He was quite as dishonest, if not so genial and corpulent, as Morley's monarch, and has been portrayed more realistically by Basil Rathbone (*If I Were King*), Walter Hampden (*The Vagabond King*), and Harry Davenport (*The Hunchback of Notre Dame*).

This last production, one of many versions of Hugo's novel, was a spectacular success in 1939, and deserved to be. It had a memorable, repulsive, and touching performance by Laughton, grotesquely made up as Quasimodo, established Maureen O'Hara (Esmeralda) and Edmond O'Brien (Gringoire) in Hollywood, and was highly praised in all its aspects, not least for its reconstruction of medieval Paris. How accurate this was I cannot say, but it looked superb, with its squalid streets, teeming crowds, ragged citizenry, and a wonderfully photographed Court of Miracles (Thomas Mitchell presiding); it convinced me that I was seeing the Middle Ages, and one cannot ask more than that.

If I were drawing up a list of historical masterpieces for this Age, I would place *Henry V* first and *Hunchback* third. In second place is a near-perfect motion picture, quite the best evocation of a folk legend ever put on the screen, *The Adventures of Robin Hood*. I call it near-perfect because I cannot think of any film which realised so well what its makers were trying to do, or so satisfied the audience's expectation. For this simply *is* Robin Hood of the ballads and childhood lore and the world's imagination. For once history does not matter. Whether, as seems probable, he was in reality a hedge-robber in Barnsdale, or a yeoman in the royal service, or a mixture of Robin Goodfellow and that Cloudsley of Cumberland who supposedly shot an apple from his son's head in the presence of Edward III (a common feat in Northern folklore), or a wandering Scottish fugitive – none of this is important. The legend is what counts, and it was the legend that Warner Brothers brought to life.

They were lucky in their players – Flynn with his impudent swagger, athletic grace, and matchless style; Rathbone's

Louis XI of France, centre, flanked by Harry Davenport in *The Hunchback of Notre Dame*, left, and Basil Rathbone in *If I Were King*.

The legend brought to life: Olivia de Havilland and Errol Flynn as Maid Marian and Robin Hood.

Gisborne like a great black cat; Claude Rains all silky villainy; Olivia de Havilland a Maid Marian out of fairytale; Alan Hale's roaring Little John, Eugene Pallette's mountainous Friar Tuck, Ian Hunter's commanding King Richard, and Melville Cooper's bombastic Sheriff. Those were the days when Technicolor was like rich velvet, Erich Wolfgang Korngold was composing heroic scores, and scriptwriters (Seton Miller and Norman Reilly Raine) knew good material when they saw it: Little John on the bridge, Friar Tuck and the river crossing, the archery contest, the escape from the scaffold, the Bishop despoiled, the meeting with King

Richard (but without the exchange of buffets, which was shot but dropped from the finished film), the arrows hissing like angry wasps, the rich robbed and the poor fed, the Merry Men uproarious in the greenwood – it was the story as everyone knew it, with dialogue to match: "This saucy fellow!" "By St Ambrose, a miracle!" "This sweet band of cutthroats", Robin and Gisborne exchanging menaces: "What's the matter, Gisborne – run out of hangings?" "I know a ripe subject for one!" It is one of the few pictures which looks and sounds even better than it did when it first appeared; with luck it will last forever as an illustration of what was meant by Merrie England, and a reminder of the curious taste of the English-speaking people whose arch-hero was a robber, a good loser, and a kindly spirit.

The Adventures is the definitive screen Robin, but he and his sons (and one daughter) have appeared in innumerable versions, with Cornel Wilde, John Derek, Russell Hicks, Jon Hall, Sean Connery, Kevin Costner, Richard Todd, Richard Greene, et al. Prince John has been a common adversary, and while no one has come close to matching the debonair wickedness of Rains, one authentic touch was added in

Claude Rains, a memorable Prince John, and the original.

Rogues of Sherwood Forest when George Macready sealed, but did not sign, Magna Carta.

The remaining English medieval screen monarch was the most formidable of them all, Edward I, "Longshanks", self-styled Hammer of the Scots and the arch-villain (very properly) of *Braveheart*, which purports to tell the story of the great Scottish patriot, William Wallace, and commits as many historical errors as can well be contained in 170 minutes. True, it does show Wallace as the dauntless leader of popular resistance to English occupation in the 1290s, the champion who inspired the war of independence which culminated in the English rout at Bannockburn, but in the process it gives a misleading picture of the man and his background, distorts history shamelessly and often risibly, and presents the knightly hero as an unkempt peasant. A footnote to the film admits that "certain incidents portrayed have been dramatised"; it would have been fairer to say that they have been thoroughly misrepresented.

Reliable information about Wallace is limited, but we know enough from Blind Harry and others to have an image of the real man, and he does not appear in *Braveheart*. For one thing, he was a Lowlander born and bred, of gentle though not noble parents, his father a landholder who was probably a knight, his mother a knight's daughter. The film depicts him ludicrously as a Highlander, occupying a squalid croft and running about the glens in a kilt, a garment as appropriate to Wallace as a grass skirt. In battle, his face is painted blue, which prompts the thought that the film-makers may have envisaged him as an early Rangers supporter, a theory reinforced by Mel Gibson's fine Drumchapel accent and the behaviour of his troops, who are straight from the Ibrox terracing – unlike the real Wallace's army, which was well organised and disciplined. It, too, was largely Lowland, but even at this date, apparently, the old Hollywood myth persists that all Scots must be kilt-swinging hairy savages – which some of them were, and still are, but not Sir William Wallace.

It is not Mel Gibson's fault that he looks not at all like

William Wallace, and opposite, Mel Gibson in *Braveheart*.

the Wallace so meticulously described by French contemporaries as being of massive stature (though possibly less than the six feet eleven inches quoted in Blind Harry), long and fair of face, with "burning brown" hair, full lips, and eyes "like diamonds full bright". Tartan nonsense apart, he plays him correctly as an implacable (and multi-lingual) foe of England whose rebellion may indeed have been triggered by the murder of his wife (or betrothed, or mistress), but not by the killing of his father, who was probably alive after Wallace took up arms in 1297. Thereafter his career was meteoric, reaching a climax with his brilliant victory at Stirling Bridge; he invaded Cumberland and Northumberland (but did not take York, as the film pretends, or any other English city), and was decisively beaten by Edward at Falkirk. He resigned his

guardianship of Scotland, visited France and possibly Rome, and was finally betrayed and executed in 1305.

The film follows this more or less, but with so many embroideries and falsifications that one ceases to take it seriously. Such small absurdities as the arrival of "the MacGregors from the next glen", or his army of Rab C. Nesbits raising their "kilts" at the English enemy, can be endured – but not the invented love-affair with Edward I's daughter-in-law, Isabella (who was an infant at the time, living in France), or the suggestion that Edward used her as a decoy, or that the future Edward II was an important figure at the time of Wallace's revolt (he was then thirteen and did not

marry Isabella until three years after Wallace's death), or that Bruce, who may have fought for Edward at Falkirk, contrived Wallace's escape after the battle, or that Bruce was an un-witting participant in Wallace's betrayal, or the classic howlers (put into Wallace's mouth) that Scotland had endured a hundred years of English rape, theft, and murder (the countries had been at peace for most of the previous century), and, if I heard aright, that Scotland had never been a free nation. Dramatisation indeed.

To do it justice, the film notes the hostility, sometimes amounting to treachery, which Wallace met with in the Scots nobles, and one cannot quarrel with Patrick McGoohan's fine performance as the iron King Edward – although whether he ever defenestrated a Piers Gaveston figure, or was the target of a murderous attack by his own son, I am inclined to doubt. Angus McFadyen's portrayal of Bruce is less convincing, mostly because it implies that he had a conscience. A hero Bruce certainly became, but he was also a shrewd and occasionally murderous opportunist. He died of leprosy, incidentally, but I don't know that his father, played by Ian Bannen, also suffered from the disease.

Braveheart's battles have been much praised, and are indeed authentically bloody, but they convey little idea of how Stirling Bridge and Falkirk were won and lost. This does less than justice to Wallace (an accomplished tactician whose development of the schiltroun was to pay its dividend at Bannockburn), if not to Edward, whose use of bowmen at the crucial moment did turn the tide at Falkirk. The large "foreign" contingent in the English army, by the way, was not Irish, but ten thousand Welshmen.

The film lingers over Wallace's hanging, drawing, and quartering, but even here there are added fantasies, with Isabella (Sophie Marceau) offering him a pain-killer in the condemned cell, and then gloatingly informing Edward, who is expiring offstage, that she is pregnant, presumably by Wallace. (In fact Edward died two years later, 300 miles away.) Bruce is among the gallows spectators, as is Wallace's Irish lieutenant (presumably inserted in the film with American audiences in mind).

Its cargo of historical nonsense aside, *Braveheart* is not a very good film, and perhaps the critic was right who suggested that it won its Oscar by being politically correct, anti-English, and far too long. The awful thing is that count-less millions, including some Scots even, will accept it as historic truth. Well, this Scot found it embarrassing and vaguely insulting – to history, to Scotland, and to William Wallace.

Edward I, in the properly tall and commanding person of Michael Rennie, makes an uncharacteristically kindly, even

sentimental appearance in *The Black Rose*, a lavish but tedious adventure yarn in which Tyrone Power and his bowman friend Jack Hawkins venture to the Orient and encounter Orson Welles intent on world conquest in a fur bonnet. Power returns to England with the secret of printing, a curva-ceous slave girl (Cecile Aubry), and gunpowder, which I should have thought Roger Bacon already knew about.

This was not Hollywood's first excursion to the ancient East: Gary Cooper had already visited the court of Kublai Khan, *c.* 1275, in *The Adventures of Marco Polo*, which took some liberties with the great Venetian's travels. More recently there has been a spectacular and almost equally romantic account of another visitor to Far Cathay – Kublai's grandfather, *Genghiz Khan*.

As played by Omar Sharif, the Mongol conqueror is a not uncivilised, wayward visionary, taken captive in childhood by a rival chief, Jamuga (Stephen Boyd), who dismembers Genghiz's father and keeps the lad in a wooden collar (inci-dents which have eluded the Khan's biographers). Genghiz escapes, and there is much kidnapping to and fro of the heroine (Francoise Dorleac) while he unites the Mongols (Telly Savalas and others) before travelling peacefully to China. There he lives at the court of the Emperor (Robert Morley in good Poo-Bah form) whom he eventually blows up in a firework display, the Mongol conquest of China and parts West is briskly covered, with the aid of narration, a resisting sultan (Eli Wallach) is disposed of, and in a final duel Jamuga is killed and Genghiz mortally wounded.

It is, admittedly, difficult to portray one of the most blood-thirsty monsters in history in his true colours, and still attract paying customers, but one does not need to present him quite so sympathetically, either. Genghiz Khan was a horror, admirable only as a military organiser; probably no one has ever mastered the art of enormous troop movement at speed as he did, or imposed such perfect discipline on an army; he may be called the inventor of blitzkrieg and total war. In brief, he united the Mongol hordes, conquered and slaugh-

Omar Sharif as Genghiz Khan, with appropriate horsetail banner, and Michael Hordern, left.

a bag of gold, in perfect safety.

None of this does the film really try to show. As a spectacle it is interesting, once one has got used to Michael Hordern going about in skins, the Chinese sequences please the eye, Stephen Boyd is a ruthless heavy, and James Mason gives a bravura performance as a courtly, lisping mandarin. Omar Sharif is sadly miscast; he does not look like a Mongol, let alone Genghiz Khan, who had reddish hair and grey-green eyes. Nor was the great warlord mortally wounded in a duel in his prime: he died in bed, aged seventy-five.

One cannot leave ancient history without acknowledging two comic asides; I could contend, seriously, that no survey of an Age is complete without an examination of what was thought to be funny about it, but *The Court Jester* and *Monty Python and the Holy Grail* need no such excuse; they stand, or fall about, on their own merits.

The Court Jester is the best fooling, when all is done, with Danny Kaye in brilliant form in Arthurian England, foiling a dithering Cecil Parker who has usurped the throne of a baby with a purple pimpernel on its left buttock. Glynis Johns is the Maid-Marian heroine, Angela Lansbury the fair princess with an iron streak, there are impostures, disguises, and splendid songs by Sylvia Fine and Sammy Cahn ("the flagon with the dragon," etc.), the pace is furious, the costumes and settings cheerful, and it is a very funny pantomime. Not the least of its pleasures is to see Basil Rathbone duelling away, as lithe and sinister as ever in his sixty-fourth year; as for Kaye, he is probably closer to the great fools like Kemp and Archie Armstrong than we realise.

After Monty Python the Arthurian legend will never be quite the same again – Graham Chapman seeking the Grail and answering fatuous riddles, the Knights jogging on foot or high-kicking in chorus, the anarcho-syndicalist peasantry, the death-dealing white rabbit, John Cleese in full armour spreadeagled against a police car . . . and for all its idiocy it has one enchanting piece of camera-work, the misty sunlit shot of Arthur's ship, straight out of heroic legend.

tered without mercy from the China Sea to the Caucasus, killing untold millions and devastating vast areas. He conquered half the known world, for no apparent reason except that it was there – lust for fame or power or territory does not seem to have been in him, only the impulse to use his vast cavalry forces for destruction. He was a genius, if an evil one, and it is said that his rule was so absolute that a girl could walk from one end of his empire to the other, carrying

After the Middle Ages, the Renaissance, which apart from a few swashbucklers and a nod towards artistic genius, had one obvious attraction for film-makers: murder and mischief in the shape of the Borgias. That they were no worse – and one of the family was certainly better – than most in their time, is irrelevant; propaganda has done its work, and to the world they are the devil's brood, and probably always will be. Rodrigo, the father, is chiefly notable as being the Pope who divided the New World between Spain and Portugal, thus paving the way indirectly for the buccaneers; his private life seems to have been as scandalous as many of his contemporaries'. Cesare, a ruthless tyrant, unscrupulous politician, and capable soldier, has been saddled with every crime in the calendar, few of which can be brought home to him. Lucrezia has suffered most of all: she is perhaps the most infamous woman in history, the arch-poisoner, intriguer, and seductress, guilty of incest with her father and two of her brothers – so runs her reputation, without the slightest evidence. In fact, she seems to have been rather a nice woman, beautiful, intelligent, and a devoted patroness of the arts.

But we would not expect the cinema to rehabilitate any of them, although Lucrezia (Paulette Goddard, looking much less angelic than the blonde original) received sympathetic treatment in *Bride of Vengeance*, which was remarkable for the appearance of Macdonald Carey as Cesare, to whose portrait he bore a close resemblance. This could not be said of Orson Welles, who played him in *Prince of Foxes*. Cesare was slim in person and feature, and said to be soft-

From left, Cesare Borgia, Lucrezia Borgia (from *The Disputation of Saint Catherine* by Pinturicchio), and Macdonald Carey and Paulette Goddard in *Bride of Vengeance*.

Tudors and Sea-Dogs

Medical historians still disagree about what killed Henry VIII. Was it cardio-renal failure, chronic sinusitis, syphilis, brain damage caused originally by jousting, or just plain obesity? Whatever the medical cause the ultimate death-blow was dealt by Charles Laughton.

He was the first screen Henry, the most memorable, and with the possible exception of Sid James, by far the worst. In terms of accurate historic portrayal, that is; his bravura performance in *The Private Life of Henry VIII* won him a deserved Academy Award and made him an international star; it is still a deplorable caricature of England's best-known and (at a safe distance) most affectionately remembered king. For Henry was both a great man and a monster – a brilliant, cruel, patriotic, selfish, talented, arrogant, megalomaniac tyrant; Laughton made him a childish posturing buffoon, a vain ranting thing without intelligence or stature. It was a comic performance relieved by one moment of genuine stricken pathos – but then, it was a comedy, to the extent that the audience was invited to laugh at the gross belching creature who strutted and postured and threw chicken-bones over his shoulder (a thing which the real Henry, who was presumably well brought up by Henry VII, would probably not have dreamed of doing).

It is said that Alexander Korda conceived the film after hearing a cockney taxi-driver singing "I'm 'Enery the Eighth I am"; if so, it was an appropriate beginning, and the stocky rotund Laughton a fitting choice. The real Henry was a giant, six feet three and broad with it; he would not have found it necessary to impress Binnie Barnes by taking on a professional wrestler. His rages, we are told, were truly terrible; Laughton's were noisy tantrums. It is doubtful if Walter Raleigh would have said of Laughton's Henry, as he did of the original, that if all the portraits of tyranny were lost to the world, they might be recreated out of this one king.

But if this Henry was without greatness, the film was an immense success – the first truly international British picture, and the foundation of this country's best years in the cinema. It launched Robert Donat and Elsa Lanchester, was pleasing to the eye, and had a chilling opening sequence in which Jane Seymour's (Wendy Barrie) wedding preparations were skilfully intercut with Anne Boleyn's (Merle Oberon) last moments before going to the block. One cannot quarrel with the film as a splendid entertainment; it is just a pity that the picture of Henry VIII impressed on two generations is of a scruffy-bearded glutton talking with his mouth full.

The great Tudor was better served by several other distinguished actors, including the ubiquitous Montagu Love, Robert Shaw, Richard Burton, Charlton Heston, and Keith Michell. Of these, Burton was for me the least convincing; he worked hard on the cruel, lustful, unscrupulous side of Henry's nature – and yet remained Richard Burton in a beard. But *Anne of the Thousand Days* had compensations; its sets and costumes looked authentic, it charted fairly the King's pursuit and conquest of Anne Boleyn, his machinations to remove Catherine of Aragon, his disillusion with Anne, the trumped-up charges of adultery and incest, and her final execution – although that Henry offered her a way out was news to me – and the playing was excellent. Genevieve Bujold was an ambitious and spirited Anne, possibly prettier than the original whom a contemporary described as "not one of the handsomest women in the world" (certainly she was no Merle Oberon), Anthony

"All the portraits of tyranny . . ." Henry VIII and his impersonators: from top clockwise, portrait of Henry (after Hans Holbein), Keith Michell, (*Henry VIII and His Six Wives*), Robert Shaw *(A Man for All Seasons)*, Charlton Heston (*The Prince and the Pauper*, 1977), and Richard Burton (*Anne of the Thousand Days*), and on facing page . . .

... Montagu Love, *(The Prince and the Pauper*, 1937), and Sid James in *Carry On, Henry*.

Quayle was an accommodating Wolsey, and John Colicos was in chilling form as Cromwell.

It was better history than most of its critics seemed to realise; one wonders just how closely they had studied the records of the time. It is a question worth asking whenever one comes across a costume picture being disparaged with vague phrases about "historical hokum", "Hollywood fantasy", "pseudo-history", and the like, uttered with a confidence that suggests intimate acquaintance with the source material of the subject under review. Well, there may be film critics whose bedside reading consists of the State Papers, Wyatt's Life, Cavendish, and the correspondence of Henry and Anne. But on whatever authority, they were less kind to *Anne of the Thousand Days* than perhaps it deserved, at least as a view of history. As a film, it might have fared better if it had not appeared only three years after the highly acclaimed *A Man for All Seasons*, which was certainly a better picture and fairly glittered with star performances.

It is probably sheer perversity, but against all the evidence in his favour I have never cared for Sir Thomas More, and it is probably a tribute to the excellence of Robert Bolt's script and Paul Scofield's portrayal that they didn't make me like him any better. That by the way, and whatever reservations one may have about More's reputation for tolerance and humanity, the film did justice to his integrity and courage in refusing to bend his conscience to his king's policy. It was not surprising that it won five Oscars, and might reasonably have had four more – to Wendy Hiller (Lady More), Orson Welles (Wolsey), Leo McKern (a fascinating contrast to Colicos as Cromwell), and Robert Shaw as Henry.

This last was an interesting piece of casting. Shaw, when he exerted himself, was a fine actor and a compelling screen presence; he was a great "looker", as he demonstrated in *The Sting*, eyeing Paul Newman across the table – it was almost worth paying money to sit opposite him at a canteen script conference and listen to him grating: "Look, you've got to give me a line!" He had a fine, smouldering fire in his eye, and it burned balefully in his Henry; this was a mad tyrant, whether fixing More with his empty stare or clapping his hands with brutal glee as his courtiers floundered in the mud.

He did not look like Henry, but there the lack of resemblance ended.

Physically, Keith Michell and Heston were ideal casting. Michell, who played Henry both on television and in the cinema, achieved the difficult feat of ageing the subject from youth to old age; if Heston is my favourite, it is for personal reasons, and also because for all his imposing height he had to overcome the disadvantage of looking not in the least like Henry Tudor. Make-up and his own immersion in the character turned him into a very proper tyrant – a hulking, gross giant, mottle-faced and lurching along on his "sorre legge", darting piggy-eyed wicked glances at his court, growling his lines, pawing at ladies-in-waiting, and dying at last defiantly in the shadows, muttering of "Monks, monks, monks!" while his jester whimpered at the foot of the bed. That, for the record, is how Henry went in fact.

Hollywood has done well by his reign visually at least; if it has had little to say about the Reformation or the Dissolution, that after all is not a realistic film-maker's province. The images have been faithful in the main – and perhaps one should not be too hard on Laughton and Korda. After all, what does the world remember about Henry VIII? Six wives, and if they were not as beautiful as Mesdames Oberon and Barnes, or as grotesquely funny as Elsa Lanchester, no one in the audience was going to object.

If there is one historic era from which Hollywood emerged with flying colours, to say nothing of blaring trumpets and thundering cannon, it was the Elizabethan Age. True, here as elsewhere the strict letter of history went by the board now and then; religious hatred, that vital ingredient of the time, was largely ignored, in obedience to one of the film industry's strictest taboos; and apart from Elizabeth herself the great figures of the time were neglected. Raleigh, for example, one recalls only briefly in the person of Vincent Price smarting furiously in his silver armour in *Elizabeth and Essex*, and my

Anne Boleyn, left, followed by Merle Oberon and Genevieve Bujold.

Sir Thomas More, (after Hans Holbein), above, and Paul Scofield in *A Man For All Seasons*.

sole recollection of Shakespeare the man is in the Globe Theatre sequence of *Henry V*, where a balding, modest figure is seen for a moment taking an unobtrusive bow.

But in two areas the film-makers triumphed. Firstly, they did Elizabeth proud; no historic figure has been represented more honestly in the cinema, or better served by her players; so far as we can know that remarkable woman, arguably the best ruler England ever had, her images on film seem to be faithful to the original. Secondly, the best of the Elizabethan movies caught the spirit of the age, when English adventurers began to look to the horizon with piratical exuberance, challenged the Spanish Goliath, and created a legend that still shines down the centuries. Hollywood, having shrewdly decided that the great theme of Elizabeth's reign was the confounding of the devildoms of Spain and the establishment of British sea-power (and who is going to say they were wrong?), went to work with a will and proved their point with some passable pictures and one quite splendid one.

Several distinguished actresses have played Elizabeth, including Sarah Bernhardt, Bette Davis, Agnes Moorehead, Athene Seyler, Florence Eldridge, and Glenda Jackson, but it is a curious fact that the one still most closely identified with the part was the least like Elizabeth physically, Flora Robson. The real Elizabeth, if we accept the likenesses by Gheeraerts, Hilliard, and others, was thin-faced and tight-lipped, with a sharp, almost beak-like nose, and not all the make-up in the world, with wigs and ruffs and farthingales thrown in, could make Dame Flora look like that. Bette Davis won the look-alike stakes hands down; she was all dangerous vinegar and snap, peering suspiciously (as we are told the real Elizabeth did), using her kerchief just so, rapping out her lines, and generally looking as though she were on her way to sit for the Armada Portrait. Yet it remains Robson's part; she had the voice, the style, the authority, the sheer physical presence of Gloriana, and when she needed it, the hidden bitterness and tormented doubt. Delivering her speech at Tilbury, hectoring her advisers, ordering King Philip's portrait out of her sight, railing at or flirting with Errol Flynn, she was just Good Queen Bess and always will be; she would have unfrocked the Bishop of Ely, by God.

Flora Robson also had the advantage of appearing in the two best Elizabethan pictures, both of which concentrated on the Armada crisis. The first was *Fire Over England*, a collector's item in that it teamed Laurence Olivier and Vivien Leigh, with Leslie Banks, Raymond Massey, James Mason, Robert Newton, and a notable performance by old Morton Selten as Lord Burghley. And by this film, made by Korda, hangs a tale which demonstrates the film industry's unhappy knack of not knowing a good thing when it sees it – in this case A. E. W. Mason's novel on which the picture was based, and which the screenwriters ditched almost completely. This although Mason was apparently a favourite author of Korda's, who filmed three of his books in as many years.

The true story of the defeat of the Spanish Armada (and no one should be deceived by those curious propagandists who seek to devalue it) is one of history's great adventures. From a film point of view it has everything – little England the last bastion against the Spanish superpower; Elizabeth scheming desperately to avoid war and yet be prepared for it; the brilliant intelligence operation of her master-spy, Walsingham, which laid the foundation of victory; Drake's daring raid on Cadiz ("We'll put on a brag, your grace") which delayed the Spaniards for a year; the great battle in the Channel when Howard's ships fought the galleons to a standstill, burned them out, and drove them north to destruction in the storm; the victorious English seamen starving in the ports; Frobisher offering to fight Drake in his shirt – all right, it would run for hours, and the budget would be horrifying, but the stuff is there.

Mason thought so, and his novel is a fine intellectual swashbuckler whose dashing hero is a conscience-torn Walsingham agent with a grudge against the Inquisition, who crippled his father. He penetrates Armada headquarters as valet to the Spanish admiral, smuggles the plans out to

Portrait of Elizabeth I (attributed to Nicholas Hilliard).

Walsingham,[1] escapes detection in a hair-raising defenestration sequence which is a stuntman's dream, duels desperately in a vain attempt to rescue crippled father, and finally sails in disguise aboard the Armada (as no fewer than six Walsingham agents actually did), blowing up a galleon in mid-Channel before swimming ashore to England, home, and the beauteous Cynthia, who has been foiling treachery on the home front.

There is the screenplay ready-made, almost as it stands, not too expensive (a mere single galleon to incinerate), and hewing faithfully to history, with a perfect cameo role for

1 This is historic fact. The forgotten hero was one Anthony Standen, an English agent who masqueraded as an Italian in order to set up surveillance in the household of Santa Cruz, the Spanish commander-in-chief, where he gained access to the Admiral's secret plans and correspondence.

Flora Robson in *Fire Over England*, with, from left, Leslie Banks, Laurence Olivier (behind), Vivien Leigh, Morton Selten as Lord Burghley. Right, Lord Burghley. Below, left to right, Bette Davis in *Elizabeth and Essex*, Florence Eldridge in *Mary of Scotland,* and Glenda Jackson in *Mary Queen of Scots.*

Elizabeth, and an excellent part for Sir Francis Walsingham. But for reasons best known to Korda, the writers ignored Mason almost entirely and concocted a commonplace tale in which an English agent penetrates the Spanish court to discover the names of assassins plotting to kill Elizabeth. This gave Olivier the chance to do a little light swashbuckling, Flora Robson set her seal on the Virgin Queen, James Wong Howe photographed some beautiful interiors, there was a haunting little tune, "The Spanish Lady", and Raymond Massey stole the show as Philip of Spain – he had evidently done his homework, and captured the dry, pedantic, inexorable Spanish monarch in a few minutes on screen. Whoever wrote his line, "That is the sand, and that the ink", muttered impassively when Olivier upset his inkstand, deserves an honourable mention. A good enough film – but not *Fire Over England*, and a great opportunity lost.

However, as Prince John once remarked to Guy of Gisborne, golden days lay ahead, and when Dame Flora resumed her reign three years later it was in the right film at the right time; seldom has a historical picture appeared in a more topical context than Warner Brothers' 1940 production of *The Sea Hawk*.

The novel which Sabatini had written a generation earlier is second only to his *Captain Blood* as a tale of pirates and blue water, and Warners had previously made it as a silent, with Milton Sills. It concerns an Elizabethan adventurer sold into slavery who rises to prominence among the Barbary Corsairs, and there is much kidnapping, betrayal, swordplay, slave-market drama, harem intrigue, and sea-fighting before villainy is confounded and true love conquers. Spirited stuff, but Seton Miller and Howard Koch sensibly decided that simple melodrama was unsuitable for war-time, and doing wisely what Korda had done unwisely, jettisoned virtually everything except Sabatini's title and substituted their own rousing story which, while fictitious in itself, was historically faithful in many respects, and caught the spirit of two "finest hours" by inviting comparison between the Armada crisis

and the Battle of Britain, which had barely ended when *The Sea Hawk* arrived on British screens.

Miller and Koch have been accused of loose plotting, but no one can say that they did not scour Elizabethan fact and fiction for their material. For once there is no written prologue: Philip of Spain (Montagu Love, who looked nothing like him but had as unctuously wicked a voice as tyrant could wish) sums up the position in 1585: Elizabeth and England have got to go, so that the map of the world can become a map of Spain – and we are treated to a dramatic shot of His Catholic Majesty's shadow looming over the map in question. Vintage Michael Curtiz, and a fitting prelude to a blistering sea-battle in which Errol Flynn, rather more tight-lipped and aloof than usual, and his sea dogs hammer a galleon into submission, taking prisoner Spanish Ambassador Claude Rains and his gorgeous niece (Brenda Marshall, who

Rogues a-plotting: Claude Rains, left, with Henry Daniell, and opposite, "English bulldogs and Spanish mastiffs" at grips in *The Sea Hawk*.

looked more like a sultry Castilian beauty than Olivia de Havilland). They also release an unkempt horde of English galley slaves in a genuinely touching sequence inspired, I would guess, by Kingsley's *Westward Ho!*, and none the worse for that. The haughty hidalga Marshall will have none of Flynn, naturally, but after a rather pretty scene in which they converse at long range, he at the quarter-deck rail, she at a rail lower down, it is obvious that all will end happily, Spaniard though she be.

The repercussions at Elizabeth's court are authentic, with the Queen outwardly alarmed and inwardly delighted, gloating over the loot her sea hawk has brought home, and cooing at his flattery, but terrified lest he provoke the Dons into a shooting war – a fair reminder of the truth which bedevilled privateers like Drake, as well as Elizabeth: Spain had to be kept at bay, but without overt official hostility. Thus when Flynn puts to sea again, it is with secret charts; little does he know that Rains and a treacherous English statesman, Wolfingham[2] (Henry Daniell) have discovered his destination. This is Panama, and the Spanish treasure train (which Drake did in fact ambush with some success). The Warners crew have no such luck; trapped in fever-ridden jungle, they are captured (their automatic flintlocks notwithstanding) and set to toil as galley slaves, until on the way to Cadiz they manage to break loose, scoop up the plans for the Armada in passing, and row a captured galley back to England in one of the most triumphantly over-the-top sequences ever filmed. I am assured that the orders they shout to each other are pure nautical gibberish, and the sight of them all in their loincloths heaving away and chanting, to Korngold's music:

> Pull on the oars!
> Strike for the shores of Dover!
> Pull with the sea, hearty and
> free, troubles will soon be over!
> Sing as you go, here we go, for
> we know that we row
> For home, sweet home!

or words very close to that effect, can only be called sublime. Never mind, it worked.

After that, it only remains for Flynn and Daniell to duel it out in the best Curtiz style – gigantic shadows fencing along the wall, iron sconces clanging on the flagstones, people rolling on the stairs, and the Queen entering dramatically[3] just after Daniell has received the mortal stuck-in, and Flynn, looking breathless but humble, is fumbling in his tunic for The Plans. At this point I was looking forward to seeing the Armada being overwhelmed, and the closing scene came as rather an anticlimax: Dame Flora giving a 1940-oriented Tilbury speech, and Alan Hale and the lads flourishing drawn rapiers and positively singing "For England – and the Queen!" while radiant beams shone down and Korngold's trumpets went wild.

The Sea Hawk was a first-class film, almost a great one – at least for the year 1940. Someone said of it that if it had been a silent film, it would have been a classic, an opinion which, if unfair to an excellent cast and conscientious writers, was a tribute to the visual splendour of the production. It had its share of anachronisms (references to "British", and Dover substituted apparently for Plymouth) and took liberties with Anglo-Spanish political relations, but its overall picture was accurate, and it came at a time when it was needed, when a beleaguered Britain was glad to welcome a reminder that what had been done once could be done again. Churchill, we are told, was deeply moved by it, and it is bracketed with *Lady Hamilton* as his favourite historical film. Plainly it was worth making, for that at least.

But it would be wrong to regard *The Sea Hawk* merely as melodramatic propaganda. It had great spirit and much

---

2 A name obviously inspired by Walsingham and an unhappy libel on a great patriot. Donald Crisp played a Burghley/Howard figure, and Frobisher and Hawkins appeared briefly, but Drake's name, significantly, was not mentioned.

3 Flora Robson later recalled how, at Flynn's suggestion, she made her entrance calling briskly: "All right, break it up, boys!" and reduced Michael Curtiz to tears.

Robert Devereux, Earl of Essex (by William Segar), and right, Errol Flynn with Bette Davis.

beauty, and some of its scenes are indelible: the thunderous sea-battle, the squalid gloom of the slave deck, the steamy oppression of the Panama swamps, the deserted warship creaking at its moorings, the typical Curtiz touch of the Spanish captain drinking his toast to the Armada and seeing, reflected in his goblet, the half-naked slaves in the doorway behind him. Best of all, it did justice to a great heroic theme.

Drake of England, although it did feature the Armada battle and was a reasonably accurate production, left no vivid impression on my nine-year-old mind, despite the fact that I sat it through twice and had to be removed from the cinema by anxious parents. Matheson Lang was not Drake as I envisaged him, which was as a sort of Devonian James Cagney – and that may not be far wrong. On the face of it Rod Taylor was better casting in *Seven Seas to Calais* but was defeated by the script and director of this curious historical fantasy in which various real events – Drake's circumnavigation, the Nombre de Dios raid, the Babington Plot, and the Armada battle – were ruth-

lessly and ineptly fictionalised. The ship models may well have been the worst ever seen.

The Private Lives of Elizabeth and Essex plays false with history by suggesting that Queen Elizabeth was middle-aged at the time of the Essex conspiracy; in fact she was sixty-seven, thirty-four years older than the dashing earl, and all the white make-up cannot make Bette Davis (thirty-one when the film was made) look older than her forties. So the relationship between the ageing queen and her favourite is distorted from the start; that she was fond and doting there is no doubt, but that is not the same as the grand romantic passion suggested by this lavish adaptation of Maxwell Anderson's play. Essex in fact was a spoiled, brilliant, ambitious soldier courtier who presumed on an old woman's favour and his own charm and popularity, sometimes openly insulting her, sulking when he did not get his way, and always underrating her; acclaimed as a hero after his attack on Cadiz in 1596, he failed utterly to deal with Tyrone's Irish rebellion and, faced with disgrace and bankruptcy, attempted a coup which ended in his death on the scaffold.

With some "telescoping" the film presents this reasonably fairly, while romanticising the relationship into a chaste love affair punctuated (and this is accurate enough) by violent quarrels, but while Bette Davis gives a fine performance it is simply out of historical context. Whether she was right to demand (unsuccessfully) Olivier instead of Flynn as Essex is a nice question; acting ability is all very well, but the great swashbuckler was better type-casting as the handsome, reckless earl. Given the basic historical flaw in the story, other liberties do not matter much – there was no suppression of their correspondence while Essex was in Ireland, so far as I know; she did not box his ears after the Cadiz expedition, but on a later occasion; his rebellion and arrest are dramatised and oversimplified, and there was no last-minute meeting before his execution – when she heard of his death the Queen was playing the virginal, and paused only a moment before continuing.

The film is a fine glossy pageant, Donald Crisp is a smooth and devious Francis Bacon, Vincent Price an imposing Raleigh, and Henry Daniell a conniving (but not deformed) Cecil. There is an interesting portrayal of the Irish leader, Tyrone, by Alan Hale, the arch-scene-stealer whose great gift as an actor was to change character without changing appearance; we have no good evidence of what Hugh O'Neill Tyrone looked like, but if he was not Hale's double, he should have been.

Before taking leave of Tudor England one should acknowledge two good performances of Elizabeth as a young woman, by Jean Simmons in *Young Bess* – which has one fine moment when the young Elizabeth, roused to fury, confronts Henry VIII (Laughton) and strikes an identical pose, feet wide-planted and arms akimbo – and by Lalla Ward, who was suitably imperious and formidable in *The Prince and the Pauper*.

But one sixteenth-century question remains unanswered: how did the cinema fail so signally with Mary Queen of Scots? Even without the romantic mist which surrounds her, she is surely still one of the most filmable women in history.

A beautiful teenage widow, six feet and red-haired, queen of two countries and pretender to a third, transported from the gayest, most sophisticated court in Europe to a gloomy, northern kingdom, married to a jealous consort whose good looks mask a repulsive nature, forced to watch the murder of a handsome courtier who may or may not have been her lover, conspiring(?) to have her husband blown up and strangled, marrying his murderer, losing her throne in bloody battle, putting herself in the power of a rival queen, conspiring in captivity, and finally being beheaded while her little pet dog scampers off the scaffold . . . Shakespeare, Daphne du Maurier, and Hollywood combined would not have dared to invent her. Perhaps she is one of those historic figures whose reality simply outstrips normal dramatic convention; in any event, the two best-known films about her have been less than successful. Vanessa Redgrave played the title role in *Mary Queen of Scots*, and won an Oscar nomination, and the film had the added advantage of Glenda Jackson as Elizabeth; still, it was a curiously lacklustre piece, which committed the cardinal (and quite unnecessary) sin of falsifying history by allowing the two to meet – something which, it is generally agreed, Elizabeth was at pains to avoid because she knew that if she once met Mary face to face she would never be able to deal ruthlessly with her thereafter. In this respect the film was false not only to fact, but to Elizabeth's character.

So was *Mary of Scotland*, which brought Katharine Hepburn, in one of her less happy performances, into confrontation with Florence Eldridge; the film was directed, at considerable expense for those days, by John Ford, and may well be the worst historical picture I have ever seen. It romanticises or distorts the characters beyond recognition, bristles with anachronisms and inaccuracies, and is just an atrocious comic strip version. To give an idea of the approach – Mary, on her arrival at Holyrood, is serenaded by a crowd of Edinburgh citizens straight off the shortbread tin, in sporrans and plaids, singing a topical version of "Loch Lomond". Into this unspeakable scene rushes none other than John Knox,

Katharine Hepburn with John Carradine as Rizzio, in *Mary of Scotland* and right, Vanessa Redgrave in *Mary Queen of Scots*.

denouncing Mary at the top of his voice; he is interrupted by Fredric March (Bothwell), in balmoral and claymore, who drowns him out with the aid of a pipe band playing "Blue Bonnets over the Border". This is one of the better scenes. Later, enter March with the deathless line: "Oh, hullo, Darnley, still hangin' around, eh?", after which he goes to the fire, lifts his kilt, and warms his behind.

Elizabeth is represented as a vicious shrew, Mary as a misty-eyed heroine. John Carradine is at least believable as Rizzio, Moroni Olsen gives a thunderous performance as Knox, Ian Keith is the Earl of Moray (sorry, Mow-Ray), but the stars are the Scottish lords, skirling and hooting in plaids (and here and there a kilt) of the Macabre tartan. For anyone who has the misfortune to see it, Bothwell murdered Darnley. Furthermore, Bothwell was a Borderer, wouldn't have known a claymore if it fell on him, which unfortunately it didn't, and never wore a kilt in his life. But there it is: from *Mary of Scotland* in 1936 to *Braveheart* in 1995, the rule apparently

persists that all Scotsmen must wear "kilts"; how else would Middle Western audiences recognise them?

In the heyday of the historicals there were few things more exciting, yet at the same time more tranquilising in their effect on the front stalls on a Saturday afternoon, than a good map, Olde Worlde for choice. Maps meant adventure in faraway places. Sometimes they heralded a British Empire movie or a saga of land exploration, and occasionally they were employed, under captions or with a spoken prologue, to give the groundlings an idea of the extent of the Roman imperial frontiers, or the vastness of the untamed American wilderness. But as often as not they came on the screen unexpectedly, after the first twenty minutes or so, in which case they were animated by a line slowly wiggling across the ocean, and the audience knew that now the talk and planning were over, and they could sit back and wait for the moment when the map dissolved or opened up on one of the loveliest sights the cinema could show – a ship under full sail, thrashing along, taffrail under, through heavy seas, or silhouetted against a distant tropic sky. Those ships were not only things of beauty, they stimulated anticipation of brave new worlds, exotic barbarians, shipwreck, and spectacular action.

There have been some memorable ships in the movies: the Bounty becalmed in the doldrums, or with the breadfruit pots bobbing in her wake; the Black Swan surging menacingly into camera and suddenly exploding in deafening broadside; the longships of *The Vikings* gliding like dark phantoms through silvery sea mist or returning in triumph with Kirk Douglas running the oars and the great horns booming; the Baghdad merchantman, its huge painted eye coming into close shot; the British fleet in stately line off Trafalgar, male voices singing "Heart of Oak" with splendid cutting to a series of weatherbeaten faces, each reading a word of Nelson's distant signal, "England expects . . . " – no wonder Winston Churchill loved it; the superb long shot of the beaked Macedonian galley racing in to ram in *Ben Hur*; the jaunty little Maggie puffing her way musically to Highland harbours; the Bismarck being slowly battered to a wreck; the waves cascading over the decks of the Mayflower; the US submarine lying undetected and silent on the floor of Tokyo Bay while a medical orderly performs an appendectomy with the aid of a textbook; Blood's Arabella grappling the Frenchmen with cannon blazing and enough toppling masts and rigging to outfit a fleet; Compass Rose driving relentlessly through the survivors in the water; Columbus's brave little caravels[4] on a sea like limitless blue glass; the Titanic going down; the Poseidon turning turtle, and an endless host of liners, windjammers, warships, clippers, pirates, South Sea traders, merchantmen,

trawlers, and stately Spanish galleons, all ploughing gamely through establishing shots, sailing into glorious Technicolor sunsets, or being pounded to pieces on storm-lashed rocks.

Most of these immortal vessels, the *nil admirari* experts are never tired of pointing out, were probably models. To your true lover of sea movies, this is irrelevant; he may well be capable of telling a model from the real thing, but in practice he does not deign to notice; to him they are all full-size ironclads crammed with bluejackets, or towering three-masters with all sail set, guns run out, and Errol on the poop exhorting Guy Kibbee to give 'em another broadside, Hagthorpe. (There have been, admittedly, some models so patently bogus that one could not help noticing – usually ocean liners in second features, with tiny twinkling light bulbs and little waves splashing jerkily against a painted horizon. The better models, undetectable to any normal eye, have been splendid scale constructions large enough to take at least one operator, and sometimes a small crew, inside their hulls.)

The sailing ship, real or not, has been an expensive and unpredictable staple of historical pictures from time immemorial, and out of all the film dramas of fighting sail, piracy, exploration, ghost ships, mad captains, bucko mates, smugglers, and the rest, the story of one small armed transport of the Royal Navy takes pride of place, as it deserves to do. The Bounty, subject of three major productions, has been part of film folklore for sixty years; it is also a classic example of the best and worst in Hollywood's treatment of history.

The true story (or rather stories) of the Bounty is an epic of the sea to be classed with the Odyssey and the voyages of the Argo, Columbus, and Magellan. Hollywood has touched only part of it, and that perforce in condensed form; the full tale of the ship and its company is so complex and sensational – and still mysterious – that it would take several films to tell it properly. It is one of the factual dramas that outstrips fiction.

For the record, the Bounty was despatched in 1787 to Tahiti to collect and transport breadfruit plants to the West Indies.

---

4 "The *Nina*, the *Pinta*, the *Santa Maria* . . . " in that order, inspired a rousing little musical number by Kurt Weill and Ira Gershwin, sung by Fred MacMurray and chorus in *Where Do We Go From Here?*, a happy little historical comedy in which MacMurray sailed with the discoverers of the New World and, if memory serves, was conned into buying Manhattan Island by two thoroughly sophisticated Indians, Anthony Quinn and June Haver.

Her young commander, William Bligh, was a fine seaman and navigator of genius, who in later years was to distinguish himself in action, win the praise of Nelson, and end his days as an admiral. His friend and protégé, Fletcher Christian, sailed in the Bounty, and was advanced by Bligh to second-in-command, though he was only twenty-two. The characters of the two men have been dissected and disputed for two centuries, without total success. Bligh was tough, brave, efficient, and (contrary to the false portrait of the first two films) a humane and considerate commander; he was also cursed with an explosive temper and a withering tongue. Christian is more of an enigma; he was inexperienced and possibly incompetent,

Top left: the real Fletcher Christian (an artist's impression based on contemporary descriptions, by Larry Learmonth), and, right, William Bligh. Bottom left, Clark Gable and Charles Laughton. Top right, Marlon Brando and Trevor Howard. Bottom right, Mel Gibson and Anthony Hopkins.

and seems to have been unstable and highly sensitive to criticism.

All went well until Tahiti, where the crew had an idyllic time of it with the native belles. Bligh seems to have let discipline slip (he was not a born manager of men), but once at sea again he bore down, and Christian, who had left a pregnant sweetheart on Tahiti, was eventually driven by Bligh's upbraidings to contemplate jumping ship; in the event, he changed his mind, apparently on the spur of the moment, and with the help of the more discontented elements aboard, mutinied, took the ship, and turned Bligh and the loyal men loose in an open boat.

It was an act of appalling cruelty, and tantamount to a slow death sentence: the nearest inhabited settlement was over 3000 miles away, and Bligh had no charts and little food. But in the most remarkable open-boat voyage in maritime history he made it to Timor, and eventually to England. A naval ship, the Pandora, was sent after the mutineers, and captured some of them, but was wrecked. Christian and his fellow mutineers took refuge on Pitcairn Island, far off the sea routes, the *Bounty* was burned, and not for nineteen years was their hiding-place discovered, by which time only one of them was left. Christian probably died on Pitcairn, although there is some remarkable evidence to suggest that he got back to England – it includes identification by a former shipmate, and a curious letter by the poet Wordsworth, who had been at school with Christian. It has even been suggested that the 'Rime of the Ancient Mariner', by Wordsworth's friend Coleridge, was inspired by the Bounty drama; it is not impossible.

Those are the barest facts. We all know what Hollywood made of them, and history, truth, and fair play took a frightful beating.

The first Bounty film had Bligh (Charles Laughton) as a sadistic tyrant who flogged and abused his crew mercilessly, and Christian (Clark Gable) as the stalwart hero driven to desperation. Their relationship was misrepresented, Bligh was made out to be dishonest as well as brutal, ludicrous nonsense about keel-hauling was introduced, a key figure, Midshipman Heywood (called Byam in the film and played by Franchot Tone), was distorted beyond recognition, the reason for the mutiny was an exaggerated nonsense. The one concession to fairness was in the tribute paid to Bligh's heroic voyage, but he was still left discredited. The film's verdict was spoken by the court-martial president, ignoring Bligh's hand: "I admire your seamanship and courage, but . . . " It was all a libel on a flawed hero, a travesty of truth – and a splendid film.

This could not be said of the 1962 remake. Bligh (Trevor Howard) was if anything even more of a villain than Laughton, and to the mutual antipathy between him and Christian a new and farcical element was added – Christian was portrayed as an aristocratic exquisite, with Marlon Brando playing him like an adenoidal Scarlet Pimpernel; Bligh was the despised commoner. (In fact both men were from good but not upper-class families, Bligh's from the West Country, Christian's from the Isle of Man.) The Bounty flogged and keel-hauled its way to Tahiti as before, the mutiny took place in a welter of silly epithets, Bligh was seen only briefly in his open boat, his court-martial was an offensive fiction (poor Henry Daniell deserved better at the end of his career), and Christian's final change of heart and gory death were, to put it mildly, in keeping with the rest of a film which seemed to go out of its way to distort history. The first film, if false to the main fact, had been credible in plot and characterisation; the second was not.

Why, we may ask, did Hollywood do it, not once but twice? The answer is probably: convention and cliché. The truth of the mutiny is a superb drama – but it is psychological drama, of two conflicting natures, one of which snapped under the strain. Why Christian went out of control we cannot know, because we do not know him, or Bligh, well enough, and we can only imagine what it was like in that unreal floating exile, years and thousands of miles from home: a crew sulking over paradise lost, a captain impatient to reassert authority, an unstable lieutenant possibly heartbroken for his girl in Tahiti, and driven beyond endurance by verbal bullying. It is made for sensitive dramatisation – and that was not what films were about in 1935. Clear, recognisable "motivation" was needed, right v. wrong, and given the unsavoury reputation that Bligh had borne unjustly for 150 years, the temptation to reshape history (with the help of a popular novel) into a spirited, easily understood tale of cruelty and rebellion, was not to be resisted. It may well be that no one on the film knew the true story, anyway. But they knew what the customers liked, and gave it to them, and the screen officers and crew of the Bounty responded with a will.

Laughton was immense, brooding and scowling, rasping his "Mis-tah Christian!" into the language; presumably only Victor McLaglen's performance in *The Informer* denied him the Oscar. Gable, who was also nominated, was first-rate, the script was a beauty, the action fast and clear, and there are images that live in the memory – Laughton, beetle-browed, sweeping his hand across his mouth, Franchot Tone draped over the crosstrees in a howling storm, Donald Crisp assaulting Ian Mac Wolfe with a fish, Hiti-hiti in his cocked hat, the solid tramp of the press-gang (the men shown being pressed were in fact volunteers), the small boats pulling Bounty in a flat calm, Bligh roaring defiance from the launch while Christian, already in doubt, watches in silence. It was all very good, and deserved its Academy Award; the pity is that it established a historical falsehood.

The industry made some amends in 1984, with *The Bounty*, which told the essential truths, and fell curiously flat. It would be tempting for a Hollywood apologist to say that here is proof of the need to reshape history for good film drama, but that won't do; the fact is that *The Bounty* was not a very good picture. This in spite of a brilliant performance by Anthony Hopkins as Bligh, and a highly creditable effort by Mel Gibson to get inside the skin of the tormented Christian. Perhaps the device of telling the story in flashback from Bligh's court-martial (well conducted by Laurence Olivier and Edward Fox) was a mistake; in the end, what came off

the screen lacked conviction. I could believe that ship and its crew in 1935; they seemed real in a way that the 1984 Bounty did not. A pity, because it was sound history, give or take a few minor details (Bligh's obsession with rounding Cape Horn was emphasised, without so far as I know any historical warranty). But once at least it came to life, in the moment of mutiny – brawling, struggling confusion, everyone yelling at once, Christian nearly hysterical, and some of the authentic recorded dialogue being used at last. (None of the films really exploited Bligh's splendid gift of invective, examples of which are to be found in the journals of survivors.[5] With all his sterling qualities, he must have been a good man to stay away from; later in life, as governor of New South Wales, he was the object of another insurrection, and his career was well summed up by a friend as "a turbulent journey".)

And so we say farewell to troubled Tahiti, but remain in Nelson's navy, and indeed with the man himself. He had been press-ganged briefly into the first *Bounty* picture, as an officer (Francis Lister) at the court-martial, and had been played in silents by Victor Varconi and Conrad Veidt, but there has only been one screen Nelson of importance, and that is Laurence Olivier.

Lady Hamilton (the US title, *That Hamilton Woman*, has that breathless gossipy flavour beloved of American exhibitors) had some historic significance in itself. It was part of Korda's war effort, made in America while that country was still neutral, and since it emphasised the similarity between Britain's stand against Napoleon and her solitary resistance to Hitler, it was widely (and rightly) regarded as propaganda. Churchill was known to be its champion, and isolationist circles found its message too strong for their taste.

5 "I'll see who will dare refuse the pumpkin, or anything else I may order to be served out! You damned scoundrels, I'll make you eat grass, or anything you can catch, before I've done with you! . . . You damned hound! . . . God damn you, you scoundrels, you are all thieves alike, and combine with the men to rob me, but I'll sweat you for it, you rascals! I'll make half of you jump overboard, before you get through Endeavour Straits!" Etc., etc.

One of Romney's portraits of Emma Hamilton, and Vivien Leigh.

And since it was about an illicit love affair, it encountered censorship problems which looked far-fetched at the time, never mind today. In spite of these checks, the film was a considerable success.

As a reflection of history it is eminently fair, bearing in mind that it deals with the love affair of Nelson and Emma Hamilton, and not with their lives. There is little of Nelson the fighting sailor, and nothing of Emma's reputed early career as barmaid, shop assistant, lady's maid, and eighteenth-century strip artist, in the course of which she had a succession of lovers. One of these passed her on to his uncle, Sir William Hamilton, British envoy at Naples, who obligingly settled the nephew's debts; whether this pretty transaction shocked Emma as much as the film suggests may be doubtful. However, she married

Hamilton, who was thirty years her senior, but quickly transferred her affections to Nelson, the budding naval hero, on his arrival at Naples. The affair caused great scandal, wrecked Nelson's marriage, and might well have blighted the career of anyone less vital to his country's survival.

Initially, Emma may just have been hunting another scalp, but that it became a deep and genuine love affair there is no doubt. How far it affected Nelson's professional conduct, and how far her considerable influence on Neapolitan politics (which mattered at the time) was of help to him and their country, has been disputed ever since. She may have been valuable; he, in turn, disobeyed orders to protect her (and Naples) in a crisis. The film makes the most of these things, but not unfairly; it is a skilful piece of work, with an intelligent, often witty script by Walter Reisch and R. C. Sherriff. They are faithful to the main course of historic events, and cope admirably with the eternal problem of how to make famous lovers talk and act when no intimate detail is available. If some critics thought the relationship over-glamourised – well, Nelson and Emma were a glamorous pair, and played by Olivier and Vivien Leigh they could hardly have been anything else.

For once, too, a film heroine was no more beautiful than her original, if Emma's portraits by Romney are anything to go by, and only a carping critic would object that by the time she met Nelson, her celebrated figure had grown "nothing short of monstrous", according to a contemporary. But he added: "Her face is beautiful", and society agreed with him. Vivien Leigh played her with skill and vivacity. Olivier, although a good deal more stalwart than Nelson, succeeded in looking uncannily like him, but it must have been a frustrating part. Nelson was a genius and man of action, an "irresistibly pleasing" hero, charming, vain, and "swallowed flattery like pap"; the film focused on Nelson the lover, not Nelson the man, and the personal magnetism of one of the great war leaders – probably only Napoleon inspired greater devotion – had little chance to come across.

Alan Mowbray, that blandest of actors, did an unobtrusive job of picture-stealing as Hamilton, the jealous-complacent husband; Gladys Cooper was all icy outrage as the betrayed Lady Nelson; Sara Allgood made Emma's mother a jolly, vulgar biddy, and Henry Wilcoxon was a properly massive and sympathetic Hardy. Model ships notwithstanding, Trafalgar was well fought and won, and the death in the cockpit was immaculately staged. Olivier has played some celebrated last moments; this was his best.

One suspects there was a little of Nelson, and a great deal of the celebrated Lord Cochrane, in C. S. Forester's contradictory and engaging hero, Hornblower, but neither was evident in *Captain Horatio Hornblower, RN*, which was a good example of Hollywood exploiting a best-selling character in

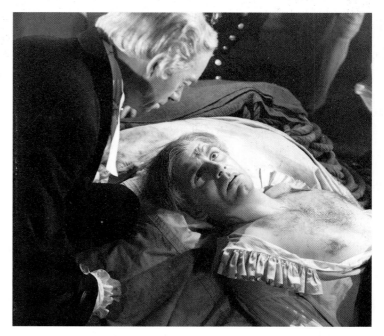

Horatio, Lord Nelson (by Lemuel Francis Abbott), and, below, Laurence Olivier in *Lady Hamilton*.

its most mundane way. Gregory Peck's casting outraged the purists, but he cleared his throat effectively and managed to give Hornblower a bit of style, which was otherwise lacking in a film which shrank three novels into two hours and told none of them satisfactorily. Virginia Mayo was decoratively bad casting as the austere Lady Barbara, James Robertson Justice galumphed about the lower deck, there were some good battle scenes, hearty dialogue was badly delivered, Hornblower's captain's cabin looked commodious enough for the First Sea Lord, and the loyal toast was drunk sitting down (as in *The Bounty*) at a time when the Royal Navy had not yet been accorded that privilege.

There was also the obligatory flogging, without which no sea movie is complete, a point made by James Agate in reviewing *The Sea Wolf*, which didn't have one and left him feeling cheated because he had been "looking forward to two hundred lashes in Technicolor". Usually the recipient is some anonymous extra, but among the starry names and character

Alan Ladd being chastised by William Bendix in *Two Years Before the Mast*, watched by Howard da Silva (arms folded), Brian Donlevy (behind da Silva), and Barry Fitzgerald (first on rail).

actors who have gritted their teeth at the gratings are Richard Harris, Gordon Jackson, Paul Henreid, Errol Flynn, Alan Ladd (twice!), Ross Alexander, Louis Jourdan and Donald Crisp.[6] By way of variety, Gary Cooper and George Raft were hung by their thumbs from the yardarm in *Souls at Sea*, Alec Craig was suspended from the Bounty's shrouds with a ship's block round his neck, William Bendix belaboured all hands with what looked like a knotted hawser in *Two Years Before the Mast*, under the cold eye of Howard da Silva, who rivalled Laughton as a maritime disciplinarian, and Barry Fitzgerald was towed through shark-infested waters in *The Sea Wolf*. John Wayne, Victor McLaglen, and Edward G. Robinson kept order aboard with their fists,[7] but of all the buckos, sadists, and martinets who have maintained the Hollywood tradition of brutality afloat (with which no historian can quarrel) by far the most chilling embodiment of wickedness was a performer who never laid a hand on anyone.

This was Robert Ryan, as the master-at-arms, Claggart, in *Billy Budd*, a curious piece from a novel by Herman Melville, about a saintly youth (Terence Stamp) on a British man-of-war who is hanged for the accidental killing of a nasty superior. This is said to be highly allegorical, and parallels have been drawn with the Crucifixion; I have not read Melville's novel, but if the film reflects it faithfully then what his ship needed was a good psychiatrist. For twisted logic and tortured conscience, the officers who sit in judgment on Billy are in a class of their own, with Peter Ustinov anguishing it up a storm; heaven knows how they came on against the French ship with which they are about to do battle as the film ends. But by that time Claggart is long gone, after a superb satanic study that should have earned at least an Oscar nomination. The word satanic is deliberately chosen: Ryan's Claggart is a spirit of

Robert Ryan, right, with Terence Stamp in *Billy Budd*.

malevolence, but it is attractive, too, and any actor who can do that is out of the ordinary. The film has no special historic interest, but that one performance distinguishes it.

There was evil enough, and passion, brutality, suspense, drama, and good acting in *The Sea Wolf*, however much it may have disappointed Agate. Jack London was a fine hand at hairy-chested psychology and Hollywood made frequent use of his books; this one has been filmed several times, but the 1941 production had the advantage of Edward G. Robinson as a mad intellectual sea-captain, Ida Lupino (fallen woman), Alexander Knox (castaway refined novelist), Gene Lockhart

6 The first two in *Mutiny on the Bounty* (1962); thereafter in *The Spanish Main, Against All Flags, Two Years Before the Mast, Botany Bay, Captain Blood, Anne of the Indies*, and *Mutiny on the Bounty* (1935).

7 In *Wake of the Red Witch, South of Pago Pago*, and *The Sea Wolf*.

Edward G. Robinson in command in *The Sea Wolf*. The respectful crew members are, left to right, John Garfield, Stanley Ridges, and Francis McDonald.

(drunken doctor – no profession has produced more lushes on film than medicine), John Garfield (rebellious crew member), and Barry Fitzgerald (vicious and homicidal ship's cook). This crew of eccentrics was directed by Michael Curtiz, and all round was a memorable study of Life At Sea When Uncle Will Was A Lad.

The purpose of the voyage escapes me, except that Captain Wolf Larsen was in mortal fear of encountering his even more abominable brother, Death Larsen. This nemesis did appear in the distance in the final reel, but by then the doctor had put on his best suit and hurled himself from the masthead, the cook had been thrown overboard and rendered one-legged by a shark, the novelist had exchanged philosophy with the mad skipper, who had recurring fits of blindness and quoted Milton, John Garfield had mutinied, the ship was sinking, and only by some miracle did Miss Lupino and Garfield survive and sail off into the mist in a small boat, presumably to complain to the Board of Trade.

Obviously the cast alone were worth the price of admission; it should be added that the atmosphere was dank and sinister and the photography first-rate; as an enjoyable sidelight on the merchant marine it is rivalled in my list only by *Slave Ship*, commanded by Warner Baxter, who made up an engaging quartet with Wallace Beery, George Sanders and Mickey Rooney.

At first glance, Hollywood and pirates would seem to be made for each other, but in fact they are not. Apart from the technical difficulty that sailing ships are nightmare machines which refuse to stay still, and even large models have their problems, there is the plain fact that pirates – the real pirates of history, the Blackbeards and Morgans and Kidds and Calico Jacks – are too bizarre, too larger-than-life, too unreal even for the cinema. That they *were* real is irrelevant; their truth is too strange for fiction, and pantomime and Peter Pan have turned the grim reality into a comic figure which usually defies attempts to fashion it for conventional drama, or even melodrama. Madmen who run about with blazing fireworks in their whiskers, eccentrics who hold religious services and prohibit swearing on their unholy cruises, red-headed hussies who put to sea disguised as men and fight duels to the death – they may do for send-up, but try to present them as they truly were, and the audience will laugh them off the screen. One should be able to make a serious historical drama out of Morgan, the gifted Welshman who led the largest private war-fleet in history and crippled Spain in the Caribbean, or about Kidd, the supposed clergyman's son who was apparently railroaded to Execution Dock to prevent a major political scandal. Excellent subjects, given the background of heroic adventure, rousing action, loot, sex, and violence – but somehow, inevitably, the colours start to run; consequently, audiences have seldom seen anything approaching historic reality. Three pictures stand head and shoulders above the rest: the original *Treasure Island*, *Captain Blood*, and *The Black Swan*, and it may be significant that all three were based on the works of the two great pirate novelists, Stevenson and Sabatini.

The beauty of *Treasure Island* is that it is faithful to R. L. S. in all but a few details – some unnecessary domestic dialogue at the beginning, and the omission from the script of the best line in pirate literature: "Take a cutlass, him that dares, and I'll see the colour of his inside before that pipe's empty." Otherwise, it is a little gem – Lionel Barrymore gloriously over the top as Billy Bones, Otto Kruger's dry Dr Livesey, Nigel Bruce trumpeting as the Squire, a noteworthy juvenile performance by Jackie Cooper as Jim Hawkins, a terrifying Blind Pew, a fine cackling Ben Gunn, and the best of the set-pieces: dark and sinister doings at the Admiral Benbow inn, the blockhouse besieged, Jim pinned to the mast by Israel Hands' dirk . . . and Wallace Beery.

Perfect casting is rare. Beery *was* Long John Silver, bluff, plausible, sly, the villain with the heart of gold plate, screwing up that "face as big as a ham" as he wheedles and conspires; Robert Newton and other successors were dwarfed by comparison. If only Stevenson could have lived to see him.

The Bloody Assizes: the notorious Judge Jeffreys, and, below, Leonard Mudie in *Captain Blood*.

Surely he would have forgiven his book's abridgement, and the slight reworking of the ending which produced one of the cinema's magic moments, when Hawkins abets Silver's escape and stands in tears at the rail while the old scoundrel rows slowly away into the darkness. Fine stuff, by the powers.

The definitive pirate movie is *Captain Blood*. Sabatini's book (and this is a highly personal opinion shared probably by nobody, and we shall have to wait a couple of hundred years to see) is one of the great unrecognised novels of the twentieth century, and as close as any modern writer has come to a prose epic. So much for that. The film held reasonably close to the original, which was based on Morgan's exploits within a fictitious framework, recounting the story of an Irish surgeon falsely accused of being a Monmouth rebel and sold into slavery, falling for the niece of his brutal owner, escaping to become a buccaneer, turning patriot in a crisis, getting the girl, and becoming Governor of Jamaica.

All in the day's work for the young hopeful from Northampton Rep, Errol Flynn, whose first leading role it was, and for Michael Curtiz (director), Basil Rathbone (all fleering French villainy), Lionel Atwill (brutal uncle), and the nineteen-year-old Olivia de Havilland. They were to do even better, but as it stands *Captain Blood* is interesting because it does put piracy in a historical context; attention is truthfully paid to the Monmouth Rebellion, the Bloody Assizes, and best of all, to the ethics of buccaneering – the drawing of articles, the code of discipline, even the curious provisions for life and accident insurance. Judge Jeffreys is memorably captured by Leonard Mudie, pale and feverish-eyed, delivering sentence in his dreadful dry whisper: "Now, fellow, we be done with witnesses . . . " (his malady, in fact, was kidney stone, not tuberculosis as diagnosed in the film), James II makes a suitably handsome and cruel appearance in the person of Vernon Steele, and the Glorious Revolution of 1688, if unseen, is properly referred to.

At a lower level, the film is reputed to abound in anachronisms of costume and detail – wigs and ships' rigging are said

A casting director's dream: Sir Henry Morgan (from Exquemelin's *Buccaneers of America*) and right, Laird Cregar – who was only twenty-six when *The Black Swan* was filmed.

to be out of period, but I can't say I noticed, possibly because Curtiz and his photographer, Hal Mohr, achieved something rare in the cinema: now and then, it was as though a window had been opened on another age. The interiors *look* candle-lit; the players seem to belong in their setting; there are few concessions to glamour; sometimes a scene looks like a Flemish painting; the slave quarters are stifling and filthy; the heat beats off the plantation and waterfront; the battles look like battles; the most famous of screen duels takes place in a half-gale (and who will ever forget Rathbone sprawled on the sand with the surf washing through his curls?) – in a

word, it looks and sounds historically real, partly because Casey Robinson had the good sense to lace the script heavily with Sabatini's dialogue. ("Don't fling your French at me!" became a playground slogan, *c.* 1935.) To the writers the laurels, to Curtiz, and to Korngold, who set a new pattern for sea-music.

The Black Swan did it all in Technicolor, turned Sabatini's claustrophobic little story into a full-blooded spectacular, came close to parody in its exuberance, and was great fun all round. Its principals were a good deal nearer to their originals than the genteel Peter Blood; they rioted and looted,

William Kidd, left, (from a sketch made at his trial by Sir James Thornhill), and, above, Charles Laughton with pirate henchman Abner Biberman in *Captain Kidd.*

Right, Binnie Barnes as the eighteenth-century female pirate Anne Bonney, in *The Spanish Main,* and on opposite page, Anne Bonney (from the Dutch edition of Defoe's General History of the Pyrates), and Jean Peters in *Anne of the Indies.*

drank heavily, and mistreated their wenches shamefully, even Maureen O'Hara (who was indispensable to seventeenth-century movies, because she was Junoesque and looked like Nell Gwynne modelling for *Vogue* under the supervision of Sir Peter Lely). Tyrone Power was a surly thug of a hero with a drooping moustache, George Sanders a shambling red-bearded monster, and Anthony Quinn wore a patch over one eye. But the picture was dominated (as his films so often were) by the imposing Laird Cregar as Sir Henry Morgan; this was the best kind of film portrait, authentic in appearance

and (one imagines) behaviour, pistolling right and left with a Welsh accent. There were rousing sea actions, tavern brawls, a furious night attack on a Spanish settlement, Tyrone stretched defiantly on the rack, and a full-blooded duel which ended with Sanders wandering about impaled on a rapier. But what stays most vividly in memory as an authentic picture is the buccaneers carousing over their spoil, pouring drink on female captives, and one bald-headed horror giggling drunkenly as he paws through his glittering plunder. Drink and the devil, indeed.

Captain Kidd paid only a little heed to history, which was a pity, for the true story is an odd one. Kidd was a former buccaneer who, with the backing of various noblemen, was commissioned to hunt down and plunder pirates; in the event he turned pirate himself and was hanged, protesting his innocence to the last. The film never got to grips with this situation but gave Charles Laughton a chance to smack his lips in oily villainy and twitch memorably beneath the gallows. It also introduced the fiction that Kidd had pretensions to gentility – in fact he was of respectable middle-class

"Blackbeard" Teach, left (from a sketch in Defoe's General History of the Pyrates), and Robert Newton as *Blackbeard the Pirate*.

background, and nothing like Laughton; the authentic portrait shows a rather distinguished, strongly featured individual. Randolph Scott, of all people, was the rapier-wielding hero, and Gilbert Roland, Abner Biberman, John Carradine, and Sheldon Leonard were a fine crew of supporting villains. Of historic interest was Henry Daniell's brief, chilly appearance as William of Orange, an imaginative piece of casting. Over the sequel in which Laughton met Abbot and Costello, decency compels us to draw a veil.

For now pirates were well into send-up, with Bob Hope's *The Princess and the Pirate*, which introduced a splendidly wicked Spanish viceroy, Walter Slezak, in a part which he was to reprise memorably in *The Spanish Main*; funny villainy is a

great gift, and he made the most of it, smirking and preening with immense style. *The Spanish Main* naturally had Maureen O'Hara, and if Paul Henreid seemed odd casting as the Dutch buccaneer hero, it was at least a timely reminder that Holland played its distinguished part in true-life piracy. The one historic figure on view was the female filibuster Anne Bonney; Binnie Barnes swaggered and duelled gamely in the part, but the dreadful harridan depicted in Defoe was probably a lot nearer the real thing.

And so the pirates sailed away. Burt Lancaster's excellent *The Crimson Pirate* was pure comedy, with hot-air balloons and wooden legs getting stuck in gratings, and *Blackbeard the Pirate* was an "Oi-be, har-har!" jamboree for Robert Newton. Oddly enough, he may well have been quite like the real Blackbeard Teach, who started life stealing wigs in Bristol, had seven wives, fired off pistols under the table at mealtimes, tried to recreate Hell by sitting in a ship's hold full of burning sulphur, was finally killed in true Hollywood style in a duel with a dashing naval lieutenant (Newton, on the other hand, was tamely drowned by disgruntled associates), and departed the scene as a severed head swinging from a yardarm. Even for Hollywood, it is too far over the top-gallant.

""Then I'll take her when you're dead!" Errol Flynn and Basil Rathbone cross swords in *Captain Blood*.

The longest duel in screen history: Stewart Granger (in the stripes) v. Mel Ferrer in *Scaramouche.*
Previous page, Dumas's Musketeers: from left, Athos (Oliver Reed), D'Artagnan (Michael York), Aramis (Richard Chamberlain), and Porthos (Frank Finlay).

FOURTH AGE
Romance and Royalty

In the introduction to this book I implied that one of the best ways of learning history, in a simple form at least, is through fiction. Perhaps a better way of putting it is to say that the smoothest introduction to the past can be performed by a story-teller (novelist, dramatist, or film-maker) who knows his subject, respects it, and uses it honestly. Such a one was Alexandre Dumas père, who decided 150 years ago that Scott and Shakespeare were on to a good thing and he could do it even better. In some ways he was right; thanks to him we have seen the early seventeenth century in all its brilliance. He has given life to one of the least glamorous periods of modern history and personified it in four young men in plumed hats and long tabards, flourishing their swords and looking for trouble.

Dumas did not invent the Musketeers; he merely im-mortalized them. They were real people whom he found in an old book by one Courtilz de Sandraz, purporting to be the memoirs of Charles de Batz de Castlemore, Comte D'Artagnan, commander of the 1st Company of the King's Musketeers. It is difficult to tell how much is fact and how much fiction – Voltaire had deep suspicions about it and Sandraz's other works – but there seems to be no doubt that the real D'Artagnan was a dashing soldier and gallant, and his English translator is probably right in describing his Memoirs as a collection of the stories told about him in his day, exagger-ated and embroidered perhaps, but based on truth. They are all there in the Memoirs – Athos, Porthos, Aramis, Jussac, Treville, and Milady ("Milédi", the beautiful Englishwoman with whom D'Artagnan confesses he was in love) – and Dumas recalled them to the colours in "The Three Musketeers", blending them artfully into Franco-English history.

There is no romance like it: the young Gascon cadet, thirsting for glory, falling foul of the indomitable Three, then standing up with them against the Cardinal's guards, saving the Queen of France's honour by retrieving the diamond studs she has unwisely bestowed on her wooer, the Duke of Buckingham, foiling the plots of the Cardinal and the wicked Milady, losing his beloved Constance, finally becoming a lieutenant in the Musketeers. The central hinge of the plot – that Cardinal Richelieu, a rejected admirer of the Queen and both a personal and political enemy of Buckingham, used the studs in an attempt to disgrace her – may be mere historical gossip by La Rochefoucauld, from whom Dumas borrowed it, but it fits neatly into the facts. Buckingham, the handsome and arrogant favourite who was virtual ruler of England, did pay court to the young French Queen and, finding himself barred from France, was preparing to risk war when he was assassinated at Portsmouth.

There have been at least six sound and many silent versions of *The Three Musketeers* (one of them a musical with the Ritz Brothers) as well as films of Dumas's other Musketeer novels. Before the war, the D'Artagnans included Walter Abel, Warren William, and Don Ameche; Milady was played by Binnie Barnes and Margot Grahame, and Richelieu by Miles Mander (who also played Aramis in *The Man in the Iron Mask* in the same year, 1939). Then in 1948 came the lavish MGM spectacular, a film of brilliant colour and costumes, staged with great panache, with Gene Kelly swashbuckling acrobatically in the Fairbanks tradition as D'Artagnan, bringing all his dancer's grace to the role; it was a splendid, almost balletic rendering of the story, and its

"More inhumanity than a thousand dagger thrusts" – Memoirs of D'Artagnan. Two Milady de Winters: left, Lana Turner, and Faye Dunaway, right.

writer, Robert Ardrey, held close to the plot of the original, and performed the considerable feat of condensing it into just over two hours without losing the essentials. MGM used their battery of star names, with Lana Turner as Milady, Vincent Price (Richelieu), Frank Morgan (Louis XIII), June Allyson (Constance), Angela Lansbury (the Queen), Keenan Wynn (Planchet), John Sutton (Buckingham), and Van Heflin, Robert Coote, and Gig Young as Athos, Aramis, and Porthos. It was a spectacular in the old studio tradition: rich, lively, glossy, romantic, and thoroughly enjoyable.

Twenty-five years is a long time in the cinema (compare 1948 with 1923, for example) and in 1973 the approach was quite different. The story was told in two films[1] totalling three and a half hours, with a mixture of comedy and realism; there was room for more of Dumas, and for historical detail – a real tennis match, the siege of La Rochelle, the extravagances of royalty in elegant palaces and the squalor of slum interiors, even an early submarine, authentic broadsword rough-housing instead of the conventional polished rapier work. The Musketeers were closer to Dumas's originals – a good deal less decorous and principled than they usually

1 The second, *The Four Musketeers*, was released in 1974.

Louis Hayward, holding mask, is supported by middle-aged Musketeers in *The Man in the Iron Mask*: from extreme left, Aramis (Miles Mander), Athos (Bert Roach), D'Artagnan (Warren William), and Porthos (Alan Hale). The furtive figure behind is Colbert (Walter Kingsford).

appear on screen. Visually, the film was beautiful, in sets and costumes, and the director, Richard Lester, filled the screen with life and spirit and fun.

These are brief, and I hope fair, descriptions of the two productions, the vivacious romance of 1948 and the realistic comedy of the twin films of 1973; they are from different generations. Obviously, as the screenwriter of the 1973 films, I belong to the latter; for me, the M3 and M4, as we called them, had the best director who ever tackled the subject, and there never have been Musketeers to match Oliver Reed (Athos), Richard Chamberlain (Aramis), Frank Finlay (Porthos), or Michael York (D'Artagnan). Nor a Milady so wickedly lovely as Faye Dunaway, a Cardinal so masterful and urbane as Heston (how one man can look so like Henry VIII *and* Richelieu remains a mystery) . . . and so on through the cast, with Raquel Welch (Constance), Spike Milligan (Bonancieux), Roy Kinnear (Planchet), Christopher Lee (Rochefort), Simon Ward (Buckingham), Jean-Pierre Cassel (King Louis), Geraldine Chaplin (the Queen), Michael

Gothard (Felton), and all the others, including the tiny girl watching the dentist at work in the Paris street. No screenwriter was ever so fortunate, or more grateful.

Dumas aged his Musketeers through a series of novels (one of which, "Son of Porthos", set a style in titles which Hollywood fastened on joyfully) covering a long period of French history. It was in the fifth that he chose a subject which is one of the true classic mysteries, and was to inspire one of the best Musketeer films, *The Man in the Iron Mask*.

Who this unfortunate was – if, indeed, he did exist – has been the subject of endless speculation since the day when, according to tradition, a masked prisoner was brought to the Bastille in 1698. One rumour was that he was a brother to Louis XIV, and the rightful heir to the throne; another, quoted in Voltaire, that he was an illegitimate son of Anne of Austria, Louis XIII's Queen, and therefore Louis XIV's half-brother; another that he was Charles II's illegitimate son, the Duke of Monmouth; yet another that he was a son of Cromwell. Various French nobles, as well as a foreign diplomat named Matthioli, were suggested as candidates; another variation had the mask made of velvet, not iron – there was no lack of stories, and Hollywood, adapting Dumas, went for the most sensational.

This has twin sons born to Louis XIII's Queen. One grows up to be a tyrannical Louis XIV, while the other, Philip, is raised as a model of virtue by D'Artagnan and his three friends; neither brother knows of the other's existence until chance brings them face to face, all is discovered, and Louis has his twin locked in the Bastille in an iron mask. The Musketeers rescue their protégé, imprison Louis in his place, and Philip is beginning a liberal reign when Louis escapes, chases and swordplay ensue, Louis is drowned, mask and all, the Musketeers die gloriously, and Philip marries Joan Bennet and becomes permanent King of France.

It is fine, romantic stuff, full of secret passages, gloomy dungeons, torture chambers, intrigue, and action, and distinguished by a remarkable performance from Louis Hayward as the twin brothers. As an actor, he was well ahead of most of his fellow swashbucklers, and in *Iron Mask* there was never a doubt which brother was on screen: the difference between Louis and Philip-impersonating-Louis was quite beautifully done. Walter Kingsford as Colbert and Joseph Schildkraut as Fouquet may not have been strict portrayals of the originals, but they played neatly off one another, Warren William was a stern and resolute D'Artagnan, and Miles Mander, Alan Hale, and Bert Roach were a well-matured trio as Aramis, Porthos, and Athos. The iron mask itself was a thing of nightmare, especially in one grim shot of the enthroned figure, a cloak about its shoulders, the hideous metal face shining dimly in the shadows. Darth Vadar never looked so horrific.

It is fitting that the Musketeers should fall chronologically at the beginning of Hollywood's Fourth Age, which runs roughly from the death of Elizabeth to the Napoleonic Wars. They typify the films set in those two hundred years which form the great romantic era of the cinema, the final flourish of real costume and pageantry and old-style gallantry,

the last great age of fairytale royalty, of gentlemen heroes and Gainsborough ladies, of cloak-and-sword picaresque, swagger and powder and patch and honour and debonair style, when the romantic flame burns all the brighter because it will soon go out. (Not that it ever quite vanished; Hollywood, preaching the sturdy values of progress and democracy and individual equality, has never shed altogether its nostalgia for the prettier shibboleths of the old days, which can lead to odd contradictions. The heroine of *Star Wars* still had to be a princess – of republican sympathies.)

But if the Musketeer spirit runs through the films of those two centuries, it is accompanied by a sense that the legendary days are past, and history is beginning to get serious. "Modern times", after all, began sometime in the seventeenth century. Before that, we have a sense that for all the spiritual upheavals and wars and great race movements, nothing basic had changed all that much over the centuries; until the 1600s the eternal foundations remained unaltered. Monarchs still ruled, more or less absolutely, as they had always done; the people were still the people, seldom looking beyond their immediate horizons; God, however He was worshipped, was in His heaven, and the lot of peasant and shopkeeper and cleric and overlord seems to us to have been not very different from what it had always been since governed society began. That is a huge, vague generalisation, but since there is no room here for the Cambridge Ancient and Modern Histories it will have to do.

But in the seventeenth century things began to change – the world's horizons opened, outwards and inwards, the English-speaking people questioned and changed their system of government, new ideas took root and grew with alarming speed, science and exploration fuelled the process, and in two long lifetimes, no more, the time had sped from Elizabeth to the steam locomotive – and that was the least of it.

So while Hollywood's interest in the years between D'Artagnan's recovery of the Queen's diamonds and Rod Steiger's defeat at Waterloo has been largely romantic, it has recognised that after 1600 history is a developing process, not something frozen in the distant past. Its treatment of the Elizabethans, the Middle Ages, Ancient Rome and Egypt, and the Bible stories, had a legendary quality; no doubt they had historic significance, but they were far off and not quite real – but set a film between 1600 and 1800 and you could not ignore that it touched on matters of real importance, like colonial expansion, the Pilgrim Fathers, the British Civil War, the contest for the New World, the rise of parliamentary government, the American War of Independence, the French Revolution, free speech, democracy, the Industrial Revolution, exploding shells, and the spread of literacy. It was beginning to look something like our own times; a pattern was becoming visible which, with a little study, could be related to the present day.

This did not change the film-makers' approach; a story is still a story, whenever it happened. But a difference is detectable between Romantic Age movies and their predecessors: the human characters are distinctly modern in outlook, speech, and general behaviour, as though anticipating the twentieth century; the costumes and courtliness may still be there, but the minds beneath the wigs are entirely in tune with our own; there is a sense of the future and continuing change. When Robin led Marian out of the great hall at Nottingham Castle, it was into a world that would never alter, but when the Scarlet Pimpernel brings his lady back from France, we know quite well that their grandchildren are going to drive cars, use zip fasteners, and get cut off on the phone.

Cardinal Richelieu, lucky man, had no inkling of this, but the vigour with which he opposed constitutional reform suggests that he may have suspected that the world was changing. I return to him now, because as history progresses the volume of films increases, and the only way to deal with the Romantic Age is to move ahead chronologically through a selection of films which either deal with great events and people, or touch, however lightly, on that romantic past.

Hollywood kept Richelieu at work not only in the Musketeer films, but in a sympathetic biography with George Arliss (*Cardinal Richelieu*), and in *Under the Red Robe*, an off-beat, atmospheric swashbuckler from the novel by Stanley J. Weyman, who revived the costume romance a hundred years ago, and with this book in particular provided a plotline which has been used time without number. Its hero is Gil de Berrault (Conrad Veidt), whose skill as a duellist has earned him the nickname The Black Death. Sentenced to hang, he is reprieved on the gallows steps by Richelieu (Raymond Massey), who employs him against Protestant rebels: he is to penetrate their leader's lonely chateau and bring him prisoner to Paris. De Berrault duly impersonates his way in, but falls for the beautiful chatelaine (Annabella) and after much heart-searching, purloining of diamonds, mistaken identity, and night alarm, decides he cannot go through with his dirty work. Being the soul of honour, he returns to Paris to be hanged, and is fortunate to find Richelieu on the verge of disgrace and, by a twist of plot, in a forgiving mood. De Berrault is pardoned, and all ends happily.

As a swaggering ruffler with a bedraggled feather in his hat, Conrad Veidt had no equal; no one could prowl with such controlled menace, or sweep a heroine off her feet with such sardonic charm. Romney Brent was a dapper, insolent henchman, and the wonder is that no one turned the pair of them into a series. Massey was a formidable if rather passionate Richelieu, and a good likeness. The sets were stone-flagged and bare, and Georges Perinal shot them in shadowy candle-light: one interior, a seedy wayside inn, with fowls clucking among the benches, and Veidt stalking in the firelight, is specially memorable, but it was all a fine evocation of period.

One of Richelieu's preoccupations, in raising France to the forefront of the Continental powers, was the Thirty Years' War, a ghastly episode little taught in English-speaking schools (British involvement was peripheral) and consequently ignored by Hollywood. It was one of the most horrible, wasting wars in European history, arising initially out of Protestant refusal to have a Catholic king on the Bohemian

Top left: Cardinal Richelieu (by Philippe de Champaigne), below left, Raymond Massey; top right, Charlton Heston, and below right, George Arliss.

throne, and spreading into a great confused religious-political struggle which achieved nothing except carnage, destruction, plague and famine on an untold scale in Germany and her neighbours. Only once, to my knowledge, has the cinema touched it, in James Clavell's *The Last Valley*.

This begins, appropriately, with mindless massacre, rape, and looting, and has Omar Sharif as a fugitive scholar persuading a band of mercenaries, led by Michael Caine, that they would do well to sit out the war in an idyllic, land-locked valley. The result is religious strife, bloodshed, personal jealousy and hatred, ambush, attempted rape, witch-burning, and much casual slaughter, in a plot which left me bewildered – in fact, the whole bloody business is probably an excellent microcosm of the Thirty Years' War, with no clear picture of what is happening and half the cast ending up dead to no purpose.

To that extent it must be rated a successful film; it confirmed, graphically, the impression I had received from Sydenham Poyntz, an English mercenary who has left us one of the few accounts of the war by an actual participant. The movie also touched accurately on military history at one point, when Caine leads his troop to the attack at the Rheinfelden bridge (1638), in which Prince Bernard's Protestants, dragging cannon along with them, rout the Imperialists at the gate, and take the city; this incident is faithfully done.

It is the sad price of publicity and typecasting that at first sight Michael Caine looks rather odd in a steel beaver helmet, yellow-bearded and German-accented, but he gives one of his best performances as the hard-bitten mercenary captain, nicely complemented by Omar Sharif as the personification of reason. Nigel Davenport is a shrewd rural headman, and the mercenaries look and sound the parts of brutal and barbarous forayers. As a drama, *The Last Valley* is not remarkable; as a reminder of what happened in Central Europe, 1618–48, and shaped the future of Germany, it reads an interesting lesson.

Among the great casualties of that war, in which he fought

Michael Caine as a mercenary of the Thirty Years' War in *The Last Valley*.

on the same side as Michael Caine, was Gustavus Adolphus, the warrior King of Sweden, who was found dead on the field of Lutzen in 1632; he had been stabbed and shot through the head, the back, and twice in the arm. This did not stop Hollywood showing him still alive when found at the beginning of *Queen Christina*, so that he could speak a few last words; the film also depicted him as elderly, bald and grey-whiskered, when in fact he was a vigorous thirty-eight. The screenplay then proceeded to dramatise the life of his daughter, but worked in a respectable amount of factual material at the same time.

Christina was a remarkable queen and woman. She ascended the throne when she was six, and began to rule with a firm hand when she was only eighteen; reared as a boy rather than as a girl – she affected men's clothes and had a passion for horses and hunting – she had her father's strong

Queen Christina of Sweden (by J. H. Elbfas), left, and Greta Garbo.

temper, intelligence, and good looks, but not his martial ambitions, and it was in large part due to her that the Thirty Years' War was ended. She was devoted to science and the arts, had six languages, and corresponded with the great minds of her day, and since in addition to being an able ruler she was also vain, capricious, and extravagant, her popularity was immense. Her people's chief complaint was her repeated refusal to marry, and finally tired of royal responsibility, she abdicated at the age of twenty-eight and devoted herself to intellectual pursuits. Years later she reapplied for her throne, and that of Poland, without success.

She is, in fact, pure Hollywood, except for her apparent indifference to romance, which robs her of acceptable "motivation": queens, especially when played by Greta Garbo, cannot abdicate simply because they are fed up and want to read. The film puts this right, with a chance meeting at a snowbound inn with the handsome Spanish Ambassador (John Gilbert); passion ensues, and the notion of marrying anyone else, like her cousin Charles Gustavus (Reginald Owen), becomes even more repugnant to the Queen than it was before. But she cannot marry her Spanish lover, who is a Catholic and therefore unacceptable as consort, so she abdicates, to the consternation of all, not least her ardent admirer, the wicked Treasurer Magnus (Ian Keith), who forces a duel on the Spaniard and mortally wounds him. In the famous closing shot Christina sails away to exile, her lover having expired on the main-deck with Akim Tamiroff standing by.

This is a real three-handkerchief movie, and in its own way, superb. Garbo, at her most beautiful, emotes as never before, and gets away with it as no other actress could; she is also excellent casting, for while it is doubtful if Christina looked quite so stunning, this is a most believable queen, imperious, strong-willed, striding about in plumed hat and jack-boots, quelling the revolting citizenry with a mixture of iron hand and gentle touch. For the record, Christina was described by the English Ambassador as "sprightly, but somewhat pale . . . her mien and carriage very noble", and by another as having "a broad and serene brow, well-shaped eyes, gentle and lively expression . . . a rather pretty mouth".

John Gilbert, whose penultimate film this was, was chosen, according to Mr Halliwell, after Garbo had turned down Olivier, Leslie Howard, and several others. He is rather a silent-screen matinée idol, but his voice is better than I had been led to believe, and he is at least adequate. The film looks splendid, there is genuine, boisterous atmosphere in its tavern sequence, the costumes are authentic – Garbo, mistaken for a man, uses her male appearance with splendid self-consciousness – and there is great charm in the scene of the Queen's accession at the age of six, the tiny girl in her long gown bustling in between ranks of bowing courtiers and clambering manfully on to the throne. And apart from the romantic aspect the film does well by history; in fact, her abdication was a long-contemplated act, but her relentless quest for peace, her distaste for a dynastic marriage, her ability, her devotion to scholarship, and her patriotism, are faithfully shown.

Christina's abdication was a tremor in Swedish history; the end of the Thirty Years' War, which she helped to achieve, was momentous for Europe; but what happened in Britain in the same generation was world-shaking. The Great Rebellion, those civil wars in which a king was deposed, tried, and executed for treason by his own subjects, was a turning-point: it was crucial in determining how the British – and by extension, much of mankind, including the United States – would govern themselves. A process began whose milestones include the 1688 Revolution, the American War of Independence, the French Revolution, and the emergence of democracies in every continent – without the great war of King and Parliament, world history would have been unimaginably different.

It is the kind of subject, obviously, that the commercial cinema can only glance at, even in its immediate political and military aspects, which must be reduced to the simplest possible terms. Which means, since films are about people, concentrating on one or two of the main characters in the drama, in this case King Charles I and Oliver Cromwell, and telling the story through them.

Cromwell is a gallant effort. It tries to serve history, and succeeds to the extent that, in broad terms, it traces the clash between King and Parliament, shows Cromwell's rise to power, and the King's trial and execution, all fairly enough, given the necessity to simplify and dramatise events. It certainly carried conviction to a highly partisan Dublin audience when I first saw it, Charles's progress to the scaffold being accompanied by groans from the stalls, and an answering cry of "Take that, ye swine!" from the balcony. Such earnest critics of history may well have approved the scenes which show Cromwell standing up for the commonalty against landed interest (which he did), and preparing to leave for America (which he once said he *might* do, in certain circumstances), but they would also be well aware that he was *not* one of the Members threatened with arrest when Charles made his famous invasion of the Commons, and they may have wondered, as I did, if he played quite such a leading role in events before the war, hectored the King, and sought the impeachment of Strafford. The film also exaggerates his role at the Battle of Edgehill (where he was humble Captain Cromwell of Troop 67) by suggesting that he played an important part, and is most unfair to Essex, the Parliamentary commander. It should also be noted that it was the Cavalier

Charles I (by Van Dyck), left, and Alec Guinness in *Cromwell*.

Sir Jacob Astley, not the Roundhead Cromwell, who breathed the memorable prayer before action: "Oh Lord, Thou knowest how busy I must be this day; if I forget Thee, do not Thou forget me."[2]

Inevitably, there are historical queries all the way through, as there are bound to be in a picture which takes its subject seriously and tries to cover so much in less than two and a half hours. The main thrust of *Cromwell* is true, it gets a great deal of history, and the sense of history, right, and in one particular it is a triumph. Alec Guinness's portrayal of Charles I is perhaps the best living image ever presented in a historical film; he is Van Dyck's portraits come to life, and if some expert points out that he is slightly too tall I can only say he doesn't look it. It is a majestic performance, in the literal sense, carriage, style, accent and all; no wonder the Dublin audience believed him.

If Richard Harris is a disappointing Cromwell, it is not his fault; he is simply miscast, and one cannot accept him any more than one could accept Clark Gable as Napoleon – he simply looks nothing like, and can give no believable impression of, that plain, burly, enigmatic Englishman who stares so dourly out of his portraits, but who had a "wonderful under-

2 One can only regret, but not complain about, the omission of a fine moment at Edgehill when the future Charles II, then twelve, flourishing a pistol and shouting "I fear them not!" had to be hurried out of harm's way.

standing in the natures and humour of men" and performed the most remarkable revolution in his country's history. We cannot know what Cromwell was like; there was no Parliamentary Boswell. But we may be sure that the force was with him, and it is not to be felt from this film. He may well be unplayable; Ralph Richardson, who looked something like him, might have done it fifty years ago – or Spencer Tracy, with his powerful presence and authority; that would have been something to see.

As it is, the most memorable appearance of Cromwell was in the glum, austere shape of John le Mesurier, seen only in a brief scene of *The Moonraker*. This was a lively cloak-and-sword adventure whose period flavour actually gained from the fact that much of it was played inside a country inn where Royalists were trying to arrange the escape of the young Charles II. There were good sets, haunting music, a most likeable fat cavalier (Paul Whitsun-Jones), and some splendid Roundheads. Hollywood has rather neglected the soldiers of the Parliament; they may have been Right but Repulsive (while the Cavaliers were Wrong but Romantic, as

the good book says), but they were great menaces on screen, striding into camera in their lobster-tail helmets and buff gauntlets to demand of the Royalist beauty where her fugitive lover is hiding, before they start smashing the panelling. In *The Moonraker* Marius Goring was the Roundhead menace to Sylvia Syms and the heroic George Baker, while Oliver Reed, close-cropped, and Lionel Jeffries were the New Model heavies in *The Scarlet Blade*, but they have been exceptions to the cinematic rule, which is to concentrate on cavaliers, and one in particular, the famous swarthy man two yards high, who, after Henry VIII, is everyone's royal favourite.

The surprising thing about Charles II, considering his legendary charm, wit, gallantry, adventurous career, and general film potential, is that he has been played so seldom, and never by one of the great swashbucklers. Gable, Flynn, Fairbanks, Rathbone, Donat, and others with aristocratic moustaches[3] have all been cast in far less likely costume

3 The Wright and Lely portraits of Charles bear a striking resemblance to Rathbone, but a later painting attributed to Hawker suggests that the real look-alike is Walter Matthau.

Left, Oliver Cromwell (by Hutchinson after S. Cooper). Richard Harris as *Cromwell*, and John le Mesurier in *The Moonraker*.

roles, but the most photogenic of monarchs remains a supporting player; only twice that I can recall has he received a substantial role in a major film.

George Sanders, who bore only a superficial resemblance, but had the necessary air of bored, good-humoured tolerance, was the nearest thing to a definitive Charles in *Forever Amber*, losing at picquet with considerable style and promenading with his spaniels ("Children, children, what distressing behaviour"). But, as always, it was Sanders first and the character nowhere, and the film did little to enhance his credibility. It was Gone with the Great Fire in dazzling Technicolor, Hollywood's dream of the Restoration, and Pepys and Evelyn would not have marked it highly for technical merit, however much it deserved for effort.

The book was a huge bestseller, daring for fifty years ago, which is to say coy by today's standards, and it paved the way for countless inferior imitations set in a fantasy world anywhere between the Middle Ages and the Crimea, in which gypsy wenches were branded for poaching at Glasgow Assizes (*sic*), Victorian landlords exercised the *droit de seigneur*, and voluptuous heroines of humble birth went through legions of rakes, cavaliers, pirates, slavers, dukes, maniacs, and Highland chiefs (who ravished them as a preliminary to the wedding haggis) and other assorted lovers on their way to a title, commercial empire, or the king's bedroom. *Forever Amber*, as I remember, was well researched in a sound historical framework, but its fictional heroine and plot had an enormous influence on pseudo-historical fiction writing which, to judge from American paperback stalls, still continues, and the film no doubt encouraged the trend.

Amber (Linda Darnell) is a Puritan girl who throws off the shackles and embarks on a career as a light lady in Restoration London, where she has a series of lovers, among them His Majesty, but loses the only man she really cares for (Cornel Wilde) who emigrates to America with their child. Along the way there are the plague, the Great Fire, duelling, elaborate court settings, sumptuous costumes, and much

Charles II and, below, Nell Gwynne, by Sir Peter Lely.

George Sanders with Linda Darnell in *Forever Amber*, and right, Vincent Price, with Virginia Field (as Nell Gwynne) in *Hudson's Bay*.

implied passion, but the striving for visual effect results in a picture of the time that is all too glossy and artificial to be true. Sometimes there is a genuine Restoration flavour, as in a spirited duel between Wilde and Glen Langan, the King's arrival at the playhouse with "Romeo and Juliet" being interrupted while the players acknowledge him, and a fine squalid prison interior, but for once Linda Darnell, usually an accomplished performer, seems mechanical, and the only notable characters are Sanders, Richard Haydn unusually cast as an unpleasant nobleman, and John Russell as a raffish highwayman.

Sanders played Charles again in *The King's Thief*, a run-of-the-mill piece memorable only for having David Niven as its villain, plying his rapier against Edmund Purdom, but neither here nor in *Amber* was he as convincing as Vincent Price in *Hudson's Bay*. Here at least was an actor who looked reasonably like Old Rowley, and combined the languid style with the athletic presence – one could imagine Price walking ten miles a day for the fun of it as King Charles did; Sanders gave no such impression. The only fault here was in the script, which gave the Merry Monarch a slightly harder edge than he perhaps deserved.

Hudson's Bay is good history in its essentials, with a little glamour thrown in – the ideal mixture for historical cinema. The fact behind it is that two French explorers and fur traders, Pierre Esprit Radisson and Chouart des Groseillers

("Gooseberry"), penetrating westward in the 1660s, realized the potential of the fur trade in the Hudson's Bay area, but met with no response from their own country; indeed, they were punished for exploring without permission from the French, who at that time held sway in Canada. So, by bureaucratic stupidity, are empires lost: Radisson took his project to the English, who had recently driven the Dutch from what is now New York, and found eager supporters, including Prince Rupert; King Charles granted a charter and the great trading company was formed which established the British foothold in Canada.

The film gives Radisson (Paul Muni) and "Gooseberry" (Laird Cregar) an English companion, Lord Crewe (John Sutton), who smooths their path at Charles II's court; his sweetheart (Gene Tierney) has a dissolute brother (Morton Lowry) who joins the trading expedition, sells drink to the Indians, and is shot on Radisson's orders – none of which interferes with the unfolding of a significant chapter of empire. Indeed, the subplot helps with the film's message, which is that commerce is fine, but not at the expense of the environment or native people – it is an irony which will probably escape modern campaigners that a movie extolling the glories of empire and capitalism (and the fur trade, of all things!) should be just as concerned about conservation and minority rights; indeed, it was preaching long before today's reformers, and may remind them that imperialism had its virtues, too.

Hudson's Bay paid the penalty for being ahead of its time; critics found it boring, and one described it as "a cock-eyed history lesson" which, overall, it is certainly not (again, one wonders how much authority there is behind some of the careless, dismissive reviews). It was a bit of a sermon, with Paul Muni preaching, but no one could do it better. He made Radisson a jaunty little rogue (which, judging from the lively style of his *Voyages*, he may have been), and the huge Cregar was an excellent foil; Nigel Bruce was an interesting Prince Rupert, and Morton Lowry (one of those film players whose face is instantly familiar, but whose name no one knows) established himself as a memorable spoiled weakling.

There was no straight history in *The Wicked Lady*, but plenty of style; like *Forever Amber* it fulfilled the popular notion of the Restoration as a time of flopping wigs and bulging bosoms (which it was) when gallants and wenches rioted in four-posters and discarded heaps of fashionable clothing. The film was shot (according to its male lead, James Mason) in twelve days, and with the British cinema's top box-office team – Margaret Lockwood played the title role – was a considerable success; it was rated the height of daring and vulgarity at the time, with Miss Lockwood being compared to Jane Russell, and cleavages having to be discreetly re-shot for the American market. It was, to quote a Restoration writer, full of sin and impudence, with Miss Lockwood stealing Griffith Jones from Patricia Roc and taking to highway robbery and a tobyman lover, Mason; there was a Tyburn hanging, much gaming and wenching and pistol-play, Felix Aylmer was an anxious old steward and Michael Rennie an imposing figure born to wear a full-bottom wig. While not a distinguished film, it managed to seem more decadent than its 1983 remake, which did it with horsewhips.

It is interesting to compare the earthy approach of *The Wicked Lady* with that of *Frenchman's Creek*, made in America a year earlier (1944). Granted that *Frenchman's Creek* was based on a Daphne du Maurier novel, its screen adaptation still had the decorous, glossy hallmark of the old romantic tradition, and yet its subject was not dissimilar to the British film's. The wicked Lady Skelton, admittedly a bad lot in the first place, was more than a match for her highwayman lover; the murderous adultress was acceptable in postwar Britain, but Hollywood, grown even more prim in the war years, would not have touched her. Its heroine was a virtuous if spirited noblewoman (Joan Fontaine) with a dull dog of a husband (Ralph Forbes) and an unwelcome rake of an admirer (Basil Rathbone). Miss Lockwood would have cuckolded the one and pegged the other out to dry when she was finished with him, but Miss Fontaine retires to Cornwall and engages in a light-hearted romance with a French pirate (Arturo de Cordova); she even joins his crew, and takes part in operations dressed as a boy. There is plenty of action and excitement, the piece is beautifully dressed (the London interiors look properly Restoration), and there is a grand melodramatic scene when the heroine, with some of the Skelton spirit briefly emerging, knifes the caddish Rathbone and clobbers him with a suit of armour. Cecil Kellaway has the acting honours as a French servant, de Cordova is thoroughly gallant, and there are no shocks of the *Wicked Lady* kind to the sensibilities.

In retrospect, the Restoration looks like a happy time; those who knew it called it Good King Charles's Golden Days, and Hollywood has reflected the image. With the passing of the Stuarts much of the carefree glamour seems to have faded, and certainly the new dynasty of Hanover could not have got off to a sadder start than it did with poor Sophia Dorothea of Zell. She is an almost-forgotten tragic figure who mothered the ancestor of our present royal family, and two and a half centuries later inspired one of the best British historical films, *Saraband for Dead Lovers*. As a screen entertainment it has never been judged remarkable; as an example of what a historical movie should be – a faithful dramatisation of fact – it is near-perfect.

Sophia Dorothea was sixteen, gay, and beautiful when she married the Elector of Hanover's son, later to be George I of England. He was a brutish and unfaithful lout, and it was not surprising that she turned for sympathy to a child-hood friend, Count Philip Konigsmark, a dashing Swedish adventurer, soldier, and former bull-fighter, now a colonel of Hanoverian dragoons. It was said that he had gained his colonelcy through his attentions to the plain but promiscuous Countess Platten, the Elector's mistress, and she, noting his attachment to Sophia, became fiercely jealous. It is doubtful if Sophia and Konigsmark were lovers, but possible that they were plotting to get her away from her obnoxious husband; Countess Platten, hoping to expose them, is believed to have

Above, Sophia Dorothea of Zell, and below, Joan Greenwood; overleaf . . .

... above, Count Philip Konigsmark, and below, Stewart Granger in *Saraband for Dead Lovers*.

Above, George I, and below, Peter Bull asserting his royal authority.

forged a note which took Konigsmark to the Princess's rooms at night, and on his return he was waylaid in the palace's Hall of Knights and killed by swordsmen posted by the vengeful Platten. Sophia Dorothea was promptly divorced, and spent the next thirty years in a fortress, where she died in 1726.

Saraband tells the story with complete fidelity, and only the smallest of romantic touches, and makes an enthralling film of it. Stewart Granger (Konigsmark) was born for this kind of costume picture, and Joan Greenwood is an appealing Sophia – the sight of her sitting up in her marriage bed awaiting her appalling husband (Peter Bull) would have melted a producer's heart. Flora Robson's acting is such that it is possible to feel sorry for her as the scheming Platten, and Françoise Rosay is a regal mother-in-law. The script is impeccable, there is a nightmare carnival scene in which Sophia is driven frantic for perhaps a little too long, but Granger is allowed to cut loose in the final swordplay with fine swashbuckling effect, until stabbed from behind by the treacherous Anthony Quayle. Best of all, the film conveys in a few brief scenes the stifling monotony of court life in a pretentious little German state; in this, too, *Saraband* is good history.

So is *Rob Roy*, the 1995 version, which is not only an excellent film in its own right, but far and away the best and most authentic picture of the old Scottish Highlands and the Highlanders that I have ever seen. From the vast opening shot of a party of kilted caterans scouting through breathtaking scenery in pursuit of a band of reivers, it is Stevenson and Scott and Neil Munro and my grandmothers' stories come to life, with not a fault that I could find in costume, weaponry, custom, behaviour, and atmosphere, and I am grateful to Michael Caton-Jones and his writer, Alan Sharp, for having done so well what Hollywood usually does so badly.

My one small regret is that the film deals with only one interlude in the great freebooter's remarkable career, but then 133 minutes could hardly encompass all his adventures, raids, thefts, pursuits, escapes, and general roguery which have passed into Scots folk-lore. Most of the tales are probably

true, although subject to interpretation: I have an infant memory of being shown Rob's grave at Balquhidder, where he lies near my own great-grandfather, and saying: "He was a robber, wasn't he?", only to be rebuked by my stern MacDonald grandmother: "He was no more a robber than those who hunted him."

Being of the outlawed Gregora, Rob Roy had banditry bred in him from birth, c.1671, and varied the trades of cattle drover and dealer with rustling and blackmail (the protection racket) until his fortieth year, when he had to take to the heather in earnest over a matter of £1000 borrowed from several noblemen for cattle purchase; whether he was let down by an associate or simply decamped with the money is uncertain, but he was certainly evicted and his wife "insulted" (as Scott tactfully puts it), whereafter he and his MacGregors waged "predatory war" against the Duke of Montrose, his principal creditor. The catalogue of his subsequent exploits, including the taking of Inversnaid fort, and assorted kidnappings, ambushes, captures and evasions, is impressive. As a Jacobite he joined the 1715 rising to the extent of attending the Battle of Sheriffmuir but declining to take part at the critical moment ("If they cannot do it without me, they cannot do it with me"); it may have been caution, or a reluctance to offend his patron and friend, the Duke of Argyll, who was on the other side, but whichever it was, Rob demonstrated his impartiality by plundering the baggage of both armies. In late middle age he finally submitted to the law, spent time in Newgate, was pardoned on the eve of being transported to Barbados, and died peacefully in 1734.

That, greatly condensed, is the received story of Rob Roy. The film concentrates on the £1000 incident and his eviction and feud with Montrose, which is worked up skilfully with plenty of blood and broadsword work, and if the old bandit is shown in the most kindly light, as a persecuted hero who makes much of his honour and is rather sterner than the cheerful rascal of popular legend, proper attention is paid to his resource, courage, courtesy, generosity to the poor, and (in a rather clever scene) his reputed reluctance to fight unless provoked beyond endurance.

Liam Neeson is a commanding and convincing "Red Rob", even if his hair is dark, his arms not nearly long enough to tie his garters without stooping, and his character rather too honest, and Jessica Lange has the right "fierce and haughty temper" as his wife. The supporting cast is immaculate: John Hurt as Montrose is the perfect Highland nobleman (that is, a polished crafty ruffian in wig and ruffles), and Andrew Keir is the great Argyll as I had always imagined him. There are two splendid villains, Brian Cox as a repulsive Killearn, and Tim Roth as an English cad who ravishes Mistress MacGregor, seduces serving-wenches, and murders supporting players, all with considerable style, before being dispatched by the avenging hero – although I cannot believe that the real Rob was as inept a swordsman as he appears in the final duel. I assume that Roth's character, Archie Cunningham (odd name for an Englishman), is based on Henry Cunningham of Stirlingshire, a mincing exquisite who was also an extremely hard man, and who in fact bested Rob Roy in a duel.

The film is gorgeous to look at, a rousing old-fashioned adventure, excellent history in its depiction of land and people, and marred only by occasional unnecessary coarseness. Which is a pity, for I should have liked to show it to my grandchildren as a faithful image of their ancestors.

Somewhere in the fictional hinterland between the seventeenth and eighteenth centuries lies another Highland tale – *The Swordsman*, unhonoured, unsung, and unnecessary except for a comparison which I shall make in a moment. Yet it has another use, too, as representing a whole school of films which cannot be called historical, although set in the past, but which I cannot leave unmentioned, either. These are the pure costume adventures, set in various centuries (and sometimes in no identifiable century or country at all), but belonging in spirit at least to the Romantic Age. I can only pass them by with a reverent bow: *The Prisoner of Zenda, The Mark of Zorro, The Count of Monte Cristo* (and all his Sons, Daughters,

Liam Neeson and Rob Roy (inset).

Returns, and Revenges), *The Corsican Brothers, The Flame and the Arrow*, and that spate of Technicolored swashbuckle of the late forties and early fifties when it was realized that costume pictures did not have to be on the grand scale, and we had gypsy wildcats in off-the-shoulder blouses, and bronzed rascals with ruffled shirts open to the waist, noble scoundrels oppressed the peasantry from Mexico to Transylvania, Maria Montez demonstrated the advantages of gauzy harem trousers, Fred Cavens and his fellow fight-arrangers staged duels with everything from rapiers to boarding-pikes, and Jon Hall, Willard Parker, Cornel Wilde, John Derek, and a young hopeful originally billed as Anthony Curtis pinked Villainy and rescued Adele Jergens and Piper Laurie in all directions. Those films are a subject in themselves, simple in plot, often lovely to look at, and professionally made, but they are not "historicals", and *The Swordsman* is just a peg to hang them on for a brief salutation.

Like many of its kind, it was a knavish piece of work, set in the Highlands of Lake Tahoe, possibly, with Larry Parks swaggering in the title role and masquerading under the name of Fraser (not that that affects my judgement) when he was really a MacArden, at feud with another clan whose name escapes me but whose eldest son was that fine actor George Macready. Ellen Drew was a Highland beauty in what looked like nylon, and they hooted and skirled and belaboured each other with broadswords, and Michael Duane was murdered, and it was all a terrible tartan horror. However, it had one use: in the following year (1948) the eminent critic Richard Winnington was able to invoke it in appraising another film of which he wrote: "Beside [it] *The Swordsman* seems like a dazzling work of veracity and art".

The other film was *Bonnie Prince Charlie*, rated as one of the great British disaster movies, and certainly one of the unhappiest historical ventures. It need not have been, for the story of the '45 is great tragic drama – the landing of the handsome prince, the rallying of the clansmen, the thunderbolt victory of Prestonpans, the advance into England, panic in London, the critical decision to retreat from Derby, the last war cry of Culloden, the escape in disguise, Flora MacDonald and over the sea to Skye. But it didn't work on film: possibly it was thought that David Niven, being a Scot, and full of charm, was natural casting in the title role; he was not, but that was a minor mistake in a film which had plainly spent its

Prince Charles Edward (by or after A. David), and David Niven as *Bonnie Prince Charlie*.

money in all the wrong directions. It was not spectacular, a simple story was poorly handled, it failed to convey what a close-run thing the rebellion actually was, it had a romantic flavour which is fine for nostalgic legend but not for historic crisis, and it cheated on not showing Culloden – one of the easiest and yet most colourful battles, from a film point of view.

Perhaps Scotland is fated in the cinema. For its size, it has produced more great historical fiction than any other country I can think of – and only once, in the Caton-Jones *Rob Roy*, has Scottish history looked good on the screen. For the rest, *Mary of Scotland, Bonnie Prince Charlie, Braveheart, Kidnapped*... perhaps Macbeth jinxed them all.

Russia has fared much better. One need cite only the case of Bonnie Prince Charlie's contemporary, the pretty little Princess Sophie of Anhalt-Zerbst – while he was removing from Culloden, followed (it is said) by cries of "There you go, for a damned cowardly Italian!", she was settling down in St Petersburg to a miserable married life with the half-witted degenerate Grand Duke Peter, future Tsar of All the Russias. Her prospects, bewildered in a foreign semi-barbaric court, must have looked almost as bleak as Charles Edward's, but even at sixteen she had an intelligence, patience, and force of character far beyond his, and it enabled her to become Catherine the Great.

Hollywood has done well by Catherine in several films – she has been portrayed by Elizabeth Bergner, Tallulah Bankhead, Francoise Rosay, Binnie Barnes, Bette Davis, and Jeanne Moreau, among others – but in none better than *The Scarlet Empress*, the ultimate success of the combined talents of Josef von Sternberg and Marlene Dietrich. This is a fantastic film, in the true and not the debased sense of the word, a mixture of dream and nightmare purportedly based on Catherine's diary (she was a prolific writer) and, despite its surreal quality, holding in the main to accepted history.

We see her childhood at a little German court where she is haunted by horrific visions of Russia, and then the young Dietrich as a most convincing teenager, arriving wide-eyed and innocent in a frightening Muscovite palace, submitting to marriage with a goggle-eyed monster of a Grand Duke (Sam Jaffe, bearing an uncanny resemblance to a malevolent Harpo Marx) and being tyrannized by the Empress, her mother-in-law. There the young Sophie, renamed Catherine, learns to endure and to wait, practising her sex appeal on her admirers, and at last, when the old Empress dies and Catherine and Russia are at the mercy of the demented Jaffe, leading the whirlwind coup which overthrows him and leaves her undisputed mistress of the Russian Empire.

It is a difficult film to describe. Von Sternberg (he of the Vestal Virgins) exploited Dietrich's icy beauty to the limit, photographing her through veils, in soft focus, in shadow, by candlelight, and in a series of exotic costumes, and let his camera range slowly over the details of a Russian court that looks like animated Hieronymous Bosch – gargoyles, skeletons, clockwork figures, tolling bells, in sets which tower in empty shadow or whirl with bizarre life, posses of ladies-in-waiting fluttering to and fro, chanting priests, gargantuan banquets, horsemen thundering into camera, the Grand Duke giggling madly as he drills his soldiers in the palace corridors – while Dietrich is gradually transformed from an awe-stricken innocent shrinking among her grotesque in-laws, into the self-assured and calculating femme fatale eyeing her parade of lovers as she prepares to usurp the throne. This, elaborating history, is a wild sequence in which Catherine, in white Hussar uniform, leads her cavalry in full career up the palace staircases, while the 1812 Overture is given full throttle.

It is probably Dietrich's best performance, and she is ably abetted by John Lodge[4] as her stalwart admirer Alexei, by Louise Dresser as the old Empress (a fine study in autocratic eccentricity), and by Sam Jaffe. Peter was not murdered on

---

4 Having played a Russian envoy in this film, Mr Lodge retired from the cinema some years later, and became United States Ambassador to Spain and the Argentine.

Catherine II, Empress of Russia (by D. G. Levitsky), and, right, Marlene Dietrich carried shoulder-high by her guardsmen in *The Scarlet Empress.* Below, Sam Jaffe and, right, The Grand Duke Peter.

the night of the coup, as shown here, but died mysteriously some time after. As for the decor, perhaps the Russian court did look like that: I am now prepared to believe it did. The script by Manuel Komroff is extremely good, with much wit, and the character of Catherine, bold, clever, and promiscuous, is just; in reality she did not look quite as immaculate as Dietrich, but the effect may not have been all that different. In her own words: "They told me I was beautiful as the dawn and very striking. To tell the truth, I never believed myself to be very beautiful. I had charm, and that, I think, was my strength."

She is given charm and to spare by Elisabeth Bergner in Korda's *Catherine the Great*, a lighter and altogether more realistic version than von Sternberg's; again, the story is taken no further than the coup which brought Catherine to the throne. Flora Robson is in imperious form as the Empress Elizabeth and Griffith Jones is a devoted Gregory Orloff, but the film is stolen by Douglas Fairbanks, junior, cast against type as the mad Grand Duke Peter, and succeeding in winning some sympathy for that dangerously unpredictable tyrant.

Catherine ruled Russia and her legions of lovers for more than thirty years, with considerable success; when she died, almost at the end of our Fourth Age, she had outlived by three years her only serious rival among the romantic rulers of the eighteenth century, Marie Antoinette of France, who went to the guillotine in 1793, and lives in popular imagination as the brilliant, frivolous symbol of the *ancien régime*. In being extravagant, short-sighted, reactionary, and insensitive she certainly embodied many of the faults which precipitated the French Revolution, but it is unlikely that she ever made the famous sick joke attributed to her,[5] and to its credit the film *Marie Antoinette* did not use it, either, possibly because

Marie Antoinette (by Vigée-Lebrun) and, below, as played by Norma Shearer.

5 If Marie Antoinette ever said "Let them eat cake" when told that the people had no bread, she was not the first. "Why don't they eat pastry?" has been attributed to Marie-Thérèse, queen to Louis XIV in the previous century, and Rousseau refers to the cake version as proverbial. It has been spoken on screen, by Ann Miller impersonating Marie Antoinette in a musical; she was immediately hit by a custard pie.

it would have been quite inconsistent with the character portrayed by Norma Shearer.

The part had been earmarked for her in 1933, five years before the film was made; in the interval Europe was scoured for antique properties, sumptuous sets and costumes were designed, and the publicity drum was beaten: I even remember a pictorial feature designed to show how closely the cast resembled their originals. I still don't think that Louis XV looked at all like John Barrymore, or that Count Axel Fersen could conceivably be mistaken for Tyrone Power. But all the effort was not wasted: *Marie Antoinette* was a great wedding cake of a film, extravagantly romantic in appearance and in the treatment of its heroine.

Like Catherine, Marie Antoinette was a foreign princess married to an unprepossessing heir apparent; it was her good fortune that the future Louis XVI, unlike Peter of Russia, was a kindly if backward soul who treated her with an affection not shared by most of Louis XV's court, who disliked her for her impatience with etiquette, her partiality to her native Austria, and for her failure to produce an heir for seven years. She also incurred the enmity of the powerful Madame du Barry, mistress of Louis XV, and was unpopular with the public for her frivolity and extravagance – after she became Queen, the affair of the famous diamond necklace (an elaborate confidence trick in which it was made to appear that she had squandered millions on jewellery which in fact she never received) did her great harm, and she was unjustly blamed for the chronic poverty of the country, and most of its other pre-revolutionary miseries. At the same time, she did have a bad influence on her weak husband's policy; her interference and resistance to reform undoubtedly helped to make a bad situation worse.

This the film soft-pedals, concentrating at inordinate length on her affair with the dashing Swede, Fersen, which in fact was innocent, if indiscreet, and far from the grand passion of Shearer and Power; seldom have sweet nothings taken up so much screen time. Her early trials at court are shown, with

Above: Count Axel Fersen, and left, Tyrone Power.
Below: Louis XVI of France (by Duplessis).

Robert Morley, right, as Louis, with Norma Shearer, and Joseph Schildkraut as Philip Egalité.

some dramatic embroidery, and the events of the Revolution suffer from some necessary "telescoping", as DeMille would have called it. But the production looks magnificent; one feels one has been at Versailles (if for a rather long stay), the revolutionaries storm about with considerable spirit, Louis puts on his cap of liberty, the imprisonment of the royal family is a good and often touching sequence, and the attempted escape to Varennes (which was indeed masterminded by Fersen) has genuine suspense. And, at the last, Marie Antoinette is as brave as, by all accounts, she was.

The star of the film is Robert Morley as Louis XVI, painfully awkward and vulnerable, a gentle unhappy man who develops his own quiet dignity; John Barrymore is himself, which is always worth seeing, although he looks nothing like forty-four years older than Morley, as history demands he should; Joseph Schildkraut is a mincing and malicious Philip Egalité, and one of the high points in the picture is his insidious voice off-screen, reciting popular grievances, while the camera cuts from Morley bearing his new-born son through the splendours of Versailles, to a wretched peasant woman with her ragged infant in the fields. It is a telling comparison, and the film could have done with more of them.

Such brief images are often all that a film can do when it touches on a great historic theme. The causes and course of the French Revolution are not to be covered in a screenplay: starving mobs and luxurious tyranny will have to do, and since they were the root of the matter, it is fair enough to show them and let it go at that. And once again, fiction has its uses: *A Tale of Two Cities*, in its screen version, gives a more vivid picture of the events of 1789 than *Marie Antoinette* could hope to do, because Dickens could plot his own course through historic events, and use his characters to personify the forces of the time: the callous Marquis in his carriage running over a child and being more concerned for his horses; his nephew, touched with the new reforming spirit; the old shoemaker imprisoned for years by aristocratic injustice; the dreadful Defarge and the Vengeance storing up their hatred – let the master storyteller weave his threads through it all, and as true a picture will emerge as any historian can paint, and a good deal brighter. *A Tale of Two Cities* is also an excellent piece of fiction, although Dickens purists do not rate it highly, finding too much contrivance in the story of the drunken lawyer who is the double of the French aristo and goes to the guillotine in his place for the sake of the woman they both love . . . well, you either accept Dickens' coincidences or you don't.

David O. Selznick did, and the result is a model of how a great novel should be filmed, and demonstrates how much better films were then than they are now. It looks and sounds and *feels* like Dickens, and is authentic in a way that no modern production could hope to be, even those adaptations of Dickens' work which were the cream of television drama in the 1980s. Why this should be, I don't know – is it black-and-white photography, or the fact that Selznick could transmit his Dickens mania, or that the cast understood better what I can only call the Dickensian state of mind? Claud Gillingwater (Jarvis Lorry) was born in the year that

Dickens died; Rathbone (the Marquis), Edna Mae Oliver (Miss Pross), Ronald Colman (Sidney Carton), and Billy Bevan (Jerry Cruncher) were brought up by people who had lived in Dickens' time – was being Victorian an advantage? Possibly, but I'm afraid that sheer ability was a greater one. Anyway, they and the adaptors made Dickens – and the French Revolution – come to life.

As a child, I was under the impression that Rathbone had started the whole thing by his treatment of the jacquerie, and I doubt if the real sans-culottes who stormed the Bastille were any more frightful than Blanche Yurka (Madame Defarge), Lucille Laverne (the Vengeance, a cackling toothless horror), and Fritz Leiber, a fine actor who frequently portrayed Franz Liszt and whose knife-like profile looked truly fearsome under a cap of liberty. The Bastille episode is on the grand scale, with vast mobs of enraged citizenry, and the military joining in; equally impressive are the scenes in which a starving crowd snatch scraps of meat from a nobleman's dogs and are sabred by dragoons; the revolutionary tribunal, with Miss Yurka denouncing like a Fury and the innocents being condemned by a jury of raucous ruffians; Carton and the little seamstress (Isobel Jewell) in the tumbril; and the exulting spectators at the guillotine. It is a true picture, and I doubt if Thomas Carlyle, whose name appears in the credits under the unusual heading "Bibliography", would have asked his agent to get it removed.

The Scarlet Pimpernel is lighter fiction, but it too has its authentic moments, especially the brilliantly photographed first fifteen minutes, with the condemned aristocrats awaiting execution: the gentlemen conversing quietly, the ladies attending to their complexions, or reading, the children playing blind man's buff, while outside the drums roll, the knitting women stare up expectantly, their needles poised, the blade falls, a hellish cheer, and the needles click again – it is all a cliché of the Revolution, thanks to this film, which is as high a compliment as one can pay; there is enough documentation of how the *ancien régime* met its fate, to confirm it.

The storming of the Bastille in *A Tale of Two Cities*.

The *Pimpernel* is how audiences remember Leslie Howard; the expression "laid-back" had not been coined in his day, but it fitted him as perfectly as Sir Percy Blakeney's flawlessly cut inexpressibles. The saunter, the quizzing-glass, the lazy voice, the ennui, the slight shock when we notice that the fop has an eye like a fish-hook; he is a hero unique in the cinema, although it is interesting to compare Zorro, Destry, and others who have hidden their steel under an ineffectual exterior. Merle Oberon is his estranged lady, and Raymond Massey the sardonic Citizen Chauvelin baffled as the Pimpernel spirits aristocrats from the shadow of the guillotine. There is some nice period detail (Mendoza did make a comeback to beat Bill Warr), Nigel Bruce is a portly Prinny, Melville Cooper looks not unlike Romney the painter, and there is one of the screen's most satisfactory reappearances when the Pimpernel strolls in on the dumfounded Chauvelin, who supposes him to have been executed by firing squad.

There were sequels, all overshadowed by the original, although Barry K. Barnes, in *The Return of the Scarlet Pimpernel*, was a pleasant Sir Percy, threatening to teach Chauvelin (Francis Lister) to play cricket, and Henry Oscar was a notable Robespierre. And having mentioned that name I cannot omit the fine Polish actor Wojciech Pszoniak, who played Robespierre in the French production *Danton*, in which the title role was taken by the remarkable Gérard Depardieu; they were brilliant performers in an outstanding picture.

Scaramouche is the last real flourish of the Romantic Age, for while I am ending this chapter with Napoleon it is in the uneasy knowledge that he doesn't really belong here, but to the nineteenth century and a world far removed from the spirit of the Musketeers; romantic he may be, in his own way, but not like Scaramouche, who is in the old D'Artagnan tradition of swordplay and high adventure, at least where the cinema is concerned. In Sabatini's original novel, he is a rather modest lawyer, turned swordsman to avenge a friend legally murdered in a duel by yet another wicked Marquis; along the way he becomes a strolling player, a fencing master, and a Revolutionary politician, and when he finally catches up with his enemy it is to discover that the unspeakable cad is his own father. There is a lovely young noblewoman, a designing actress, and a painless lecture in Revolutionary history, and the book's opening sentence found its way into anthologies of quotations.[6]

Hollywood skipped the history but kept the quotation and the outline of the plot, the main difference being that Scaramouche's aristocratic quarry was changed from his father to his brother, a more credible relationship for Stewart Granger and Mel Ferrer. Janet Leigh was the aristocratic sweetheart and Eleanor Parker the actress, and the costumes would have caused raised eyebrows among Sabatini's Commedia dell'Arte theatrical troupe, but the swordplay made up for

6 "He was born with a gift of laughter and a sense that the world was mad." The authorities of Yale University, assuming that such a memorable saying must be a translation from classical literature, paid Sabatini the back-handed compliment of having it inscribed in stone on a college building.

everything. Granger, in astonishing tights, cut and thrust like an acrobat, he and Ferrer fought all over a crowded theatre, and when the last thrust went home (nearly) they had been at it for close on seven minutes, which is said to be the longest single combat ever shown on the screen.

It was great fun, and the whole film looked dazzling. Speaking as an old swordsman who couldn't even beat his fourteen-year-old daughter, I would place its final duel first for sheer spectacle among cinema thrust-outs, but for aesthetic satisfaction it must take third place behind Tony Curtis v. Ross Martin (*The Great Race*) and Power v. Rathbone (*The Mark of Zorro*). Flynn v. Rathbone (*Captain Blood*) belongs in some swordsmen's Valhalla of its own, and I have a personal affection for Michael York v. Christopher Lee (*The Four Musketeers*).[7]

Ah, well, there they go, fencing like fury, and we should be grateful not only to the perspiring actors and their doubles, but to people like Cavens and Hobbs and Ralph Faulkner and Sol Gorss, who made it look so exciting. And to the ladies who bit their lips and quivered in anxiety as they twisted their fans and hankies and backed away against the wall.

Even Napoleon is an anti-climax, but he half-belongs in the romantic era because one of his screen personae is the historical lover, a role in which Hollywood probably preferred him, love-scenes being much easier than battles. He has been most frequently seen in supporting roles, the Man of Destiny brooding in front of a map or outlining plans for a new campaign,[8] as background to some costume adventure, but there have been enough major studies to make selection difficult. There are four memorable English-speaking Napoleons:

7 Dick Lester was the director, and Bill Hobbs the fight-arranger, and I think it may be the only hero-villain sword-fight ever staged in a church – this because as a child I was fascinated by the sight of figures moving in and out of the coloured rays from Carlisle Cathedral's great medieval East Window, an effect which Dick Lester used in the film.

8 Or even interviewing the double who is to impersonate him, as in Woody Allen's *Love and Death*; the interview ends in the background of the scene, with Napoleon and the double falling to blows.

Symbol of the Revolution: the guillotine in D.W. Griffiths's 1921 silent film, *Orphans of the Storm*.

Herbert Lom (*The Young Mr Pitt* and *War and Peace*), Marlon Brando (*Desirée*), Charles Boyer (*Marie Walewska*), and Rod Steiger (*Waterloo*), and I choose the two last simply because I thought them the best.

Boyer not only looked uncannily like the portraits by David and others; he also epitomized the man described by countless biographers: the quick, abrupt manner, the restless energy, the direct stare, the sudden passions, the occasional "uncommon expression of sweetness", but always the impatient dynamo underneath. I suspect that anyone who saw *Marie Walewska* immediately thinks of Boyer when Napoleon is mentioned, which speaks for itself.

The prologue to the film admits "imaginative details supplied by the dramatist" but claims it does not violate the spirit

From left, Napoleon (by Jacques Louis David),
Marlon Brando in *Desirée,* and
Rod Steiger in *Waterloo.*

of "the immortal romance". It is not an unfair claim; allowing for invented conversations, the screenplay keeps close to the facts, which are dramatic enough in themselves. Marie Walewska was married to a Polish nobleman forty-nine years older than she was (the difference between Henry Stephenson and Garbo was exactly half that), and worshipped Napoleon as Poland's potential liberator even before she met him, presenting him with flowers as he passed near her home. They met again at a ball, he admired her, and Polish politicians, eager for Napoleon's protection, hinted to her delicately that she was in a unique position to serve her country – which she did, quite probably unwillingly at first. By her own account, Napoleon stamped on his watch and vowed to serve Poland

the same way unless she became his mistress; it may well be true, but there is no doubt that they came to love each other, she bore him a son, and no woman in his life showed him more devotion.

The film differs from truth only in minute details (Napoleon had met his son by Marie long before he was exiled on Elba, and she was not present when he finally surrendered to the Bellerophon), and if there is an abundance of billing and cooing Boyer and Garbo make it more palatable than most. There is a lovely little scene between Boyer and Maria Ouspenskaya, playing an eccentric old grand dame who has never heard of Napoleon; she catches him cheating at cards, and announces in a passion that she is going to count

Marie Walewska (after Lefèvre), and right, Greta Garbo with Charles Boyer in *Marie Walewska*.

the silver.[9] There are good performances from Stephenson, Leif Erickson as Marie's brother, George Zucco as the Polish chancellor, and Reginal Owen as a rather robust Talleyrand.

In his own way Rod Steiger is every bit as good as Boyer. He is the Napoleon of *Waterloo*, which is quite the best battle film ever made, both as a motion picture and as a piece of history. It is enormous and spectacular and looks like the clash of two huge armies in a perfect welter of cannon smoke, thundering cavalry, masses of infantry, vivid individual detail, and exciting action; it is also a true picture of what happened in one of the great battles of history, and for once it is possible to understand what is happening, and why it mattered.

Waterloo is, admittedly, an easy battle, with no complex manoeuvres to baffle the uninitiated. In its *very* simplest terms, the French occupied a slope facing the British and their allies on the crest opposite; Napoleon delivered a left hook at Hougoumont, a farmhouse on the British right front, and was stopped by the Guards; he assaulted across the valley throughout the day, with cavalry and infantry, and the British held on; with the Prussians under Blücher arriving, Napoleon made a

9 Napoleon habitually cheated at games. Wellington, as a schoolboy, preferred not to join in games, but took great satisfaction in watching – and detecting cheating.

Above, the Duke of Wellington (by H. P. Bone after T. Lawrence),
and below, Christopher Plummer in *Waterloo*.

last dramatic effort, launching the Old Guard at the allied centre, the British Guards drove them back, Wellington said: "Oh, dammit, in for a penny, in for a pound!" and advanced his whole force, and that was the Battle of Waterloo. A pounding match, as it was called, and "a damned near-run thing, the nearest-run thing you ever saw in your life". It lasted seven hours in fact, and about an hour on screen, and they got the highlights right – the Hougoumont assault, the charge of the Greys, Ney's cavalry streaming round the battered British infantry squares (this sequence has no equal in the cinema), the magnificent ranks of the Old Guard advancing up the hill, being met by Wellington's "Now, Maitland – now's your time!", being repulsed, Blucher urging his Prussians to keep his word for him, the demand for surrender, Cambronne's famous reply: "Merde!" (which he later denied), and the Duke riding from the battlefield in silence.

The principals are excellent. Christopher Plummer has a kinder face than Wellington, but he is a convincing Duke, and many of the right quotes are there ("He has humbugged me, by God!" "Generals have better things to do than shoot at each other", and the famous exchange with Uxbridge: "By God, I've lost my leg!" "By God, so you have!"). Steiger is just Napoleonic, and again the quotes are right ("If you want to kill your Emperor, here I am", "Those grey horses are frightening", and so on). The business of cutting from one commander to the other is dramatic, and the only thing I would seriously query is the film's suggestion that Napoleon was ill on the day, and at one point almost collapsed: this has been much discussed, but I believe the best evidence is that he was perfectly well. A few misplaced quotes don't matter, but I doubt if Wellington ever promoted anyone for looting, and I'm positive there was no deathly hush over the battlefield afterwards; there were too many wounded for that. It is a ghastly film, as a depiction of war; it is also a very honest one, and a credit to all who made it.

It says something about modern taste that a film depicting a middle-aged monarch's descent into madness, replete with often disgusting detail and harping on bodily functions, should win popular and critical acclaim, to say nothing of awards. After all, it is not a subject that would have appealed to Korda or DeMille; Louis B. Mayer and John Ford would have recoiled. Perhaps that is irrelevant; times change, and standards with them, but whatever its merits, *The Madness of King George*[10] is an unpleasant and curiously pointless picture based on the unhappy man's first major lapse into insanity in 1788–9 (he had shown signs of mental disturbance before) when his fitness to reign was called in question and regency became a possibility. That is the film's compass; with the earlier follies of the most disastrous of the Hanoverians, his ambition to rule rather than reign, the stupid obstinacy which cost Britain its American colonies, etc., it has nothing to do, nor with his final relapse into madness twenty years later.

A picture which is confined to one year of a sixty-year reign, and is nothing if not intimate, is not an easy subject for historical comparisons. We see the King (Nigel Hawthorne) slipping from eccentricity into derangement, racing about in his nightshirt, babbling and raving, tortured by incompetent physicians, treated by the pioneering Dr Francis Willis (Ian Holm), and restored to temporary normality in the nick of time before the ambitious Prince of Wales can step into his shoes. Fair enough, although I had always understood that Queen Charlotte (Helen Mirren), far from being denied access to him as the film has it, actually took charge of the King during his illness, and Ian Holm's Willis is a harsher tyrant than the humane septuagenarian doctor-clergyman whom Fanny Burney called lighthearted and innocent, and Hannah More described as "a good plain old-fashioned country parson". And did his majesty, who as everyone knows complained of the sad stuff in Shakespeare, really convalesce on "King Lear" – or is this dramatic subtlety?

Nigel Hawthorne in *The Madness of King George*.

The costumes, settings, and style of the film are elaborate, and somehow gave me the impression of watching a portrayal not of real people, but of caricatures by Gillray and Rowlandson, which may be why, quite aside from a distaste for the subject, I was not moved by it. Plainly this is a minority view; others found it delightful, loving, and wonderfully funny. Am I alone in wondering if the presentation of the royal madness as entertainment is not uncomfortably close to the exhibition of lunatics in Bedlam for the public amusement?

10 It is said that the title of the original play, *The Madness of George III*, was changed for the screen in case cinema audiences wondered what had happened to the films *The Madness of George I* and *The Madness of George II*.

Anna Neagle and Anton Walbrook in *Victoria the Great*, and, inset, Queen Victoria and Prince Albert (from the painting by Winterhalter). Previous page, British soldiers in the Crimea marching to the Alma, from *The Charge of the Light Brigade*, 1968.

Rule, Britannia

No historical films seem so dated as those about the British Empire. This is not strange; although it is barely fifty years since one quarter of the human race lived under the Union Jack, in that short time the British nation's view of itself and its place in the world has been altered as never before; perhaps no other nation has ever experienced such a sudden and drastic convulsion in its national outlook – even war, occupation, and subjection, however terrible their effects, do not bring a change in national philosophy of the kind experienced by the British since the 1940s. Rome took centuries to crumble; with the British Empire it was almost overnight.

It is probably impossible for anyone born since 1950 to understand what it was like to be, and to think, British of the 1930s; equally impossible for anyone over sixty-five to conceive what it is like to be young today and have no imperial outlook. This is something far beyond the generation gap, which has always existed; every generation is brainwashed, and brainwashes itself, but never before in Britain have there been two such diametrically opposed brainwashes inside half a century. The child of 1930 had an imperial view, whatever his class (it is a massive error to suppose that imperialism was confined to the upper and middle classes; if anything, it was stronger among the working class, and I speak from personal experience of the old Raj, where a colonel's imperialism was as nothing compared to the private soldier's). The British child of 1930 thought the Empire was terrific, giving him and his country a status beyond all other nations – and he had the evidence to prove it on a world map that was one-fifth pink. The child of 1997 has no such evidence, but being a nationalist (and rationalist) of his own

time, he takes his country's status as he finds it, without an Empire, so who needs it? It is a natural point of view, in which he may be encouraged by those revisionists who hold that imperialism was not quite respectable, and even positively evil.

The screen is a good barometer of the change in outlook. Watch a modern TV documentary reappraising the British Raj, or the British role in Africa – and then take a look at *Sanders of the River* or *The Drum*. The difference in pictorial images is trivial compared to the difference in viewpoint: the television journalist's attitudes, his standards of judgement, the whole cast of his mind, could not be further from the philosophy of the two old movies if he was a man from Mars. And if he were asked to comment on the two old films he would, at the very least, express pious relief that we had progressed since those days. (If he didn't, he wouldn't last long in television.) Ask an old child of 1930 what he thought of the TV documentary, on the other hand, and his reply might be anything from surprise at so much ignorance, to smashing the set.

This revolution in fashionable outlooks (because that is all they are) should be remembered when looking at the films of Empire. Those of pre-1950 were mostly made by people who, like the 1930 child, were imperialists and/or took imperialism for granted; the few productions since have tended, progressively, to reflect the change in attitude. All of them may be regarded as a sort of propaganda, just like the modern TV reappraisals. There is not necessarily anything sinister about this; the most telling propaganda is not that which is manufactured by the mischievous, but that which the author genuinely accepts himself. The old films, and modern TV documentaries, merely give the audience the current wisdom, and only a fool or a politician would claim either to be absolute universal truth. But our main concern is to see how well, or badly, the films of Empire deal with history; so far as the film-makers' outlook is part of that history, we will deal with that too.

Film-makers' outlooks, incidentally, can be eccentric. I wrote a film (no matter which) containing a rather patriotic speech; viewing the rough-cut I noticed that the producer, who was not British, became restless during the speech, and afterwards he buttonholed me, worried. "I dunno about that landa hope'n'glory bit," he said. "It's kinda old hat, know what I mean? The Empire's long gone; I don't see American kids identifying with that kinda thing." I said I thought they would understand it in its context in the film.

"Context, my ass!" he cried, waving his arms. "They won't buy it, I tell you! Christ, have you seen the state of the pound this morning?"

I managed to convince him, the speech stayed in, and Young America did not throw eggs at the screen, the weakness of sterling notwithstanding. But such a conversation would hardly have taken place in Hollywood of the old days, for of all the champions of Empire there were none more staunch than the American moguls. No doubt the importance of the British market had something to do with this, but there were other reasons. Even the Old West did not have the exotic glamour of the Northwest Frontier, the China Seas, Darkest Africa, and other imperial outposts (all easily reconstructed in and around Burbank), and in the instinctive feeling of America for Britain (whatever the differences and rivalries) there was a special thread for the Hollywood bosses: many of them were Jews who foresaw that the fate of Europe, and their kinsfolk, would rest on the Empire and the Royal Navy that had guaranteed America's eastern coast for more than a century. But the best reason was probably that they just liked the Empire and what it stood for, and knew that America liked it also.

So out of the dream factory came the Bengal Lancers and the Light Brigade and the Mounties and the White Ensign and endless marching columns of Central Casting Highlanders (never mind establishing shots, one bar of "Hundred Pipers" and the audience knew that the Soldiers of the Queen were at it again, about to be ambushed in the first reel, but storming in firing Vickers guns from the hip in the finale). Meanwhile, on this side of the Atlantic, another ardent imperialist, the Hungarian Alexander Korda, was unfurling the Union Jack in glorious Technicolor, and the British film industry was flourishing around Omdurman and the Khyber.

There are interesting differences between British and American imperial epics. The British were undoubtedly better historical reconstructions or (since some of the films were contemporary) representations of the imperial scene. There were no zip fasteners on Korda's kilts, the technical advisers often worked from first-hand experience, and none of his troops responded to the command "Left face!" The Americans were less meticulous in detail, more prone to take liberties with historic truth, altogether more relaxed in approach. They put across the Imperial message just as strongly, but more casually; in British prewar films there is just a hint of self-conscious tendency to show the flag for its own sake, to slip in the quick sermon, to stiffen the upper lip until it touches caricature. Mind you, the British in real life have a tendency to caricature themselves, and nowhere more than in the Indian Army; if any young viewer of today thinks that the behaviour of some screen Sahibs is a little over the top, and that no one was ever really as clipped-and-Carruthers in real life, he may rest assured that many of them were. Even send-up does not always exaggerate reality, as can be shown by a comparison of *Carry On Up the Khyber* with the unvarnished truth of one imperial incident.

In the Carry On film there is a lovely take-off of the stiff upper lip. At a residency dinner party the Governor and his lady (Sid James and Joan Sims) and their guests continue unruffled with their meal while the residency is under attack, ignoring the shells bursting in the dining room, windows crashing in, and the chandelier descending in showers of plaster; polite behaviour and protocol are strictly observed – which of course could not happen in such life-and-death circumstances, could it? Compare the case of Brigadier Shelton, held prisoner on top of an Afghan tower during the Retreat from Kabul in 1842, in which a British army of 14,000 was wiped out. An earth tremor struck, the tower was

about to collapse in ruins, and Shelton's only companion, a junior officer, rushed down the stairs, followed by his chief. They escaped, and that night, after a day of fearful peril, Shelton rebuked his subordinate: "By the way, Mackenzie, you came downstairs *in front* of me this morning." Even Talbot Rothwell couldn't top that.

In all imperial films, especially the British productions, there is much that will give offence to modern liberals – the

Confronting the restless natives: from left, Julian Holloway, Sid James, Joan Sims, Peter Butterworth, Angela Douglas, and Roy Castle in *Carry On Up the Khyber*.

imperial attitude in itself, of course, and the apparent patronising of natives. They are entitled to object, provided disapproval does not interfere with truth. Sentiments are expressed in *Sanders of the River*, for example, which would send a race relations officer into a decline – which is not to say that it was wrong to have them in the film, or to show the film, which is a true picture of its time, whatever may be thought of it today. There is sometimes a disturbing ambivalence about attitudes to this subject: on the one hand an eagerness to seize on "racism" as a weapon of anti-imperial polemic, and at the same time a strange reluctance to face truth because the objector finds it uncomfortable. I will give an example.

In the film *Northwest Frontier*, set in the Raj *c.* 1905, that fine Indian actor, I. S. Johar, played an engine-driver, and played him extremely well: it was a true rendering of a type imitated successfully by Peter Sellers and others, the

Kenneth More and I. S. Johar in *Northwest Frontier.*

quaintly-spoken "Oh-jollee-good-Sahib" funny Indian – a genuine character familiar to everyone who knows the subcontinent. One critic took violent exception to Johar's performance: it was a disgraceful caricature, and Johar should be ashamed of himself. I'd like to believe the critic thought that was true, but I doubt it. I suspect the critic knew Johar's portrayal was absolutely faithful, but preferred to pretend it wasn't because the critic found it embarrassing, and didn't like to think that Indians ever really behaved like that – or if they did, it shouldn't be shown on screen. In other words, damn the truth if it doesn't fit with what one would like to believe is true – an attitude which, honesty aside, seems to me offensively patronising. I would be less contemptuous of such critics if I thought they would be equally outraged at, say, a British general being portrayed as a pompous, arrogant, blustering clown – which has happened, and some of them were, God knows, so portray them by all means.

With these thoughts in mind, *Sanders of the River* is a good starting point, since this was imperialism at its most paternal. The book, first of an enormously popular series by Edgar Wallace, and continued by Francis Gerard, appeared in 1910, at the zenith of Empire. Like most of its successors, it is a series of short stories about Mr Commissioner Sanders who supervises and keeps the peace among the savage tribes in a British African territory. To call it illiberal and racist by today's standards is like describing *Hamlet* as a family row; Sanders is an absolute ruler who treats his subjects as dangerous children from whom he demands total obedience; he likes and admires them in their primitive state and has no use for Westernised Africans – in short, he has the views of his time. Wallace wrote from African experience, drew an accurate background, and glamourised it heavily. Probably no colonial writer except Haggard so shaped Western imagination of Africa and its people, for better or worse. The film of 1935 had Leslie Banks in the title role (bad casting to Sanders fans, who knew that their hero looked more like Roland Young, being small, spare and quiet), but the star was Paul

Robeson as Bosambo, a friendly chief whom Wallace depicted as a likeable rogue. Robeson played him straight and also sang magnificently, which was the film's main box-office attraction. It is a middling picture, with some good African location shots and a rather vague plot in which Sanders, assisted by Bosambo, is pitted against a powerful tribal king who turns his enemies into drumskins; there is fine spear work, much dancing, love interest for Bosambo with Nina Mae McKinney, last-minute rescue, and some bad back-projection, notably in the famous Canoe Song, in which Robeson thunders out "Ai-ee-o-go" while his warriors paddle away (a scene greeted in Oxford cinemas with rapturous cries of "Well rowed, Balliol!"). There was also a fairly toe-curling homily from Banks about the benefits of British rule, which must have gone down well with Jomo Kenyatta, later President of Kenya, who was one of the extras.

Robeson was disappointed with the film, reasonably enough, since he had hoped it would give the black man some dignity. One who took the same view was my father, an old Africa hand who, while a staunch imperialist, had his own quiet, decided view on Africa and its people, formed by soldiering there at a time when Nairobi had not long ceased to be a waterhole, and having his life saved by a Kikuyu warrior (whom I never met, but whose name I record simply because I want to. It was Wakibi). All of which was not without influence on my young mind, although it does not affect my judgement of *Sanders of the River* as a film and as a valuable picture of Africa. But I admit it is not one of my favourites; it prompts too many questions which I cannot answer. It is patronising. It is also about an unidentified part of Africa whose locality one can only try to deduce from Wallace's stories, which suggest that the territory where Sanders successfully kept the peace may have been that region now called Biafra.

My father and Robeson could have found nothing to complain of in *Zulu*, which in its way is the best African historical, and one of the best in the imperial canon. Purely

An ironic moment from *Sanders of the River* as Mr Commissioner Sanders (Leslie Banks) lays down the law to one of his subject chiefs played by Jomo Kenyatta, who later became President of Kenya.

as a battle picture it compares, on its smaller scale, with *Waterloo* as a piece of meticulous recreation. I suspect that Stanley Baker, who co-produced and played the lead, was inspired by Welsh patriotism, and it shows. The film depicts the defence of Rorke's Drift in 1879, where 130 British soldiers stood off 4000 Zulus for a day and a night following

Isandhlwana, the most catastrophic defeat in imperial history, in which 1600 of Lord Chelmsford's invading army had been wiped out by Cetewayo's impis.[1] Rorke's Drift became a Victorian legend, as it deserved to; eleven Victoria Crosses were awarded, mostly to South Wales Borderers, as well as to Lieutenants Chard and Bromhead, who commanded the little garrison. Half of the film is a splendid build-up: the stricken field of Isandhlwana, with the terrifying plumed and gartered black warriors striding through the burning wreckage, and then a long tranquil sequence at the unsuspecting post on Buffalo River, the troops loafing in the sun or grumbling in the hospital before the message of disaster arrives, and the stillness is broken by the distant ominous rumble of the advancing impis. There are memorable shots of the massed Zulu ranks, chanting and beating on their shields before launching themselves into attack, and of the post with its red-coated riflemen thinly spread behind their makeshift barricades; the course of the fighting is charted faithfully – the repeated charges driven off with fearful loss, the desperate hand-to-hand fighting in the burning hospital, and the last stand at the mealie-bag redoubts where the Zulu onslaught was finally stopped by the steady volley-firing of the Welsh. This, by all accounts, is exactly how it was.

Naturally, the characters are dramatised, and elements of temperament introduced to charge the atmosphere; so far as I know there is no evidence of differences between Chard (Baker) and Bromhead (Michael Caine, making a striking star debut) in fact, either on the score of Chard's supposed "amateurism" as a Royal Engineer(!) or on the question of command; Chard was undisputed senior.[2] And was the Rev. Witt present at all, and was he a drinker? There was a clergyman, the Rev. George Smith, among the defenders; he distinguished himself, but is not in the film. The singing of "Men of Harlech" I assume is borrowed from the incident of

1 The subject of another film, *Zulu Dawn*.
2 He was commissioned in July 1868, not in February 1872 as the film suggests.

The heroes of Rorke's Drift, Lt John Chard, left, and Lt Gonville Bromhead. Below, Stanley Baker and Michael Caine in *Zulu*.

Inside the redoubt at Rorke's Drift: an action scene from *Zulu*.

the Shangani Patrol, who are supposed to have sung "God Save the Queen" in similar desperate circumstances, but it made a splendid scene in *Zulu* and if it is fiction it is one of the liberties a scriptwriter is entitled to take.

All these are trivial points, and in no way affect the film's authenticity, but I do have reservations about opinions being attributed to Chard and Bromhead which seem to reflect modern attitudes to war rather than the views of Victorian soldiers. After Rorke's Drift the film has Bromhead viewing the carnage and saying he feels ashamed. I doubt if Bromhead really felt or said any such thing; he had no cause to. I question, too, whether Chard expressed such repugnance. They were professional soldiers, doing their duty, and when it was done I would guess they just felt very tired, very relieved, and not a little elated. That may be hard for modern audiences to take, but it is how British soldiers were. I'm sure Chard and

Bromhead felt great admiration for the Zulus, but shame, or disenchantment with the profession of arms? No. They continued to serve in the Army until their deaths, by which time they were both colonels. Baker and Caine were not bad lookalikes, save for Chard's moustache and Bromhead's superb whiskers.

The acting was excellent, with Nigel Green outstanding as the Colour Sergeant; he *was* the old British Army, so much so that one viewer wanted to know why he was not among the eleven VCs in the film. The real Colour-Sergeant was in fact decorated, although not with the VC. There was another interesting piece of casting: King Cetewayo was played by Chief Buthelezi.

Zulu is thoroughly good history, and so, up to a point, is *Stanley and Livingstone*, but it falls far short of the expecta-tions raised by its title, and does justice to neither of these remarkable men. Livingstone, the giant of African explo-ration, is a supporting player; the film is about how Stanley found him, and was inspired to carry on the great man's missionary role – which is not what he did. That apart, the film missed a glorious opportunity, for Stanley's career was an extraordinary one. He was born John Rowlands (or Rollant) in Wales in 1841, orphaned, beat up his schoolmaster, worked his passage to America as a cabin boy, was adopted by a New Orleans cotton broker named Stanley, enlisted in the Confederate Army, was captured, changed sides, deserted from the Union Navy, became a journalist, covered various campaigns, and was sent to find Livingstone. This success made him famous, and he continued to explore (though not in the missionary sense), founded the state which later

F. C. Selous, the hunter and scout who was the model for Rider Haggard's Allan Quatermain (by Livia Mary Bryden), and right, Cedric Hardwicke in *King Solomon's Mines*.

became the Belgian Congo, rescued Emin Pasha (who, like Livingstone, stood in no great need of rescuing) from the Mahdists, became MP for North Lambeth, and was knighted in 1899, five years before his death.

Something might have been made of this, for the Livingstone search, once the famous greeting has been spoken, is not really enough to sustain a film; some embroidery was necessary, before and after, and it was not very gripping. There was some fine African photography, Spencer Tracy was an acceptable Stanley, but for once Cedric Hardwicke (Livingstone) seemed miscast, and for a film about two such adventurers, it was strangely unexciting.

So, alas, was another film which had even less excuse. *King Solomon's Mines* is one of the adventure classics, written for a bet by Rider Haggard to prove that he could match the success of *Treasure Island*, and filmed more than once. The 1937 version was the best; it too had Hardwicke, much more at home in the role of Alan Quatermain, with John Loder and Roland Young as his companions, Curtis and Good, and Anna Lee was taken along for love interest – why this was thought necessary is a mystery. The story of the trek into unexplored territory in search of the fabulous diamond mines, the discovery that the explorers' black comrade is the rightful king of the lost land, the subsequent adventures with Gagool the witch, the entrapment in the mines – this needs no romantic embellishment, or if it did, they could have lifted one of Haggard's mysterious African queens from another book for Curtis to fall in love with. Again, the photography is splendid (as it was in the remake, which featured the giant Watutsi as the lost tribe), but the film is really a vehicle for the splendid singing of Paul Robeson, as the claimant king, with pleasing glimpses of wildlife along the way.

Indeed, with the honourable exception of *Zulu*, most African films tend to have a travelogue look about them (*Tarzan* included[3]), and if some student of the future had to rely solely on Hollywood's efforts, he would learn a great deal more about the continent's fauna than about its history. South of the equator, that is; the Sudan has been the scene of two imperial epics, historically linked, and the first deals with the last adventure of one of the great Victorian heroes, Charles Gordon.

He was a weird one, "half-cracked", "mad", "a wild man", according to contemporaries, almost removed from military college for throwing a man downstairs and stabbing another with a fork, asking complete strangers if they believed in Jesus, leading his Chinese storming parties smoking a cigar and carrying a cane, an eccentric military near-genius who administered territories, fought irregular campaigns, combated slavers, and whom a nervous British Government was reluctant to put in charge of anything until they sent him, in desperation and without written orders, to evacuate the Sudan, which was being overrun by the Mahdi's army of fanatics. Gordon was cut off in Khartoum and held it for ten months before it fell and he was killed – two days before help arrived.

Khartoum is a spectacular devoted to this last mission, and as an action picture has its share of good blood-and-thunder sequences, is extremely well acted, and contains beautiful photography of the Nile – turn a movie camera loose anywhere in Africa and the wonder of the place has a beguiling effect on producers, if not on audiences. History has had to be simplified considerably – for example, the decision to send Gordon is taken in Cabinet, Gladstone sees him secretly, Gordon says yes, and that is that. In fact, the discussions took almost two months, and Gordon and Gladstone did not meet. Again, Gordon's screen relations with Stewart, his staff officer, are shown as initially antagonistic; the truth is that Gordon had *asked* for Stewart, they took to each other at

---

3 Fortunately, perhaps, Lord Greystoke is not a historical figure, and raises only one question of academic interest. Ivor Novello is credited with the dialogue for *Tarzan, the Ape Man*, the first sound film in the series, which makes one wonder if the author of so many romantic musicals was the inventor of Tarzan's famous jungle call.

General Charles Gordon (by Lady Abercromby), and right, Charlton Heston (who is a head taller than the real Gordon) in *Khartoum*.

once, and apart from one quarrel, got on very well. During the siege of Khartoum, Gordon twice goes to see the Mahdi; in fact, there were no such meetings.

These things, even the last-named, do not involve as much tampering with history as might appear. Gordon and the Mahdi were in correspondence during the siege, so there is no question of inventing a relationship which did not exist; the film simply makes them talk to each other instead of writing. Obviously this has dramatic value, and no producer could be expected to forego the opportunity of having Charlton Heston (Gordon) and Laurence Olivier (the Mahdi) confront each other. It may not be historic fact, but it does not involve the distortion of historic sense implicit in bringing Elizabeth and Mary Stuart face to face. All told, *Khartoum* does well by history in the broad sense, and great pains have been taken with small detail, giving the film an authentic period quality.

Heston looks like Gordon, and sounds suitably British (which is a matter of style and manner as much as accent). How close he comes to the eccentric hero of Khartoum, who knows? Gordon's writing during the siege, and what we know of his behaviour, suggest a very complex character indeed, but one thing is certain: however erratic, unpredictable, perhaps even devious he was, his sense of honour was unshakeable, and it was that which kept him in Khartoum. This the film brings out fully. As to his death, there are different versions, and the film accepts the popular one showing him being killed, unresisting, on the palace stairs. This is the legendary image beloved by the Victorians, of the stern Christian soldier-martyr, but it rests on unreliable evidence. Khalil, Gordon's attendant, and a Mahdist soldier(both eye-witnesses) told a different story – that Gordon fought on the stairs, was wounded in the shoulder, fired until his revolver was empty, and was laying about him with his sword when he was shot down. It sounds much more like Chinese Gordon.

Olivier's Mahdi I have heard dismissed as a mere repeat of his Othello (what did they expect, Hamlet?). I thought he was excellent, possibly because I was looking for the Mahdi, not for Olivier. Ralph Richardson did not look much like Gladstone, and while the GOM was no doubt as unprincipled as the next politician, I wonder if he ever appeared quite as cynical as this? Nigel Green was "all Sir Garnet" as Wolseley but did not appear to have a blind eye, and Richard Johnson was a forceful Stewart.

Gordon's death provoked the famous open telegram of rebuke from Queen Victoria to Gladstone, but it was another thirteen years before Kitchener avenged him, by defeating

Above, Laurence Olivier in *Khartoum,* and right, the Mahdi. Below: W. E. Gladstone (photo by Eveleen Myers), right, Ralph Richardson.

the Mahdi's successor, the Khalifa, at Omdurman in 1898. This campaign is the background to *The Four Feathers*, a lavish Korda production based on A. E. W. Mason's novel. The film is imperial melodrama with a vengeance, with young Harry Faversham (John Clements), doubting his own martial ardour and resigning when his regiment is ordered overseas. Predictably, three other officers, including Durrance (Ralph Richardson), send him white feathers, his fiancée (June Duprez) adds a fourth, and her father (C. Aubrey Smith) opens the french windows in Faversham's presence, presumably to let out the smell. Mortified, Harry goes to Egypt, and has himself branded with the mark of a tribe who have no tongues, thus cunningly enabling himself to pass as a dumb native. Exactly what he has in mind does not appear, but by a fine coincidence he is able to rescue Durrance, who has gone blind and survived a massacre of British troops. Durrance only realises much later who his rescuer is (Harry has slipped a feather into his wallet), but before then our hero has staged a break-out from the Khalifa's jail, and Kitchener has won the war. Durrance, all set to marry Miss Duprez, gives her up, and she, the rehabilitated Harry, and a beaming Aubrey Smith are reunited.

It still looks good sixty years later, with Clements sternly determined, Richardson cool, June Duprez exotic, Aubrey Smith's eyebrows at their crustiest, and John Laurie raving marvellously as the Khalifa. There is a proper *fin de siècle* appearance to the costumes and settings in England, a rousing troop embarkation, huge shots of Kitchener's river fleet being dragged up the Nile (by Clements among others), the famous sequence in which Richardson loses his topi, an eerily filmed night attack by fuzzy wuzzies, and a spectacular charge by the Khalifa's mounted hordes as the action finale. The cavalry skirmish in which Winston Churchill took part is not seen, but the historical element is sound, and the picture is really what the cinema of Empire was all about – duty, derring-do, and the Pax Britannica. It is a long way from Band Aid.

It seems only right, before leaving Africa, to travel a few thousand miles west from Khartoum and take a last look at the corpse-propped ramparts of Fort Zinderneuf. For *Beau Geste* has more historical interest than appears at first sight; rightly or wrongly, it imprinted the French Foreign Legion on the world's imagination, and as both book and film it embodied an imperial ideal, and a state of mind which seems to have vanished altogether, except possibly in the Soviet Union, where the notion of grand imperial mission appeared still to exist until quite recently.

The author, P. C. Wren, *was* Beau Geste, the English gentleman incarnate – he also claimed to have been a prize-fighter, sailor, schoolmaster, soldier, miner, tramp, and justice of the peace, and may well have set a style for all those novelists whose variety of exotic occupations used to appear in their blurbs. He belonged to that school of Victorian-Edwardian soldiers of fortune who looked on the world as a great adventure playground, and this is the spirit of his books, of which *Beau Geste* was the great bestseller. By modern standards Wren was a snob, racist, and reactionary beside whom Buchan and Sapper look like Social Democrats, but any disgust and fury which his works might arouse at this late date would be mild compared to the feelings entertained towards him by the Foreign Legion hierarchy of seventy years ago; in their eyes he had glamourised and publicised their famous corps and distorted it out of all recognition in the process. Perhaps he did; on the other hand, he claimed to have served in the Legion before his critics' time, and maintained that the background to his fictions was accurate. That background is part of the screen *Beau Geste*, and true or false it is the best visual image we have of the old Foreign Legion.

The film, if it needs saying, is the story of three brothers who enlist in the Legion after the eldest, Beau (Gary Cooper) has stolen the family sapphire to protect the honour of his aunt (Heather Thatcher). Evil Sergeant Markoff[4] (Brian Donlevy) plans to steal the stone, and there is an exciting denouement in

4 In the novel the sergeant's name is Lejeaune; Russian names were popular for villains of the Thirties.

The Foreign Legion martinet personified by Brian Donlevy in *Beau Geste*, with a suitably distraught J. Carrol Naish.

a desert fort besieged by Arabs, Beau and Markoff are killed, middle brother Digby (Robert Preston) sets the fort on fire and is subsequently shot by a stray Arab, and only youngest brother John (Ray Milland) gets back to England with the Truth, and marries Isobel (Susan Hayward). By which time one has begun to see, if not to sympathise with, the Legion hierarchy's point of view; not the least of Wren's talents was the stretching of improbability to the point of insanity and making the public like it. *Beau Geste* is old-fashioned melodrama, full of suspense and action laced with duty,

devotion, and self-sacrificial brotherly love; it won Donlevy an Oscar nomination, and somehow the brothers made it credible, even if two of them (including the English public schoolboy Cooper) were unashamedly American. There have been other versions, but this is the one that established the famous image of the line of kepi'd corpses lolling in the embrasures of the mysterious silent fort: it says something for Hollywood and Wren that whenever the Foreign Legion is mentioned, that is the picture that comes to mind.

Imperial African movies are fairly evenly divided between

Robert Clive (by N. Dance), and right, Ronald Colman in *Clive of India*.

fact and fiction; it is remarkable that films of India are almost entirely from fictional sources, with *Clive of India* at the beginning, and *Gandhi* at the end being important exceptions.[5] At least it seems remarkable, until one reflects that Indian history does not offer all that many opportunities to the commercial movie-maker (the most obvious, the Mutiny, being fraught with hazards), and that Kipling so overshadows the subcontinent that producers looking for Indian projects turn to him almost by reflex action. This came home to me only after I had chosen eight Indian films for this Age, and

then realised that no fewer than four of them were Kipling-inspired. Not that they are faithful versions by any means, but they exploited his name, and his India, and at least one of them, I think, would have delighted him.

This reliance on fiction must influence one's consideration of Indian films as "historicals"; it becomes not a question of comparing them with written records, but of seeing how well they reflect the country, its people, Indian and British, and that mysterious institution, the Raj, which is now fast fading beyond recall. Even so, there are many who knew and remember it far better than I, so I must observe again that these are personal views, based on first-hand knowledge of only the last few years of Empire.

After which I may as well plunge straight in at the deep end and say that no film evokes India more strongly, for me, than one which (while it included what the publicists called

5 I comment on neither film, for different reasons. The first I have not seen for fifty years and can say only that Clive did not look like Ronald Colman. I have seen *Gandhi*, but my knowledge is superficial; I heard more of him when I was a child in the Thirties than I did as a soldier in India, when he was never even thought of at my level. So it would be presumptuous in me to offer an opinion, except to say that Ben Kingsley's performance was such that I forgot I was watching an actor.

"spectacular Indian footage") was, I believe, largely California studio-based, *The Lives of a Bengal Lancer*. I can't help that – it still feels like India, although its story is straight tuppenny blood stuff, and owes more to Hollywood imagination than to F. Yeats-Brown's book. It is about a colonel's son (Richard Cromwell) who hasn't really got the right stuff, and is a disappointment to his father (Guy Standing) despite the efforts of the insubordinate Captain Macgregor (Gary Cooper playing a Canadian, a common device to justify American accents) to bring them together. Light relief is provided by Lieutenant Forsyth (Franchot Tone), but when the son falls into the toils of an adventuress (Kathleen Burke) and is kidnapped by a wily frontier chief (Douglas Dumbrille at his smoothest), the action moves to a mountain stronghold where there is suspense, torture (under which the colonel's son inevitably cracks, but not Tone and Cooper), and thunderous action, Cooper being killed in an act of heroism which turns the tide, and the colonel's son redeeming himself by knifing the frontier chief. DSOs for the son and Tone, and a posthumous VC for Cooper.

It is a first-rate action movie, and saving its blood-and-thunder I can only say that its domestic atmosphere is more evocative for me than any other film of India. It has none of the magnificent panoramas of the real India and its people to be seen in *Gandhi* or *The Drum*; but it does have bungalows and tents just like the ones I lived in, and dusty *maidans*, and long-tailed puggarees and glittering lance-heads like those of the lancer barracks where we drilled, and what looks awfully like waitabit thorn but probably isn't, and the actors (even the Americans) seem truer to type than those of other films. Perhaps it is that I remember India in black and white; I can only say that *Bengal Lancer* has an atmosphere that still strikes me as true.

Purely as entertainment, it was surpassed by the film which I think Kipling would have liked, *Gunga Din*. He had an affection for films (as well he might have done, considering

Mahatma Gandhi, and right, Ben Kingsley in *Gandhi*.

Kipling on screen: from left, Douglas Fairbanks, jnr, Victor McLaglen, Eduardo Ciannelli, Cary Grant; behind, Sam Jaffe as the regimental bhisti, *Gunga Din*.

the number based on his work) and *Gunga Din* was a splendid piece of adventure which combined two Kipling elements, the poem and "Soldiers Three". I am told that Cary Grant, who played in the picture, was the moving spirit behind it, and it must have justified his hopes beyond telling.

Cutter (Grant), McChesney (Victor McLaglen), and Ballantyne (Douglas Fairbanks, junior) bear no close resemblance to Mulvaney, Ortheris, and Learoyd, and their treatment of the lowly water-carrier, Gunga Din (Sam Jaffe) is a good deal kinder than Kipling subjected him to in verse, but the picture is a well-balanced mixture of spectacle, comedy, adventure, and genuine pathos. There were never, so

far as I know, any Thugs on the frontier, but as led by Eduardo Ciannelli, with Abner Biberman in close support, they provide menacing opposition to the Raj and are a welcome change from bearded extras plunging off rocks. There is a romantic interest, with Fairbanks intent on leaving the army to marry Joan Fontaine, to the dismay of his comrades; there is slapstick brawling, high jinks with elephants and a bowl of doctored punch, sinister ritual in a Thug temple, and high excitement with the three sergeants on the brink of a snake-pit, but all gives way before Gunga Din's heroic end, sounding a bugle-call to warn the relief column (who have never heard of scouts, apparently) of an enemy ambush. Gunga Din is posthumously promoted corporal, and the wraith of the uniformed Sam Jaffe, saluting with such conscious pride as the colonel (Montagu Love) reads the last verse of Kipling's poem, is one of the most touching sights you will ever see in the cinema. It brought a lump to the throat of Bertolt Brecht, of all people, although as a devout anti-imperialist he knew it shouldn't. You cannot do better than that.

Of historical interest, in its way, is the performance of Victor McLaglen. Soldiers are fatally easy characters to mis-play, especially those of Kipling's army; McLaglen had the advantage of being the genuine article, a Life Guardsman who rose to the rank of captain and was Provost Marshal of Baghdad in the First World War. (He may also have been one of the best British heavyweights of the twentieth century, since he survived six rounds against the world champion Jack Johnson in 1909.) As a screen soldier, whatever liberties his parts demanded, he was proof of the old saying "Once a Guardsman, always a Guardsman". Sergeants were his speciality, and the outposts his province, as in *Wee Willie Winkie*, an

Victor McLaglen and Shirley Temple in *Wee Willie Winkie*.

extremely free translation of the Kipling story which the author did not live to see, fortunately perhaps. Or perhaps not. Shirley Temple could do precious little wrong in the Thirties, and as the small heroine of this Frontier adventure she was at her irrepressible sweetest. Kipling's Winkie is a boy; little Shirley is the granddaughter of a peppery old colonel (C. Aubrey Smith, naturally) who in her infant innocence softens the heart of the Border rebel (Cesar Romero), but not before her friend and protector, Sergeant MacDuff (McLaglen) has been shot by a sniper. This led to one of those amazing scenes which can only be described (comment being superfluous), in which McLaglen expires with a beatific smile on his battered face while Miss Temple sings "Auld Lang Syne". Whether it was this scene, or the film as a whole, that enraged Graham Greene as critic to the point where libel proceedings were instituted, I do not know. Maybe it was McLaglen's Scottish accent – it was one of his charms that whether called on to play an Englishman (which he was), an American, a Scot, or an Irishman, his voice never lost the clipped rasp of the old British Army, with its occasional "d" for "th"; it is a genuine pity that no enterprising recording company ever got him to tape *Barrack-Room Ballads* for posterity, for his was one of those screen voices – like those of Aubrey Smith, A. E. Matthews, and Mrs Patrick Campbell – that had the authentic quality of the Victorian era.

It was inevitable that *Kim* would be filmed sooner or later, and just as inevitable that it would fail. Like many boys of my generation, I had a resistance to the book, begotten of parental enthusiasm for it, probably, but I can see why it would excite a film-maker. Here is the great Indian novel, full of the sights and sounds of the Grand Trunk Road and the bazaars and the high hills, with the British boy growing up as a native, acting as disciple to a saintly old Lama, helping Mahbub Ali, the red-bearded super-spy, being put to school among his own people, learning the Great Game of espi-onage and intrigue, going into the mountains in search of the Russian agents, the old Lama accomplishing his quest –

it is all there, on the face of it, but Kipling himself described it as "nakedly picaresque and plotless", and it is just one of those great pieces of writing that does not translate well to the screen.

Kim was a film project for many years (with Mickey Rooney and Freddie Bartholomew in mind at different times) but eventually the part went to Dean Stockwell, and while Paul Lukas was an endearing enough lama, and Errol Flynn played Mahbub Ali with some swagger, the film could not encompass the spirit of the book. It tried hard – the script is one of the few to dare to employ second-person singular in conversation, and it says something for the players that the device never seems artificial – but while some of the Indian locations are pleasing to look at, the overall result is rather flat.

Today, when television cameras and long-distance lenses can bring the ends of the earth in close-up into the living room (and in colour, too), *Elephant Boy* looks tame stuff, but it wasn't in 1937. Critics probably expected better from Robert Flaherty, but to audiences it was a reassuring glimpse of British

Sabu as Toomai in *Elephant Boy*.

India, with spectacular shots of elephants thrown in, and it introduced one of the most engaging of all child stars in Sabu. At a time when some of the biggest box-office draws were juveniles – Durbin, Temple, Bartholomew, Rooney, et al – the little stable-boy from Mysore, with his brilliant smile and natural air was an exotic novelty; his acting was simple, and he carried *Elephant Boy* on his small shoulders without effort. Based on Kipling, the film follows the adventures of Toomai, a little mahout taken on a hunt for wild elephants by a government officer (Walter Hudd, the personification of what British audiences expected a Sahib to be – kindly, firm and slightly stuffy). Toomai's father is killed by a tiger, his pet elephant runs amok under a new brutal keeper, and the small hero and the huge beast take to the jungle where, fortunately, they run across the wild herd which the expedition had despaired of finding. All ends happily, after some spectacular shots of vast elephant herds lumbering about (and even dancing), and Alexander Korda found himself with a major star on his hands and the problem of what to put him in next.

He solved it by turning to a trusted stand-by, A. E. W. Mason (*Fire Over England, The Four Feathers*) and the result was *The Drum*, which has a good claim to be *the* imperial film. It is a lavish spectacular of the Northwest Frontier which celebrates the forces of Empire in their role as military diplomatic peace-keepers and defenders of benevolent rule – a genuine role which revisionist critics of the Indian Army and Civil Service are careful to overlook nowadays. At the same time, *The Drum* has all the ingredients beloved by readers of the Wolf of Kabul and the *Boy's Own Paper*. Sabu is Prince Azim, heir to the frontier kingdom of Tokot, to which a British military mission headed by Captain Carruthers (Roger Livesey) is sent to negotiate a treaty. The British force includes a boy soldier (Desmond Tester) who, after an initial quarrel with Azim, becomes his firm friend and teaches him to play a military drum. When the British withdraw, Azim's wicked uncle, Ghul (fitting name for a fanatical Raymond Massey) usurps the throne, and the prince flees to India

Valerie Hobson and Sabu in *The Drum.*

where he is saved from Ghul's assassins by Mrs Carruthers (Valerie Hobson). She and Carruthers return to Tokot with the British military presence, and Ghul's secret plan for a general massacre and frontier rising is foiled by Azim, whose drum signal alerts Carruthers in the nick of time. Hectic action follows, with Carruthers machine-gunning away in a dinner jacket, Highlanders and Pathans have a splendid set-to, Ghul is shot by a member of the Tokot royal family whom he has been torturing to pass the time, and Azim is restored to his throne.

The Drum's virtues as a film are a cast of high quality, excellent photography, good incident, pace, and the friendship of Azim and the drummer-boy, which is sincere and funny and had an immediate appeal for young audiences fed up with the over-sentimental mush which Hollywood tended to spread over its infant prodigies.

With the disintegration of empire one might have expected films of the *Drum* and *Four Feathers* variety to pass quietly from the screen, but twenty years later *Northwest*

Frontier made its appearance, with considerable success. It was an excellent cliff-hanger, set in 1905, with a British officer (Kenneth More) having to smuggle a young Indian prince out of a city besieged by Muslim tribesmen. They escape in an ancient steam train with an assortment of passengers – an independent American woman (Lauren Bacall), a Eurasian journalist (Herbert Lom), a civil servant (Wilfrid Hyde-White), a cynical arms peddler (Eugene Deckers), the governor's lady (Ursula Jeans), two sepoys, and the great I. S. Johar at the controls. A sort of steam *Stagecoach,* in effect, with hordes of bearded bandits in the way instead of Apaches. There is ambush, engine failure, massacre, a hair-raising crossing over a half-collapsed bridge, sporadic rifle fire, and Kenneth More sings the Eton Boating Song, which seems a bit much – Roger Livesey wouldn't have dreamed of it. And one of the passengers (but who?) is obviously up to no good. The imperial question is discussed in the intervals of mayhem, and Mr More and Miss Bacall strike up a happy relationship, despite his singing and quoting Kipling at journey's end.

In fact, More was very good at this sort of thing; he had a cheery truculence which was much closer to the real imperial type than the conventional stiff upper lip. The period detail was excellent – that train (and I. S. Johar) made me quite homesick. The one flaw was the title; I remarked to the technical adviser, a senior ex-Indian Army officer, that it seemed odd, having a Hindu prince up yonder, and he replied that he had no idea where the film was meant to be taking place, but wherever it was, it was not the Frontier.

But there is a special magic about that grim borderline, and Hollywood has been at some odd shifts to exploit it. The original *Charge of the Light Brigade* (1936) is set, for most of its running time, in the Frontier region (shot in California), and is a fine example of the film industry's getting the best of all possible worlds. It has two lancer brothers (Errol Flynn and Patric Knowles) in love with Olivia de Havilland, who is engaged to Flynn but prefers Knowles and doesn't like to say so. Meanwhile, a dastardly prince, Surat Khan (C. Henry Gordon), having had his government subsidy stopped, is flirting with the Russians and taking out his spite on the British by massacring a frontier garrison. He then moves mysteriously to Russia, and is thus conveniently on hand when Flynn and the lancers, who have been sent to the Crimean War, turn up thirsting for his blood. The famous charge takes place, then, for no better reason than to stick C. Henry Gordon full of lances, which is duly done, Flynn perishing gloriously in the forefront – he has seen to it, noble fellow, that Knowles is kept out of danger and safe for Miss de Havilland.

Such historical rubbish would not bear examination but for two things. The first is that the script, holding nothing sacred, has plundered Indian Mutiny history at one point – and got it right. Surat Khan's slaughter of the frontier garrison is almost step for step with the true story of the Cawnpore siege and massacre, when the British garrison surrendered to Nana Sahib, who then broke his promise and wiped out men, women, and children indiscriminately. It is all in this film – the barrack-room defence, the white flag, the dispute about the garrison keeping their arms, the embarkation in river-boats, the sudden hail of fire, the boats burning, the survivors being herded ashore and butchered. Only the historical context has been changed.

The other saving grace is the charge itself. All the stops are pulled out, Tennyson's poem being superimposed on the screen at intervals as the six hundred ride into the Russian guns in a very fair substitute for the Balaclava valley, and for spectacular cavalry action it is unsurpassed. It has attracted its share of cinema legends, all no doubt true – this is where, according to David Niven, Michael Curtiz issued his famous order to "bring on the empty horses", and where Flynn protested against the trip-wires which were maiming the unfortunate animals, and had his set-to with an extra who had unseated him before the charge

From the left: the 7th Earl of Cardigan, Trevor Howard, and John Gielgud as Lord Raglan, in *The Charge of The Light Brigade,* 1968.

began.[6] However it was achieved, the charge was a tour de force of film-making, and far outshone the remake of 32 years later. This second version was disappointing, although it kept closer to the facts, of which the most vital remains an unsolved mystery. Much has been made of the general incompetence with which the Crimean campaign was conducted, of the stupidity of Cardigan, who commanded the Light Brigade, and of his bad relations with his superior, Lucan. The trouble is that while all these things are true, none of them caused the charge, which would almost certainly still have taken place if the general conduct of the war had been normally competent, Cardigan had been a first-class mind, and he and Lucan the best of friends. It happened by the horrible coincidence of, first, a vaguely-worded order scribbled in haste, and, second, a genuine misunderstanding caused by an impetuous junior officer, Nolan. Cardigan, admittedly an idiot, only did what he was bound to do.

By concentrating a good deal on the preliminaries to the campaign and to the charge itself, with no great clarity, the film really does not help the seeker after truth; it seems more intent on correcting the popular view of Balaclava as a glorious catastrophe, and taking an altogether sourer view. God knows there is enough about the Crimea to make anyone sour, but not, I would suggest, the charge of the Light Brigade. One leaves the film feeling that the six hundred deserved something better.

Trevor Howard is an outstanding success as Cardigan, whom he closely resembles; Lord Raglan, the army commander, was an ass, but not the kind of an ass John Gielgud makes him. I don't know on what authority Mrs Duberley[7] can be accused of misconduct, but if none exists (and I have

heard of none) then her portrayal in the film is inexcusable.

The imperial cinema was not exclusively concerned with battlefields, or even with the Middle and Far East. *Hudson's Bay*, already mentioned, is a film of empire, and Hollywood did not neglect those resolute and colourful keepers of the Queen's Peace, the Canadian Mounties. They have figured in any number of screen fictions, frequently bursting into song, and there was a rugged redcoat in the Forties called Renfrew, who figured in choice vignettes with titles like *Crashing Thru* and *Fighting Mad*. Factual history was vaguely touched on in *Pony Soldier*, with Tyrone Power, inasmuch as this mediocre film was inspired by the remarkable exploit of Constable Daniel "Peaches" Davis, who in 1879 escorted a band of several hundred renegade Sioux and Crees through the country of their hereditary enemies, the Blackfeet. He had collected them, single-handed, from the American cavalry, and after a hair-raising journey delivered them to their reservation intact – a considerable feat, on that wild frontier, for a young man of twenty-four.

The Mounties received the DeMille treatment in *Northwest Mounted Police*, produced on a vast scale and with an impressive cast. It was based on the Riel Rebellion in 1885, in which Louis Riel led his half-breed Metis people in an armed insurrection in Saskatchewan, following unsuccessful attempts to have their grievances redressed by the government. The Mounted Police were thinly stretched, and suffered one stinging reverse from the Metis, but although Riel tried to incite a general Indian uprising the rebellion was finally crushed and he was captured and hanged.

DeMille glamourised this, his first film in colour, by involving a Texas Ranger (Gary Cooper) on the trail of one of the Metis leaders (George Bancroft); distracted by the rebellion and Madeleine Carroll, Cooper also has to deal with a rugged Mountie sergeant (Preston Foster), and a shiftless constable (Robert Preston) who forgets his duty in his pursuit of a half-breed wench (Paulette Goddard). Light relief is provided by a Scotch trapper (Lynne Overman) and his Metis

---

6 Why Niven should have been present for the filming of the actual charge is a mystery, since the character he played had perished gallantly earlier in the picture – unless Warner Brothers were being thrifty and using him to make up the numbers.

7 Mrs Fanny Duberley, wife of an officer in the Light Brigade, accompanied the army to the Crimea, and wrote *A Journal Kept During the Russian War, 1856*.

DeMille's version of the Riel rising, *Northwest Mounted Police:* from left, Lynne Overman, Preston Foster, Gary Cooper, Walter Hampden and George Bancroft.

rival (Akim Tamiroff), the Mounties are ambushed in dramatic fashion at Duck Lake (not quite according to history, in the opinion of one of the survivors, whom I interviewed in Regina almost fifty years ago[8]), and while Gary Cooper foils the Metis, Preston Foster talks the Indians out of taking the warpath. The scenery is magnificent, the costumes and minute details immaculate, and of some historical interest

is the portrayal of Riel by Francis C. McDonald, one of the great veterans of the cinema, who never seems to be mentioned in works of film reference, although his face is familiar from many screen spectaculars and countless B pictures.

Having looked through

Francis McDonald, silent matinee idol, "villain", and character actor.

8 His name was William Jones, he was in his nineties, and as a souvenir of his service as a scout in the frontier wars he carried the scar of an Indian arrowhead across his hand.

the cinema's eyes at the British Empire, it seems only proper to look at that Empire's personification, Queen Victoria herself, as she has been portrayed on the screen. But here there is a difficulty. Until now, my method has been to compare, briefly, a film with the true history it purports to show, or on which it touches; obviously this is not practical where *Victoria the Great* is concerned, since it covers her entire reign, so I can say only that it is a fair, not unduly romanticised, chronicle of highlights, distinguished by an excellent central performance. Anna Neagle is not the great queen's double, either in youth or age, but she is always credible; Anton Walbrook is ideal casting as Albert, although possibly more genial than the real Prince Consort. Only to two details could I take exception: the miscasting of the austere Felix Aylmer as the ebullient Palmerston, and the portrayal of Wellington with an Irish accent – as the Duke would certainly

have said, if you'll believe that you'll believe anything.

The casting and playing of *The Mudlark*, or the other hand, are impeccable. The film is a cheerful fairytale, from a novel by Theodore Bonnet, about a riverside waif (Andrew Ray) who breaks into Windsor Castle in the 1870s in the hope of seeing the ageing Queen Victoria (Irene Dunne). He succeeds, after various adventures, and wins not only her heart but that of her rugged and frequently intoxicated Highland retainer, John Brown (Finlay Currie), as well as the tolerance of Disraeli (Alec Guinness), who artfully uses the situation to persuade the Queen to give up her long seclusion in mourning for the late Prince Albert, and go out in public again. All three characters are shown in a most amiable light . . . well, perhaps confronted with such an appealing urchin as Andrew Ray they would have been just like that. Irene Dunne is a convincing Widow of Windsor,

John Brown, and centre, Finlay Currie with Irene Dunne in *The Mudlark*. Right, Queen Victoria in middle age.

Guinness a witty and urbane Disraeli, laying on flattery, as Disraeli himself put it, with a trowel, and Currie plainly had the time of his life. How faithful a picture it gives of the home life of her late majesty is really by the way; Nunnally Johnson's script and Jean Negulesco's direction make the cosy, enjoyable tale perfectly believable.

The incident on which book and film were presumably based had a less sentimental outcome. According to Lytton Strachey, "the boy Jones", as the young intruder was called (he was 17, but small for his age, and of a "most repulsive appearance") had made his first entry into Buckingham Palace (not Windsor) in 1838, disguised as a chimney sweep. Two years later, shortly after the 21-year-old Queen had given birth to her first child, he paid a return visit, and spent three days hiding under beds and living on foraged food before he was found beneath a sofa; by his own account he had seen the Queen and sat on the Throne. They sent him to a reformatory, twice, for he persisted in his attempts to return to the palace, and he was finally packed off to sea in the Royal Navy. He seems to have been last heard of in 1844 when he jumped overboard in the Mediterranean, apparently for fun, and had to be rescued. Now, all *that* would have made a movie.

Finally, to the last great imperialist, Winston Churchill, whose adventurous young manhood, based on his own autobiography, was brought to the screen in *Young Winston*. It is a nice blending of styles, from semi-documentary to *Four Feathers*, the military detail is first-rate, and if the tone is romantic, that is accurate enough, for the man himself was as romantic as they come. Simon Ward, faced with a part as

Benjamin Disraeli, left, with three of his impersonators: right, John Gielgud (*The Prime Minister*), and opposite, Alec Guinness (The *Mudlark*), and right, George Arliss (*Disraeli*).

formidable as any in the history of cinema biography, acquits himself splendidly, and there are excellent portraits by Robert Shaw as Lord Randolph, Anthony Hopkins as Lloyd George, and Robert Hardy as a most Victorian pedagogue.

There we have to leave the Empire, and with it the rest of the nineteenth century (except for those American aspects of it which are covered in the next Age). This is a pity; it would be nice to consider how well Hollywood has reflected the last century's social, political, literary, scientific, and artistic scenes, for example, but it would take volumes. I wish there were room to discuss Sydney Greenstreet's portrayal of Thackeray, or Edward G. Robinson (Reuter), Anna Neagle (Florence Nightingale), Clark Gable and Robert Donat (Parnell), Don Ameche (Alexander Graham Bell), Christopher Plummer (Kipling), Robert Morley (Charles James Fox), Tyrone Power (de Lesseps), Norma Shearer and Fredric March (the

Brownings), Walter Hudd (Faraday), Cornel Wilde (Chopin), Oliver Reed (Bismarck), Merle Oberon (George Sand), Danny Kaye (Hans Andersen), Jean-Pierre Aumont (Rimsky-Korsakov), Laird Cregar (Jack the Ripper), Kirk Douglas (Van Gogh), Joseph Schildkraut (Dreyfus), Mick Jagger (Ned Kelly), and Paul Muni (practically everyone else[9]). Or to survey those Victorian music halls in which Alice Faye outshone the Chicago Fire, Dick Haymes wrote "When Irish Eyes are Smiling", Tommy Trinder sang as Champagne Charlie, and Betty Grable shimmied like her sister Kate. And what of those grimy London streets, perpetually shrouded in artificial fog, through which Basil Rathbone quested eagerly with Nigel Bruce grumbling in his wake? All I can do is acknowledge them gratefully, and pass on.

9 Zola, Juarez, Pasteur . . .

Nineteenth-century People and their Players

William Pitt the Younger, and Robert Donat in *The Young Mr Pitt*.

Left, Kirk Douglas with van Gogh's self-portrait in *Lust for Life*.

The Bronte Sisters (left to right Emily, Charlotte, Anne), with left to right, Nancy Coleman (Anne), Ida Lupino (Emily), and Olivia de Havilland (Charlotte), in *Devotion*.

Above, Otto von Bismarck, and below, Oliver Reed in *Royal Flash*.

Above, Charles James Fox, and below, Robert Morley in *The Young Mr Pitt*.

Above, Emil Zola, and below, Paul Muni in *The Life of Emil Zola*.

Above, Frederic Chopin, and below,
Cornel Wilde in *A Song to Remember*.

Above, Franz Liszt, and below, Fritz Leiber,
who played Liszt in *The Phantom of the
Opera*.

Above, Nikolay Rimsky-Korsakov, and below,
Jean-Pierre Aumont in *Song of Scheherezade*.

Above, Hans Christian Andersen and below, Danny Kaye, in *Hans Christian Andersen.*

Above, Rudyard Kipling, and below, Christopher Plummer in *The Man Who Would Be King.*

Above, W. M. Thackeray, and below, Sydney Greenstreet in *Devotion.*

THE SIXTH AGE
New World, Old West

Rogers's Rangers bound for St Francis in *Northwest Passage*.
Previous page, "Westward the course of empire takes it way": an American symbol from *The Covered Wagon*.

SIXTH AGE

New World, Old West

America is the most modern, forward-looking country in the world and yet, judged by its films, no country has shown such an obsession with its past. The proportion of American movies set before 1900 is enormous compared to the costume-film output of any other country, the reason being that no one else has a national equivalent of the Western – which is, like it or not, a historical film. Leave it out of account, and America's cinematic interest in its old days is in no way remarkable. Why this should be – why the United States should have had this apparent massive addiction to Western pictures – is a question to which profound answers have been given, invoking the pioneer spirit, the private enterprise system, the country's dissenting and revolutionary origins, subconscious centaur worship, guilt complex about American expansion, post-revolutionary insecurity, and just about everything except sunspots.

Personally, I doubt if the number of Westerns turned out in the past century has really reflected any deep-seated psychological hunger in the American public. The Westerner was a folk hero long before the cinema, but he hardly dominated popular entertainment, even after the Wild West shows began in the 1880s. So why, in the twentieth century, should John Wayne and company have taken up so much screen space? The answer, I believe, is not profound at all. People tend to like, or at least to accept, what they are given, and it was both easy and convenient to give America cowboy pictures; the materials were all to hand in profusion, the subject was congenial and familiar to a captive audience, an appetite was created, and the Western film industry grew from its own momentum. Certainly it touched primitive chords (and not only in the US), but I suggest that the main reason why America loved the Western was, eventually, because it was there, a national institution born of Hollywood which had created, rather than responded to, a national demand.

If I am wrong, if the real reason was something deeper, then it has vanished almost overnight. The Western, so ubiquitous in the early days of television, has been pitched unceremoniously off the small screen, and has a dwindling share of the large one. If the Cosby-type show is the modern equivalent of Blondie and the Jones Family, and *Hill Street Blues* of the gangster picture, then I suppose the Western's lineal descendants are the Ewings and Colbys and others of the rich-family-business-sex-and-money culture. Whatever the reason, American popular entertainment is suddenly contemporary, and the Western has ridden slowly into the sunset, lamented and much-loved, but clearly expendable. That, too, may furnish material for a few doctoral theses; my cynical view is that Hollywood simply realised (as with the Western) that it had the ingredients for *Dynasty–Dallas* sagas right there in Bel Air and Rodeo Drive, and that the Century City towers would make an acceptable substitute for Monument Valley.

That is another story; I am concerned with films about bygone America, and the daunting fact is that about 90 per cent of them are Westerns, which is ridiculous when one considers that American history, for practical purposes, has lasted about 400 years, and the period celebrated in Western films amounts to only one-tenth of that time, from the Civil War to the Nineties. It may be objected that Westerns, for the most part, are not "historical", but I hope to demonstrate that they are, in a very important sense – which does not mean that 90 per cent of this chapter is going to be devoted to them. Far from it; Billy the Kid may have had ten times more film

President Andrew Jackson (from the painting by Asher B. Durand), and right, Charlton Heston in *The Buccaneer*.

attention than George Washington, but not on that account are we going to lose our sense of perspective and give the little squirt undue space.

At the same time, I have to adjust the framework. For the historian, America's past splits neatly into three – the colonial era, Revolution to Civil War, and the modern age. That is not practical for this book; American history in the cinema has to be divided into two: pre-Western and Western – which is to give the latter a share out of all proportion to its importance, in historic if not in cinematic terms.

In surveying those two and a half centuries of pre-Western American history, and bearing in mind the justifiable pride that Americans take in their national heritage, I find it odd that so few films have been devoted to the most vital episodes and to the great men. Hollywood, which has given ample coverage to the Armada crisis, the French Revolution, and the birth of

Christianity, has seemed comparatively reluctant to volunteer for the War of Independence or the Civil War; there have been films that touched them, or skirted round their edges, but really not all that many in view of the opportunities they offer the patriotic film-maker, or their importance in history and folklore. Perhaps the Revolution has been just too big and emotive a subject, and too sensitive for the British market (ironically, the one attempt to tackle it head-on came, recently, from Britain); as to the Civil War, while it is common to see Yankees and Johnny Rebs come chest to chest in Westerns, it may be that the great conflict itself is still too close for comfort, especially in the South. However that may be, it remains that while Hollywood has never hesitated to give full treatment to Elizabeth, Napoleon, Nelson, Catherine the Great, and Henry VIII, there have been no corresponding major films about Washington, Jefferson, Franklin, Andrew

Jackson, Generals Lee and Grant, Stonewall Jackson, Jeb Stuart, Paul Revere, Mad Anthony Wayne, or even Benedict Arnold who saved the Revolution and then betrayed it.[1]

Many of these worthies have appeared in films, but almost always in supporting or even bit parts;[2] apart from *John Paul Jones* (with Robert Stack), and Davy Crockett, the only great American from this period to be given star treatment on the Elizabethan-Napoleonic scale is Abraham Lincoln. On the whole, considering American domination of the cinema, it does seem as though the country's earlier history has been under-exploited; this is not to say that it has not inspired some splendid pictures, but I am just surprised that there have not been many more to celebrate one of the most brilliant and exciting chapters in the human story.

It can be said that it started with the Vikings, already noted, or with *Christopher Columbus* (Fredric March, in a film which looked well but failed to live up to the grandeur of its subject). But it really began in the little village of Scrooby, Nottinghamshire, in 1608, when a group of Puritan families left for Holland so that they might worship as they chose; they found it uncongenial there, and in 1620 they returned to England and sailed for the New World from Southampton in two small ships, Speedwell and Mayflower. With them went

other Dissenters, Anglicans, and adventurers; they had formed a company, not without difficulty, with the help of Thomas Weston, a London Puritan merchant, under a charter from the Virginia Company, but at the last minute there were disagreements about terms, and Weston left them to their own devices. They sailed anyway, but the Speedwell proved unseaworthy, and in the end only the Mayflower put out, from Plymouth. She was commanded by Thomas (or Christopher) Jones, and carried about a hundred English men, women, and children – William Brewster and William Bradford of Scrooby, Myles Standish of Lancashire, soldier and captain-general, John Robinson, and others called Fuller, Hopkins, Alden, Billington, and Winslow (let Americans never forget the names) who eventually were among the forty-one who signed the "Mayflower Compact". The journey was uneventful, although they landed not in Virginia, but in Massachusetts, where they had no legal title. They stayed, losing forty-four in their first winter, and they have been there ever since.

Plymouth Adventure has been criticised as a dull film. Some of the great moments in history are dull, in themselves; it is the consequences that matter. The film tries to inject drama by making Captain Jones (Spencer Tracy) a hostile, derisive scoundrel who conspires with Weston (Rhys Williams) to land the colonists in the wrong place, and it gingers up the emotions by having Jones falling in love with Mrs Bradford (Gene Tierney), who appears to commit suicide, torn as she is between Jones and her husband (Leo Genn). The hardships of the journey are emphasised, but apart from a beautifully filmed storm and occasional fisticuffs between Alden (Van Johnson) and crew members, it all passes off quietly enough, with Jones undergoing a change of heart and helping to see the settlers through their first winter. Which may not be very exciting, but shows a responsibility in the producers who chose to present a fairly factual account rather than some glamourised fiction. The film is perhaps a little unfair in depicting Weston as a villain; he did eventually come out to the settlement and helped to legalise it. In other respects it is a fair

---

1 If my judgement on Benedict Arnold seems contentious I can only put forward the proposition that if he had not been present at Saratoga the Stars and Stripes would not be flying over the United States today – or if it were, it would be in a very different form.

2 Andrew Jackson has, admittedly, done his bit on the screen, with Lionel Barrymore (*The Gorgeous Hussy, Lone Star*), Charlton Heston (*The Buccaneer, The President's Lady*), Brian Donlevy (*The Remarkable Andrew*) and several others, but my point is that none of the films has made a memorable impact, and his name is hardly one to conjure with in the cinema. Washington I recall only twice, played briefly by Richard Gaines in *Unconquered,* and by Douglas Dumbrille in *Monsieur Beaucaire*. Orson Welles and Charles Coburn have played Franklin (in *Lafayette* and *John Paul Jones*). Grant and Lee have made innumerable appearances as supporting players, and while Errol Flynn was portraying Jeb Stuart in *Santa Fe Trail*, the audience were probably none the wiser. Edward Arnold played Daniel Webster in *Daniel and the Devil,* a film notable only for the performance of Walter Huston, who played the other half of the title.

Spencer Tracy as Captain Jones, with Lloyd Bridges in *Plymouth Adventure*.

despises Indians and has no thought but gold. His brutal approach leads to conflict with Powhatan's tribe, and peace is restored only when Pocahontas saves the life of Smith, the Governor's lieutenant. Ratcliffe is deposed, the wounded Smith is shipped back to England, and Pocahontas is left lamenting her lost love, but with the consolation, presumably, that the idyllic life of her people can continue.

Partly true, but not the whole truth, which is much more interesting. John Smith was a remarkable soldier of fortune who, by his own account (which is probably substantially true), had fought as a mercenary in the Low Countries and Balkans, been thrown overboard in the Mediterranean, rescued by pirates whom he joined, captured and sold as a slave, escaped with the help of a Turkish lady, reached England after more adventures, and sailed with the Jamestown colonists to Virginia in 1607, when he was 27.

Pace Disney, the settlers were attacked by Indians almost as soon as they had landed (within hours, by one account, but after twelve days according to Samuel Eliot Morison). Ratcliffe (whose real name was Sicklemore) was not the original Governor, but attained the post with Smith's help, only to lose it after a disastrous period in which half the colonists died of disease and starvation. Ratcliffe was sent home "lest the company should cut his throat", and Smith took charge and saved the colony.

So much for agreed fact; now comes a moment of legend which may well be true. Smith was captured by Powhatan's Indians and only escaped a grisly death by the intervention of Pocahontas, the chief's 12-year-old daughter, whereafter peace was restored, for the moment anyway. Pocahontas ("Frisky") was a beautiful and engaging child, and used to visit Jamestown to play with the settlers' children; she was also a forceful personality and was to prove an invaluable intermediary, arranging supplies for the needy immigrants ("She, under God, was the instrument to preserve this colony," Smith wrote), and when she was detained (or kidnapped?) by the Governor as a hostage for English prisoners in Indian

account of how ordinary folk did a small thing which changed the course of history.

There had been earlier British settlements in America, but the film industry ignored them until the recent Disney production of *Pocahontas* – a remarkable neglect, for the story of John Smith and the Indian princess is pure Hollywood, with everything that the Plymouth episode lacks: romance, true love, high adventure, massacre, and the excitement of racial and cultural collision. It even has a happy ending (depending where you stop), and would have made an excellent big-screen epic rather than a children's cartoon, charming (and only mildly inaccurate in the interests of fashionable prejudice) though the latter was.

The Disney version has English settlers landing at Jamestown under the leadership of wicked Governor Ratcliffe, who

Fact and fantasy: Pocahontas as a lady of fashion (from an engraving made during her visit to London), and right, as imagined by Disney's artists.

hands, she eventually became a willing captive, for she and John Rolfe, an English planter, fell in love and were married, with the blessing of the Governor and Powhatan, who sent wedding presents.

She was a nine-day wonder when she visited London in 1616, "carried herself as the daughter of a king", was received at Court and feted by leading citizens, accompanied the Queen to Ben Jonson's Twelfth Night Masque, and had a brief reunion with John Smith, who had returned to England. In the following year she was preparing to go back to Virginia when she fell ill, possibly with smallpox, and died at Gravesend, where she was buried. She was 21.

The peace she had done so much to keep for Jamestown did not last; indeed, it had been frequently interrupted, with blame attaching to both sides – a point well made in the Disney film, where a scene of the settlers preparing to attack and chanting "Savages, savages!" is intercut with the Indians arming themselves and chanting the same words – and John Rolfe may have been one of the 374 victims, one-third of the colony, killed in the Indian massacre of 1622. Rolfe, incidentally, was the man who popularised tobacco in England, despite the opposition of that well-known non-smoker, James I. His son by Pocahontas, Thomas Rolfe, has descendants living in Virginia.

Stranger than fiction, the little Indian princess was commemorated by a statue at Gravesend, but Belle Sauvage Yard in the City, named in her honour, vanished in the Blitz. Perhaps she has a more lasting memorial – "The Tempest" was inspired by the wreck of a Jamestown ship on Bermuda in 1609, and it is quite possible that Shakespeare heard of her from Smith at the same time. It would be nice to think that Pocahontas lived on in Miranda.

For more than a century or so after the arrival of the Pilgrim Fathers, nothing much happened so far as Hollywood was concerned (one exception, *Hudson's Bay*, has already been noted) until the outbreak of the Seven Years' War (1756–63), known in America as the French and Indian War. This, a vital chapter in the long struggle between Britain and France, decided the fate of North America, and the film industry took notice accordingly with four major productions, all based on novels which in turn were well rooted in history. Two of the films were drawn from one of the best-known (and least read) books in American literature, *The Last of the Mohicans*.

Its author, J. Fenimore Cooper, thought up superb stories but did not write them very well, which hardly mattered to the English-speaking world of 1826, for he gave them something new and terrifying which held them spellbound – the American Indian. Cooper did not create the Indian bogyman; that was something already driven deep into the American conscious-ness by bitter experience, but he was the first to realise the noble savage, in all his beauty, cruelty, courage, and mystery, as one of the most fascinating menaces in fiction. In "The Last of the Mohicans" Cooper showed the Indian at his best and worst by drawing his plot from an incident infamous in colonial history, the massacre of Fort William Henry, where in 1757 a British garrison under Colonel Monro was besieged by twelve thousand French and Indian troops under Montcalm. With more than 300 killed and wounded, and smallpox raging in the fort, Monro finally surrendered on Montcalm's promise of safe conduct; in the event, the Indians butchered at least fifty of the prisoners, and carried off six hundred, almost half of whom were never heard of again.

The 1936 film, more or less faithful to Cooper's version, has Colonel Monro's two daughters, Alice and Cora (Binnie Barnes and Heather Angel) being escorted through the woods by an English officer, Hayward (Henry Wilcoxon), with the treacherous Huron brave Magua (Bruce Cabot) as guide. Sure enough he betrays them, but Hawkeye (Randolph Scott) and his Mohican allies, Chingachgook and Uncas (Robert Barratt and Philip Reed) arrive to the rescue, and there is frantic flight through the forest and down-river with howling braves in pursuit, before safety is reached. By that time Uncas, the younger Mohican, and Cora are in love, and Hawkeye and Hayward are at loggerheads, partly because of Alice, partly because of that natural antipathy which is going to lead to the

American Revolution twenty years later. The fort massacre throws things into confusion, and there are spectacular toma-hawk duels on cliff-tops, with Magua killing Uncas, and Chingachgook killing Magua, and Cora committing suicide, and Hawkeye about to be burned at the stake when help arrives in the nick of time. I need hardly add that it was yet another of those films from which, as a lad, I had to be removed by alarmed parents who had let me go to the matinée and started to get anxious about 9.30 p.m.

Apart from being an interesting lesson in colonial history, the film was my generation's first real view of those splendid Leatherstocking Indians of the forest, so much more impres-sive and terrifying than their cousins of the Plains. I doubt if many real Indians were used in the film, yet even today it remains one of the most atmospheric of historicals, mainly because of those splendid gleaming figures with their painted faces, shaven heads, and scalp-locks, slipping through the trees round the beleaguered fort. It is well photographed and costumed – and still runs continuously in a room of the reconstructed Fort William Henry on Lake George, New York State, for the benefit of visitors to that historic site.

I dare say the fault lies with me and my sentimental recol-lections, but I found the 1992 version of Cooper's story unexciting by comparison, and less historically enlightening. It had the doubtful advantage of being in colour, and probably the detail of costume, weaponry, and Indian[3] culture was more faithful than in the first film, but where a clear plot-line and strong characters came across in 1936, in images which remain undimmed after sixty years, the only impression I retain of the remake is of Daniel Day-Lewis running hell-for-leather through the woods.

Two years after Fort William Henry, the war had turned Britain's way, and Wolfe took Quebec in September 1759. In

3 "Indian" is a term no longer approved by the politically correct, who insist on "native American" – an odd and illogical expression since it obviously applies to anyone born in America, of whatever race. It is ironic that Theodore Roosevelt should have used it a century ago to describe Americans of British and Dutch descent.

"In the hands of the Redskins" ... The Indian as menace, popularised by Fenimore Cooper. The buckskin victim is Henry Wilcoxon in *The Last of the Mohicans*.

the same month a force of two hundred of the King's Rangers, an early commando unit of colonial troops and British regulars, skilled in frontier fighting and commanded by Major Robert Rogers, was sent against the Abenaki Indians of St Francis, who for seventy years had been the scourge of the colonial settlements. Rogers' force, after a perilous journey by boat and on foot, destroyed the Indian camp in a dawn raid, killing 200 warriors; they found 600 white scalps in the village. Pursued by French and Indians,

they took to the woods, and after a journey of incredible hardship, reached a rendezvous where food should have been waiting;[4] it was not, and Rogers and a few companions had to make their way, almost starving, to a British fort farther on, from which relief was sent back to his exhausted main force.

This exploit was shown in *Northwest Passage*, from the novel

4 Rogers' journey was through a forest wilderness that has to be seen to be believed. A few years ago I tried to find his rendezvous, with signal lack of success.

Major Robert Rogers of the King's Rangers (from a contemporary print), and right, Spencer Tracy in *Northwest Passage*.

by Kenneth Roberts, a most scholarly presentation of history as fiction. The film dealt faithfully with both, with Spencer Tracy as the indomitable Rogers, and Robert Young as the young Harvard student who enlists in the Rangers to escape arrest for sedition. It is a film of memorable images: the Rangers lying doggo on a wooded slope as French boats patrol the lake beneath; the Indian village at dawn, with the green buckskin figures stealing through the shadows; the starving survivors sprawled in the ruined fort while Rogers croaks out a mixture of pep talk and prayer; the closing shot of the Rangers marching away to find the fabled "Northwest Passage" to the Pacific – which never happened either in the book or in fact. The second half of Roberts' novel, in which Rogers fails in the quest which Alexander Mackenzie was to complete thirty years later, was never filmed.

With Montcalm's defeat at Quebec, Britain had effectively won the struggle with France in North America, but her hard-won possessions were not to remain intact within the Empire for long. Montcalm himself, dying at Quebec, is said to have predicted that, with the French danger now removed, it would not be long before the British colonists declared their independence from a home country whose protection they no longer needed. So they did, seventeen years later, but in the meantime there was another imminent menace; the Indian tribes, who had on the whole been closer to the French, rightly feared that the victorious British would expand westward, and in 1763 began the great warpath of tribes from as far apart as the Gulf of Mexico and the Great Lakes, led by Pontiac, the Ottawa chief who had fought for the French in the Seven Years' War.

The Indian onslaught hit the frontier outposts like a thunderbolt. Within one summer month fort after fort went down along a thousand-mile front, war parties stormed the settlements and outlying farms, and more colonists are believed to have died than at the height of the French War. Fort Niagara and Detroit were besieged, a force of British Regulars and Rogers' Rangers was badly beaten at Bloody Run, and to the south a little fort at the junction of the Allegheny and Monongahela rivers, occupied by 300 soldiers and frontiersmen and as many women and children, held out against repeated attacks for five days and nights; it was Fort Pitt, now known as Pittsburgh. Called on to surrender by the Indians, the fort commander, a Swiss mercenary named Ecuyer, refused with the significant phrase: "This is our home", and after a month's siege the fort was relieved by a force of Black Watch and backwoodsmen who lost more than 150 men in fighting their way through.

To DeMille this had everything, especially the element of Anglo-American cooperation, which had just been demonstrated in the Second World War. He decked out the story with a Virginian gentleman (Gary Cooper) falling in love with a bondswoman transported from England (Paulette Goddard), cast Howard da Silva as a renegade, made Boris Karloff chief of the besieging Indians, and turned them loose on Fort Pitt with deafening effect. There was massacre, suspense, fire-arrows, canoes plunging over waterfalls, and Miss Goddard was almost burned at the stake, but the Black Watch turned up on time (mostly dead), and the happy couple went off to prepare for the War of Independence. The film, *Unconquered*, received the usual critical mauling, and the public went to it in droves. For the anglophile DeMille it was a labour of love, and an enormous budget for that time was expended; it paid off in spectacle and some superb colour photography, and the

quality of the historical detail was high. Whatever its artistic defects, *Unconquered* is a good visual impression of the colonial frontier.

The Indian war ended, and a treaty was made with the tribes. In an effort to gain their goodwill, presents were sent to them under the care of an official named Croghan, and

Boris Karloff in the unlikely role of Guyasuta, the Seneca chief, with Gary Cooper in *Unconquered*.

several traders attached themselves to his train, hoping to resume commerce with the Indians. To some of the settlers this was rank betrayal, and a celebrated frontiersman, Jim Smith (described as an Englishman educated in Dublin) ambushed the train with his "Black Boys", a group of forest rangers disguised as Indians. The despoiled traders complained to the nearest British military commander, who made indiscriminate arrests, only to find himself besieged by a rising of angry settlers with Smith at their head. The prisoners were released, but the commander gave further offence by confiscating rifles, and was taken captive by the enraged settlers. All was smoothed over, but there was never good will between the British military and the local people again.

This curious incident was dramatised as *Allegheny Uprising,* a disastrous picture all round, and especially for John Wayne and Claire Trevor in the wake of their spectacular success in *Stagecoach*. It elaborates the story considerably, with Smith (Wayne) being tried for a murder committed by the villainous leader of the traders (Brian Donlevy), and there is a painful performance by that fine actor Wilfrid Lawson as a loony Scotch frontiersman, while George Sanders is a British martinet of quite staggering arrogance. But it is of some historical interest, as a fairly true picture of the kind of incident which helped pave the way to 1776, and as a prime example of Hollywood's view of Anglo-American colonial relations.

In this film, as in *The Last of the Mohicans* and in scores of others up to the movies of the Second World War, we see the same stock figures: the sturdy, independent American, impatient of restriction, who gets down to cases with gritty integrity, and the snobbish, hidebound, often thick-headed Briton blinded by a sort of feudal mist to the realities of life. Variations of this "confrontational" theme are legion, not only in films but in popular American views of history; compare Patton and Montgomery or Stilwell and Mountbatten. At its simplest, this view serves to explain the War of Independence – and there is something in it. Of course, it is not the whole truth; vested interests were at work in 1776 as well as British

stupidity, but they are not a heroic aspect of history, and Hollywood is not concerned with them, or with examining the difference between political independence and the fine emotional blanket-word "freedom" – which seems a curious, almost insulting term to use about the aspirations of the colonial Americans, who enjoyed a greater measure of real freedom before 1776 than their British cousins, or indeed any other people in the world, before or since. But for the cinema, simple terms and explanations have to do, and John Wayne and George Sanders must embody them.

They are the stereotypes, but while they were developed in films of the colonial era, and have been employed frequently elsewhere, Hollywood has been extremely tactful about using them in films about the American Revolution, or indeed about making revolutionary films at all. Quite the best of them, *Drums Along the Mohawk*, never once identifies Britain as the enemy, which I find significant, since it was directed by John Ford, whom I have seen described as an anglophobe. In my view, he was no such thing; like many Irishmen of the old school, he probably combined a fervent Irish nationalism with a romantic attachment to that Britain of which Ireland had once been a part, and in whose history she had played so proud a role. Anglophobes don't make films like *Patrol* and *Wee Willie Winkie* or superimpose a fluttering White Ensign over an act of heroism in *The Long Voyage Home*.

Drums Along the Mohawk is the story of a patriot community in the Mohawk Valley in 1776, to which Gilbert Martin (Henry Fonda) has brought his lady wife (Claudette Colbert), who reacts with dismay at her primitive surroundings and goes into hysterics at the sight of an Indian. No sooner has she grown accustomed to the hardships of frontier farming than the Revolution reaches the valley, which is subjected to terrible Indian raids led by the sinister John Carradine in an eye-patch. Their farm is burned, and the young couple are forced to hire out to a redoubtable widow (Edna Mae Oliver at her best). More Indian attacks follow, the community are beleaguered in their little fort, and Martin has to run for help – literally, with

"Tory" Indians attacking a settlement in *Drums Along the Mohawk*.

three Indians racing in pursuit in a splendid sustained chase sequence. Of course he gets through, and the fort is relieved just as the Indians are breaking in.

That is the outline of a beautifully observed study of frontier life. Ford can let his camera range over a room, picking up tiny details of furnishing, or over a church service, with its eccentric minister (Arthur Shields) praying and advertising in one breath, and tell more about a period than an hour-long lecture. It is a gentle, pastoral film for the most

part, which makes its violent passages all the more telling, and at the end of it one begins to understand what it must have been like to try to make a home on the edge of the wilderness, and the price that had to be paid for survival. I said that Britain is not identified as the enemy, who are described throughout as "Tories" – quite correctly, so far as those Americans who fought against the Revolution are concerned. Indeed, when the film came out in 1939, I doubt if British audiences realised they were watching a phase of the

Revolution at all, especially since the raising of the Stars and Stripes at the end is accompanied by the ambiguous strains of "God Save the King/My Country 'Tis of Thee".

The Howards of Virginia is a modest film about a family divided in the Revolutionary War, the respective factions being headed by Cary Grant and Cedric Hardwicke, with no prizes being offered for guessing who was on which side. *Revolution*, the recent British offering on the subject, is clear neither in plot nor in photography, and offers little of historical interest.

The next Anglo-American conflict was the War of 1812, remembered for the burning of Washington and the defeat of the British at New Orleans, events celebrated (twice) in *The Buccaneer*, the story of Jean Lafitte, a dashing and handsome French pirate who preyed on Spanish shipping from his stronghold of Barataria, near the Mississippi mouth. Britain, anxious to enlist Lafitte in the war, offered him a naval commission and $30,000; Lafitte, loyal to his adopted country, refused and forwarded the offer to New Orleans as proof that the British were about to attack the city, but the American authorities regarded the papers as forgeries, and even sent naval ships to destroy Lafitte's base and imprison his followers. Despite this, he offered his help to Andrew Jackson, who had the sense to release the captured pirates, and employ them and Lafitte in the ensuing battle, in which they played a major part in halting the British advance. Lafitte was pardoned by a grateful American government – and a few years later he sailed away, no one knows where.

It is one of those truths that read like romantic fiction, and DeMille only had to add a dash of love interest and any amount of hearty yo-ho-hoing, plus a treacherous senator (Ian Keith) for Fredric March (Lafitte) to duel with. Montagu Love duly burned Washington, Franciska Gaal and Margot Grahame competed for Lafitte's attention, and Akim Tamiroff had the time of his life as an unshaven pirate lieutenant. It was rousing stuff, more faithful to history than one might have expected; the remake twenty years later, with Yul Brynner in a toupé, was a mere Technicolor shadow.

Above: Davy Crockett, and below, John Wayne in *The Alamo*.

Above: James Bowie, and, below Richard Widmark.

Less than a generation after the successful defence of New Orleans an infinitely more important siege took place six hundred miles to westward. From 23 February to 6 March 1836, a garrison of 183 Americans and assorted immigrants held the Alamo mission buildings of San Antonio de Bexar against 2500 Mexican regular troops before being overwhelmed. This was the finest hour of the "Texicans'" struggle for independence, and one of the most heroic pages in American history; needless to say, it has been disputed over ever since, with some of the heroisms being called into question by revisionists and indignantly defended by admirers. None of the debated points matters much, nor do the occasional liberties taken in John Wayne's production, *The Alamo*, which was a worthy celebration of a noble deed. And if I disagree with the review which declared that the film is "doggedly faithful to historical fact" it is simply because the purpose of this book is to compare film versions with historic truth, so far as the latter can be discovered.

The last qualification is necessary, because there are things about the Alamo which probably cannot be proved now, one way or the other, beyond all doubt. There is the question which is the most sensitive of all: did Davy Crockett die fighting, or was he shot after surrendering? Even to mention it, I gather, is to court apoplectic denial from some quarters, but it has been asked by competent historians. The film shows Crockett (Wayne) battling to the last, and since there is no conclusive eye-witness evidence, that is fair enough.

Where the film does stray from fact is in suggesting that bad blood existed between Travis (Laurence Harvey) and Bowie (Richard Widmark); the truth is that after one drunken outburst by Bowie they worked well together as joint commanders, which meant that Travis was effectively in charge, since Bowie was too ill to take much active part in the defence, although he fought from his bed in the last moments. The film's suggestion that Travis offended Bowie over a letter from Bowie's wife is remarkable, since she had died years before. Sam Houston (Richard Boone) is shown early in the

Santa Anna's troops storming the Alamo.

picture brooding over the Alamo's possible fate; in fact, he had sent Bowie to have it blown up and the garrison withdrawn, but once on the spot Bowie decided to fight it out. Lastly, while cattle were herded into the Alamo in the rush to get inside when the Mexican advance was sighted, was there also a night sortie for livestock after the siege began?

These are small points. The main sweep of the film is authentic, and if it wastes far too much time in preliminaries, and gives Crockett more solemn platitudes than that cheery adventurer might have cared for, its spirit cannot be faulted.

John Ford lent uncredited assistance on the picture, and sometimes one wonders where the historical cinema would have been without him and Cecil DeMille; their names come up again and again, as does that of Henry Fonda where Americana is concerned. So there is an inevitability about the teaming of Ford and Fonda on the best film about the most loved and revered of all Americans, *Young Mr Lincoln*. For me, it is Fonda's best performance, and how he failed to get even an Oscar nomination for it is a mystery.

There have been a score of other screen Lincolns, notably

Raymond Massey and Walter Huston, while Frank McGlynn senior made almost a career of playing him in cameos before the war; they were all Lincoln as the man of destiny, but Fonda is the struggling young lawyer in Springfield in the late 1830s. No photographs exist of Lincoln in that period, but Fonda, with a false nose, bears a close resemblance to the first portrait of 1846; indeed, after a few minutes one forgets it is Fonda, and an actor cannot do better than that. Without overplaying, he is the slow, gangling, country boy already touched with greatness – there is one perfect Ford shot of him seated in court, thinking, and it comes as a shock to realise that it is exactly the figure of the Lincoln Memorial.

We see him studying Blackstone, splitting rails, courting Ann Rutledge (who died young), judging pie-making contests, and living the life of a small-town lawyer who was notoriously casual about fees and had a talent for composing quarrels before they came to court. All of which is true; the main thread of the plot, in which he defends two brothers on a murder charge, appears to be based on the Armstrong case which he actually conducted twenty years later, and the opportunity is taken to bring in other court-room incidents and quotations from his career – a very harmless device which does not affect the integrity of the portrait. The crux of the trial, in which Lincoln breaks a key witness (Ward Bond) by proving that there was no moonlight on the night of the murder, is factual.

As a film portrait, it can rank with any in these pages, but it does not overshadow two first-rate supporting performances, by Donald Meek as the prosecutor and Ward Bond as a shifty perjurer, while John Ford's brother, Francis, does his usual scene-stealing as a drunken juryman.

Lincoln has "walked on" in countless dramas touching on the Civil War, and it seems odd that he does not appear – indeed I don't think he is even mentioned – in the three films I have chosen to represent the great conflict of 1861–65, but two of them are concerned with military operations, and the third is set in the South. Indeed, for most cinemagoers it *is* the South, and as faithful a picture as they could wish for, as well as

The earliest known picture of Abraham Lincoln as a young Congressman (photograph by Mathew Brady), above, and Henry Fonda in *Young Mr Lincoln*.

being the most famous film ever made, *Gone With the Wind*.

To comment on it as a piece of history seems superfluous. Not being an authority on the subject, I can say only that in almost sixty years I have never heard or read any criticism of its dialogue, decor, costumes, atmosphere, or historic setting, and since David Selznick was not in the habit of getting things wrong we must assume that there are no faults to be found. The fictional story marries neatly with the course of the war, and the only point I can think of that has not been made a hundred times already is that if Selznick had trouble with the Hays Office over Clark Gable's closing line he might have pointed out that the "dam" which Rhett Butler didn't give is a small piece of metal used by tinkers for mending pots, and is not to be confused with the oath "damn". In other words, he wasn't swearing – but in view of the publicity that Selznick got from that one word, I don't imagine he would have thanked anyone for the information.

The Red Badge of Courage is a very good war picture. The

Scarlett O'Hara (Vivien Leigh) among the wounded in *Gone With the Wind*.

A convincing image of the US Civil War: John Huston's *The Red Badge of Courage*.

author of the book, Stephen Crane, wrote it without having heard a shot fired in anger (he was not born until 1871, and did not see action as a war correspondent before it was published), but it was highly praised by Civil War survivors, and John Huston did a faithful screen version, so we may accept it as authentic. Young Fleming (Audie Murphy) is a Union private who runs away from his first battle but manages to rejoin his unit with his desertion unsuspected, and there-after distinguishes himself by his bravery; he confesses his shame to a comrade (Bill Mauldin), who in turn admits that he, too, fled from the first action. It is a beautifully simple film, distinguished by excellent period dialogue and a fine performance by Murphy as the coward-hero which is specially intriguing in view of the fact that he was the most decorated American soldier of the Second World War. The battle scenes are impressively realistic – the platoon waiting for

The cadets advance into action in *The Horse Soldiers*.

the Confederate advance, stopping it by rifle-fire, exulting, and then realising that the brutes are coming in again, and look like getting there this time. This is the point where Fleming runs, unnecessarily as it turns out; it is interesting that his heroism is performed in much more trying circumstances, when he and his comrades have to advance against an entrenched opposition. There are some lovely military moments – the General cracking the same joke to different units, Fleming's long-range conversation with an unseen Confederate sentry, the badinage among the soldiers, of whom John Dierkes, Arthur Hunnicutt, and Andy Devine are outstanding.

The Horse Soldiers has John Ford dispatching John Wayne on a long-range cavalry operation behind Confederate lines,

the object being to destroy a vital railway junction. This is barely enough to fill out two hours, so Wayne is saddled with a medical officer (William Holden) at whom he snarls continually, and a Southern belle (Constance Towers) who is in a position to betray the operation and has to be carried along, to the inevitable romantic conclusion. The one point of historical interest is the regiment's encounter with an opposing force of small boys from a Southern military academy, which is based on a real incident; Wayne's troops flee in disorder, leaving the infants in possession of the field. The film is another example of Hollywood's insistence on the ancient cliché of two officers who can't abide each other (*cf. The Alamo*); obviously this does happen in war, occasionally, but civilians should not be misled into thinking that military operations are carried out to a constant chorus of mutual insult and insubordination, as the cinema would have them believe. American films are not alone in this; British military jaws are outthrust just as truculently at each other, possibly because producers feel that war is a pretty humdrum business and needs livening up with a bit of personal rancour.

And there we have to leave the Civil War, with some regret that there is no space to do more than mention Errol Flynn's escape from Libby Prison (*Virginia City*, with Humphrey Bogart as a Mexican *bandido* complete with sombrero and accent), or *The Tall Target*, a factually-based thriller with Dick Powell thwarting Adolphe Menjou's attempt to assassinate Lincoln on a railway train, or *Salome, Where She Danced*, which touched the war only briefly with General Robert E. Lee (John Litel) riding home from Appomattox, and thereafter took off into an absolute joyride involving Yvonne de Carlo, the Franco-Prussian War, stagecoach robbery, Abner Biberman playing a Chinese medical man with a Scots accent, and a rapier duel in a Western cow-town between Albert Dekker and David Bruce – why do they never make such films nowadays, for the sheer fun of it? But the History of America, Part One, has to end here; Part Two lies out there, beyond the wide Missouri.

The Westerns, those often-derided "horse operas" and second features, are the best historical films ever made. Not that they are much concerned with history in the usual sense of recorded chronological fact, but rather with visions of the past – both the semi-legendary Western past which they have created and perpetuated, and the real past which they have captured with a clarity and completeness beyond anything achieved in other areas of costume film-making. No bygone period has been shown to us in such minute detail and in such profusion. Thanks to Hollywood we know exactly what the old American West looked like, and with only a little imagination we can understand what it felt like.

At the same time, they tell us remarkably little (and then usually inaccurately) about those political and military events which, by historical convention, we are taught to regard as important, or about those celebrities, famous and infamous, who are looked on, often mistakenly, as the embodiments of an age. Hollywood's practice is to shape and adapt such events and people to make them conform to romantic legend; in short, while presenting a marvellous and authentic picture of that West which was peopled by ordinary folk, it has shown scant respect for the big milestones, and paid abject homage to romance where the well-known figures are concerned. Seldom has it made more than a token effort to give a true portrait of a Western hero (who was frequently a villain) or heroine; at the most elementary level of physical resemblance, the portraits on these pages prove that glamour has beaten reality hands down. But the anonymous farmer, the cowboy, the frontier mother, the Indian brave, the soldier, the storekeeper, the gambler, the school-teacher, the desperado, the preacher – they and their families and the strange outlandish world they lived in have been dealt with faithfully.

In this respect the Western is of real historic value, and we can forgive the cavalier treatment of record – and the concentration on petty criminals – for those deathless images of the vast cruel country with its endless sky, its stark ugliness and breathtaking beauty, the crude log cabin in the lee of the hill with its makeshift fence and vegetable plot, its worn, hardy, ill-clad people struggling to survive; the little town with its raised boardwalk and unmade street, the signs, the hitching-rails, the women in poke bonnets, the loafers gossiping outside the swinging doors of the saloon, the small boys playing at the livery stable, the aproned blacksmith pausing to watch the stranger in battered hat and dusty clothes riding in, the man with the badge and cradled shotgun surveying the scene; the stuffy front room with its texts and precious furniture and fading photographs; the blanketed Indian squatting in the sun, or sitting on his pony on the ridge, lance in hand, watching the distant wagons like toys on the great plain; the lonely railroad and the silhouetted telegraph wire; the hard, earnest faces singing in the wooden church, and the great trail-herds lowing; the camp fire with its coffee pot and blanket rolls; the wild cowhands hurrahing into town, blazing away, the bearded faces at the bar and the reclining nude above it – all these things we know are authentic, from photographs and the paintings of Russell and Seltzer and Remington, and the descriptions of Twain, Stevenson, and scores of others. Hollywood has given them life, a thousand times – perhaps not with invariable accuracy; Victorian materials were not quite as creaseless as they sometimes appear, and the hostesses and soiled doves of the saloons were never as glossy as Ann Sheridan in *Dodge City* or the pert misses shaving the customers in *Honky Tonk*. But to be fair, the serious Westerns have been scrupulous in costume and settings, and have got even better with the passage of time; the saloon harpies of *The Life and Times of Judge Roy Bean* were a raddled lot, and the cabin interiors of *Will Penny* made no bones about the hardship and squalor of frontier life.

So far so good, but all too often authenticity takes wing as soon as the characters open their mouths. There seems to be a convention that screen Westerners should speak with the vocabulary and style of the twentieth century. Occasional honourable efforts are made to get a genuine period flavour into dialogue – the John Ford and DeMille pictures are usually conscientious exceptions, and films like *Shane, The Gunfighter, The Shootist*, and that little gem of a B-picture, *Comanche Station*, do seem to be peopled by real Victorians; *True Grit*'s dialogue has a delightful antique ring to it. No doubt only eccentrics like me wince when a cowhand (in *The Magnificent Seven*) says "For real", and it may seem unimportant when people of the 1880s use dialogue which could be lifted straight into a World War Two picture or a TV commercial. Still, it seems a pity when there are such invaluable guides to Western speech and deportment as Twain, Bret Harte, Henty, Lewis Garrard, Mayne Reid, R. M. Ballantyne, and Owen Wister.

Perhaps producers fear that the macho image of the Westerner will suffer if he talks in an "old-fashioned" way, or maybe it would destroy the illusion which I suspect exists – that the Old West is still going on out there. In any event, the convention is so well established that I should hesitate to try to work into a screenplay the recorded exchange between Wild Bill Hickok and John Wesley Hardin in 1871:

"You can't hurrah me. I won't have it."

"I haven't come to hurrah you, Mr Hickok. But I am going to stay in Abilene."

No modern Western director would wear it (but the irony is that Wayne or Fonda or Cooper could have made it memorable). On the whole Americans seem to like to see the American past in their own image, as I discovered when I tried to convince the late Steve McQueen that it was perfectly in order for him to use the word "rascal" in a nineteenth-century film. He thought it sounded "too European", and when I assured him that his grandfather wouldn't have thought so I received the meditative blue-eyed stare while he considered and finally said: "Rascal. Rascal. Do I have to say it? Maybe I can just 'look' it." He was, in fact, a great "looker" who could use a glance where another actor would have had to speak a line, and he may have been right: audiences might have found "rascal" odd coming from him – but they would certainly have enjoyed seeing him "look" it.

But whatever he sounds like, against his authentic background, the screen Westerner is a true figure who also fulfils a romantic ideal; as has frequently been pointed out, he is the "man alone", self-sufficient, independent, answerable to no one. Those who set about to explain his significance are fond of pretending that he is unique. He isn't anything of the sort. He is the pirate and the outlaw and the pioneer in another guise, the free spirit, nothing more. "I live where I hang my hat," says Liberty Valance, and in that the screen Westerner is faithful to his original.

There are two main Western hero types, the John Wayne and the Randolph Scott, and the difference is marked. Scott is the old-fashioned ideal, quiet, slightly grim, self-possessed, eyes on the horizon, unfailingly courteous, touching his hat-brim to ladies and calling them "ma'am" (he could even remove a note from Marlene Dietrich's garter with perfect good breeding), meeting trouble with a poker face and a lightning draw. Was he ever heard to swear? I doubt it. Wayne was a harder article altogether, a rugged expansionist with a short fuse, given to strong language and physical violence; even when complimenting a school-marm on her cooking he did it with a deep-breathing deliberation which suggested that he was preparing to go out and wreck a saloon, preferably with Scott inside it.[5] Wayne was a purposeful lurching menace, bred in a hard school, viewing the world with a stern suspicious eye and waiting hopefully for trouble. Where Scott, riding superbly, scanned the distance with serenity, Wayne sat on his horse as though it were hard work, and brooded about the Apaches. Scott smiled with tight-lipped tolerance; Wayne occasionally roared with laughter or beamed on small children, but kept an eye on the door. As a rule there was nothing between them for granite integrity (Scott had occasional lapses into villainy), but Wayne's was of the great outdoors; Scott's was genteel. Asked to define their screen religions, I should have put down Scott as an Episcopalian and Wayne as a lapsed Presbyterian. Of the two, I have no doubt that Wayne's was a commoner type in the Old West, but both, being arch-types, had their originals.

In their films, and hundreds like them (including the horse operas of Buck Jones and Hopalong Cassidy), we can see at least a social history of the West, what it and its people looked like, how it lived, worked, fought, and worshipped, its homes, clothing, furniture, and recreations – all this has been well done, and perhaps it is the best kind of history. Of the course

5 I can recall their being teamed together only twice, in *The Spoilers* (a "Northern" rather than a Western, since it was set in Alaska), and in *Pittsburgh*. In the first film they had the most tremendous set-to which began in a bedroom, with Scott hurling a spitoon, and progressed in a welter of broken furniture downstairs and out into the street. Wayne won, but Scott triumphed in the re-match in *Pittsburgh*, where they contested with iron bars and lumps of coal at the bottom of a mine. These two classic encounters inspired Robert Service, author of *The Shooting of Dan McGrew*, to compose a poem entitled simply "John Wayne and Randolph Scott".

John Wayne and, below, Randolph Scott.

"The dear familiar creatures" . . . Indians attack a wagon train in *How the West Was Won*.

of events from the 1840s to the end of the century we receive a much hazier impression – gold in California in '49; emigrant trains westward, miners on the California trail, farmers to Oregon; overland stages, the Pony Express, the telegraph and the railroad; the resisting Indians, bewildered by invaders with whom they shared a mutual hostility, being defeated and confined; struggles for land and water and mining rights, and through it all a constant thunder of gunplay, Indian raid and reprisal, cavalry to the rescue, banditry on the large scale, and a yearning from the respectable community for law and order, which eventually arrived, usually with statehood.

Well, it is not an inaccurate impression, give or take over-emphasis here and there, and much simplification (and ignoring) of great issues. Some points need to be made. The West was a violent place, but brigandage and shoot-outs and Indian fighting were a drop in the ocean of sheer hard work – clearing, planting, building, mining, cattle-raising and driving – which was the thing that really won the West. A stranger with no knowledge of US history save what he got from films might not appreciate this; he might also conclude, mistakenly, that the more celebrated villains of the time were more sinned against than sinning. He would be puzzled at the change in status of the Indians, from the perpetual enemy, a mixture of noble savages and murderin' red varmints, into oppressed and cheated defenders of a precious culture – the conflicting images are all true, but the fashionable viewpoint has changed. Our stranger would also not realise that when a real gunfight occurred, it took place in clouds of dense smoke (black powder had this effect), that the fast draw was far less important than shooting carefully and straight, and that the quality of marksmanship was less deadly than the cinema suggests.

Hickok may have been able to group five revolver shots within a few inches at fifty yards, but if so he was an exception; it was no easier then to hit a human target at twenty yards with a heavy-calibre pistol in an emergency than it is now. Nor is a rider to be dropped with a single rifle shot at long range as a matter of course. Finally, a man hit with a .44 or .45 bullet seldom takes much further interest; if he does not die of his wound or of shock, he is probably maimed for life. He does not wince and carry on shooting, riding, or leaping off hotel verandahs. Which poses the question: does the total of those killed in screen gunfights exceed the number of fatalities in real shoot-outs between, say, 1865 and 1890? I would guess that it does, enormously.

Out of many hundreds of Westerns, I have chosen three handfuls; first, a few which touch on true historic events; second, some of the best illustrations of Western themes; and third, a clutch of personalities. Again I must remark that some of the most admired Westerns are of no special historical interest, while some apparently odd choices repay study. We start on the large scale, with a general and episodic impression of the Westward movement, *How the West was Won*, a spectacular epic which follows an emigrant family through four generations, from the Erie Canal in the Thirties to their settled home in the West half a century later. On the way they encounter river pirates led by Walter Brennan, and escape with the help of a Mountain Man (James Stewart, a very sanitary specimen of the breed) who subsequently marries one of the daughters (Carroll Baker). The paterfamilias (Karl Malden) is killed on a foundering raft, and the other daughter (Debbie Reynolds) becomes a theatre dancer and catches the eye of a genteel young adventurer (Gregory Peck). They cross the plains together in a wagon train, and Peck makes and loses a fortune in California; meanwhile the Mountain Man has turned farmer and soldier and been killed at the Battle of Shiloh. The next generation (George Peppard) is involved in the building of the railroad (Richard Widmark supervising), and subsequently as a peace officer fighting bandits (Eli Wallach and gang). By this time Debbie Reynolds is the very old lady of the family, having survived long enough to see the dream of settlement realised, but not, mercifully, the aerial shots of the Los Angeles traffic with which the film ends.

The film was shot in Cinerama, and there are impressive journeys down rapids, Indian attacks, buffalo stampedes, and train wrecks; the course of empire tends to take a back seat to the family's domestic affairs and romantic entanglements, but it is instructive enough, and there are such dramatic compensations as the nocturnal meeting of Generals Grant and Sherman (Harry Morgan and John Wayne) while a Union soldier (Peppard) and a Confederate (Russ Tamblyn) discuss the war at a humbler level in the background.

From the Forties onwards the emigrants travelled by wagon or by ship around the Horn; some even walked across the continent pushing hand carts. Then came the stage lines, well dealt with in *Wells Fargo*, which works in some history along with the obligatory love affair (Joel McCrea and Frances Dee); it is at least a good deal more factual than *Pony Express*, a fiction which has Buffalo Bill Cody (Charlton Heston) and Wild Bill Hickok (Forrest Tucker) establishing the famous messenger service. In fact, Cody did ride for the Pony Express when he was fifteen and weighed about eight stone – few of the riders were more than twenty-one, and the upper weight limit was less than ten stone. Mr Heston stands six and a quarter feet and is well built; they would not have let him near an Express mount. That small detail apart, it is a pity that the brief and glorious story of the Pony Express has not been factually treated by Hollywood; it lasted only eighteen months, 1860–61, in which time its juvenile riders carried the mail across America at breakneck speed through the perils of wilderness, savage weather, and Indian pursuit, and set a standard for reliability and courage which, as Abraham Lincoln said, "can only be equalled, never excelled".

As the Pony Express died, the first telegraph line across the continent was completed, an event celebrated in *Western Union*, adapted from a Zane Grey novel which puts a romantic gloss on the story but is none the worse for that. Vance Shaw (Randolph Scott) is an erstwhile badman recruited by Dean Jagger as a trouble-shooter for the telegraph company in their transcontinental operation; Confederate renegades disguised as Indians sabotage the line; they are led by the evil Jack Slade (Barton McLane) who turns out to be Shaw's brother, and this leads to a fratricidal encounter which many consider to be the ultimate Western gunfight. When the film was first released *Picture Post* was so impressed that it did an extensive spread of stills captioned with extracts from the screenplay; the sequence became known as "the Barber Shop scene", and has lost nothing in more than fifty years – Scott unwrapping the bandages from his burned hands, confronting McLane who is seated half-shaved with a gun drawn beneath his apron and his associates concealed around the shop, the shooting breaking out, supporting villains biting the dust,

The pioneer family raft-borne in *How The West Was Won*: from left, Karl Malden, Carroll Baker, Debbie Reynolds, and Agnes Moorhead.

and then – horror of horrors – Scott expiring on the board-walk. I can still remember the appalled hush of disbelief that fell on the minors' matinée as the unspeakable McLane, scowl-ing through his lather, turned the hero's corpse over with his boot. The impossible had happened, Villainy had triumphed, the code of the West had been shattered – and no one believed it for a minute when the tenderfoot Robert Young appeared to give McLane his quietus before going off to marry Virginia Gilmore. Its breaking of sacred tradition apart, the Barber Shop scene is a fine piece of dramatic photography, and remains unsurpassed of its kind.

White movement westward, gradual in colonial times and gathering momentum after Independence, became a flood from the 1840s onwards, with dire consequences for the Indians. The problem had been recognised a century earlier, when the British Government had optimistically decided that all west of the Appalachians should be Indian land; the American government inherited the problem and the idea of an Indian boundary, but the emigration surge made the keeping of frontier treaties impossible, and guaranteed Indian hunting grounds began to dwindle. It is easy to blame Washington, but less easy to see what they could have done to stop the westward tide; they made treaties, no doubt with good intentions, and broke them – with less apparent reluc-tance as time went on. Some tribes submitted quietly, but the lords of the Plains, the great Sioux confederacy and their Cheyenne allies, were prepared to fight for their countryside. Through the 1860s the war raged sporadically – the Little Crow rising in which hundreds of settlers were killed, the Chivington massacre of almost 300 Cheyenne men, women and children, and scores of smaller raids and reprisals. The current fashion is to overlook or condone Indian atrocities, and hold the American army and invading settlers guilty, and indeed America had much to answer for in its treatment of the tribes. But it has to be remembered that those soldiers and settlers were the grandchildren of Fort William Henry and Fort Pitt and the Mohawk Valley, and with such a folk-memory

Villainy triumphs in the Barber Shop scene from *Western Union*. Barton McLane stands over the body of Randolph Scott.

it is possible to understand why they regarded Indians as they did. That is not to excuse them, but merely to point out that they cannot fairly be blamed for not seeing things from the academic viewpoint of the 1990s. They had the feeling of their time – as did the Indians.

The final encirclement of the Plains Tribes took place on 8 May 1869, when the last spike was driven at Promontory Point, Utah, in the Central and Union Pacific rail link across the continent. It was the kind of historic achievement to inspire DeMille, and the result was *Union Pacific*, a stirring spectacular in his best style, with the usual mixture of fact and fantasy. An unscrupulous Eastern tycoon (Henry Kolker) is out to sabotage the railroad being built by General Dodge (Francis McDonald), and who better to do the dirty work than Brian Donlevy, who proclaims his villainy by dipping his

Laying the tracks in *Union Pacific*.

cigars in whisky and reading the Police Gazette. He and his gambler partner (Robert Preston) seduce the railroad workers with drink, cards and wild women along the way; they also steal a payroll under the nose of Joel McCrea, the railroad trouble-shooter, who is Preston's rival for the favours of Barbara Stanwyck, a tomboy postmistress, and there is much gunplay, Irish sentiment, hearty comedy from Lynne Overman and Akim Tamiroff as McCrea's henchmen, and love scenes of interminable length. To which is added a satisfying documentary of railway building – Union Pacific themselves cooperated with period rolling stock, etc., and DeMille photographed it in loving detail and with his usual sure touch in handling action on the grand scale. His players, his saloon interiors, his railway gangs, look as though they belong in the 1860s; there is an impressive train-wreck by marauding Sioux, and genuine suspense as his principals lie hidden in a shattered coach, telegraphing for help while the looting goes on around them. The most convincing shock is provided by a scene in which two gamblers casually shoot a harmless Indian for a bet, to cries of mild regret from a bevy of prostitutes, and indignation from no one (except McCrea, obviously); that is an all-too-authentic incident from the Old West. Its embroideries apart, *Union Pacific* is a fine historical image and, incidentally, a reminder of what a good actor Robert Preston was without apparent effort.

As the transcontinental railway was being completed, two other Western legends were parting company. William Frederick Cody and James Butler Hickok had first met (according to Cody) during the Civil War, when Cody was a young Union soldier and Hickok was operating, disguised as a Confederate, behind the enemy lines. They became firm friends and, after the war, served as Army scouts on the Western frontier, sharing occasional adventures (of which the film *Pony Express* was not one) before Hickok left the service in 1869 to begin his career as peace officer of Hays City and Abilene. At about the same time Cody, whose prowess as a buffalo hunter and Indian fighter had already made him famous, was elevated

to new heights by the novelist, Ned Buntline, and began the stage career which was to lead to his famous "Wild West Show". From time to time he returned to the frontier, and it was while scouting in the Sioux War that he killed the Cheyenne leader, Yellow Hair, in single combat and took his scalp.

Two films have been devoted to Cody. Joel McCrea played him in *Buffalo Bill*, with Maureen O'Hara as his wife Louisa, Thomas Mitchell as Buntline, and Anthony Quinn as the unfortunate Yellow Hair (called Yellow Hand in the picture). It is a mixture of fact and romance – but then, so was Cody's whole career; he was a great showman and self-publicist, who was not above allowing his legend to be embroidered, and this has led revisionists to suggest that there was little under the surface, a point taken up by *Buffalo Bill and the Indians*, in which Paul Newman played Cody the entrepreneur. It is a sour, dull piece which does less than justice to its subject, who in his day was a brave scout, hunter, and frontier fighter.

The many faces of Buffalo Bill: from left clockwise, Colonel W. F. Cody himself, with Joel Macrea (in *Buffalo Bill*), Paul Newman *(Buffalo Bill and the Indians),* Louis Calhern (*Annie Get Your Gun*), and James Ellison *(The Plainsman).*

James Butler ("Wild Bill") Hickock, left, and Gary Cooper in *The Plainsman*.

Hickok has suffered something of the same fate. Like Cody he was a genuine adventurer whose legend became so inflated (partly as a result of his talent for telling tall stories) that a reaction was inevitable. In fact he distinguished himself as a spy for the Union Army, was an expert guide and scout, and (to his lasting notoriety) a gunfighter of matchless skill. It is unlikely that he was romantically attached to the celebrated Martha ("Calamity Jane") Canarray, a coarse and drunken hoyden who had worked as a mule driver and, to her credit, was a fearless nurse of smallpox victims during an epidemic. She lived into the present century, and at her own request was buried beside Hickok, who was shot from behind by one Jack McCall in a Deadwood saloon in 1876.

They have had one major film, *The Plainsman*, a historical fantasy "telescoped" by DeMille with rare abandon. Calamity Jane (an immaculately-coiffured Jean Arthur) is in loving pursuit of Hickok (Gary Cooper, clean-shaven), but he will have none of her, since he is bent on tracking down Latimer (Charles Bickford) who is selling guns to the Indians, and also on wooing back to scouting service the newly married Cody (James Ellison) who has come West to start a hotel (something which the Codys actually did early in their marriage). Subsequently Hickok and Calamity Jane are captured by Indians, and she saves him from being burned alive by betraying the whereabouts of an ammunition convoy which Cody is leading to a beleaguered fort. Far from being grateful, Hickok spurns her yet again, rides to warn Cody, is involved in an Indian ambush, emerges to resume his pursuit of Latimer, shoots three soldiers who have been hired to kill him, has to flee the wrath of the Army, who despatch Cody to track him down (I'm sorry, it is this sort of plot), catches up with Latimer and shoots him, and finally (with DeMille's conscience presumably driving him back to historical truth) is himself shot in the back by McCall (Porter Hall), with Miss Arther embracing the corpse.

It is an awful, brilliant picture, for all this nonsense is played out against a background which is a model of period authenticity and splendid staging. DeMille can make a production out of such a simple thing as a steamboat casting off, or find genuine beauty in a long shot of a wounded scout slumped in his saddle under a leafless tree; his crowd scenes are like Remington pictures come to life, his Indian battle, with hordes of painted braves charging up a shallow river, is a splendid spectacle, and the moment when Calamity Jane and Mrs Cody are alone in a cabin at night, and the Indian faces appear at the window, is truly frightening. Some of his asides may seem a little dated now (President Lincoln is interrupted by his wife with the words: "We'll be late for the theatre"), but the main regret is that so much good historic detail was expended on such romanticised fiction. Cooper's is an interesting performance; he didn't like Hickok, and this is perhaps the only time that he appeared unsympathetic.

Only a few weeks before Hickok's death an event of far greater importance had shocked the American public. On a sunny June afternoon the celebrated Major-General George Armstrong Custer and two hundred odd men of his Seventh Cavalry had been surrounded and wiped out on the Greasy

Grass slope above Little Big Horn River. It is the most contentious subject in Western history, a debate which has been much confused, in the words of a leading authority, by the Great American Faker and the Great American Liar, and much nonsense has been written (and filmed) about it. It has it mysteries still, but the main facts are clear enough.

Following abortive treaty negotiations over the Black Hills of Dakota, the sacred place of the Sioux and the target of white gold-seekers, the Indian recalcitrants led by Sitting Bull and Crazy Horse had withdrawn into the wild country south of the Yellowstone River. There they had beaten off a force under General Crook on the Rosebud Creek, but with the arrival of General Terry's army it was assumed that they would be forced to surrender. Their exact position and numbers were unknown, and Terry despatched Custer to find them, the intention being that he should then wait until Terry's full force had come up. Custer, a dashing and experienced commander, was determined to deal with the Sioux himself; his career had been under a cloud and he hoped to

Martha Jane Canarray – plain Calamity Jane, left, and as the cinema presented her: centre, Doris Day in *Calamity Jane*, right Jean Arthur in *The Plainsman*.

win credit and glory which, it is believed, would have helped him further his political ambitions. Nearing the Indian camp he split his force into three, ordering Major Reno to deliver the main attack while Custer, with 200 riders, took them in flank; only when the camp came into view did Custer realise that the Indians were in great force; he began his attack, was pushed back and quickly surrounded, and he and his men wiped out. Reno withdrew, and presently the Sioux did likewise.

Custer was not as big an ass as he sounds, but he did blunder badly. So did Hollywood when they put his story on film in *They Died With Their Boots On*, a historical mess which bore little resemblance to Custer, the battle, or the reasons for it. Custer has been played by fifteen actors in sound films, and this, being the Errol Flynn version, was the definitive big-budget one. It traces Custer's career from West Point to his death, and to enumerate its inaccuracies would take more

space than it deserves. My chief complaint was that the terrain chosen bore no resemblance to Little Big Horn, which is a lovely spot, with bluffs and a fine slope down to a wooded river; one can see easily what happened, if not why: Custer's command was neatly sandwiched by Gall's dismounted warriors and Crazy Horse's cavalry, but their tactical brilliance is not even noticed in the film, in which mobs of mounted Sioux simply appear in meaningless fashion and mop up Flynn's lot in the conventional Hollywood style. To pick up just a few of the other errors – Flynn is shown as the last man on his feet, which Custer was not (he may even have been among the first killed, although I personally don't believe he was); there were no sabres at Little Big Horn; Custer's hair was close-cropped; Butler the Englishman (the last man killed in fact) was a sergeant, not a captain, and he did not teach Custer the tune "Garryowen"; Custer was not promoted by accident; he was not, as portrayed by Flynn, a

Major-General George Armstrong Custer, left, has been played by Errol Flynn, right, in *They Died With Their Boots On*, and, on facing page . . .

. . . by Ronald Reagan, left, in *Santa Fe Trail*, Robert Shaw, centre, in *Custer of the West,* and, right, Richard Mulligan in *Little Big Man.*

simple upright soldier but a rather devious manic-depressive of irrational tendencies; whatever his motives and behaviour before the battle, they did not include shanghaiing a former comrade (Arthur Kennedy) who had been selling guns to the Sioux and liquor to the military . . . but why continue? It is typical Hollywood dream-rubbish of the worst kind, and why on earth do they do it when the truth is so much more interesting?

As fiction, it is a moderate film, but too long. It is marginally better than *Custer of the West*, in which Robert Shaw plays the lead even less convincingly than Flynn, and the battle is still further misrepresented. *Little Big Man*, in which Dustin Hoffman plays a 121-year-old survivor of the massacre, is an offbeat comic fantasy of little help to the history student; it has a good lookalike Wild Bill in Jeff Corey, and a manic Custer in Richard Mulligan, and while it makes a black send-up of the battle, in one respect it is faithful: the battle location is so good that I wouldn't be surprised to learn that it

was Little Big Horn; it certainly looks like it. And one cannot leave the film without mentioning Chief Dan George as an endearing Indian patriarch.

The most unusual of Custers was Ronald Reagan, who played him with considerable good nature in *Santa Fe Trail*, a film which has little to do with the Trail in question, being about John Brown (he of the body) the fanatical abolitionist who seized the Harper's Ferry Arsenal with intent to arm a slave uprising. The hero here is Flynn again, playing "Jeb" Stuart, the famous cavalry leader who did in fact take part against Brown in the Harper's Ferry siege. There are three points of historical interest about the picture. First, it takes place in 1859, and Custer (who is depicted as Stuart's comrade) didn't even graduate from West Point until 1861. Second, the tone of the film is sympathetic to the slave-owning Stuart, and against the abolitionist Brown and his villainous associate, Van Heflin – this seemed odd in 1940, and even odder now. Third, the Harper's Ferry siege is reasonably accurate history, and Raymond Massey's John Brown is a real wrath-of-God zealot and a splendid portrayal of the strange, half-crazed crusader who became a legendary figure in the war against slavery.

Custer at Harper's Ferry may be romance; his defeat at Little Big Horn was, for white America, a stunning reality, but for the Plains Indians it was the end. They had beaten American troops in pitched battle, and lost the long struggle which had been foregone from the beginning. The rest was tragedy, exemplified by an incident which took place two years later, in 1878. It inspired a film from John Ford, *Cheyenne Autumn*, which forms a convenient bridge from "history" films into those illustrating frontier themes.

Even more than the Sioux, the Cheyenne ("The People", as they called themselves) were the aristocrats of the Plains, and none more so than Little Wolf of the Northern Cheyenne, a veteran of Rosebud and Little Big Horn, and the most renowned warrior of his nation. *Cheyenne Autumn* describes how his band, sent to a reservation far from their homeland, suffered a year of neglect and suffering before striking out for the north. In the film version they are accompanied by a teacher (Carroll Baker) and followed by a sympathetic army captain (Richard Widmark) who tries to prevent punitive action, without success. There are clashes with the troops along the Cheyenne's line of march; eventually their leaders, Little Wolf (Ricardo Montalban) and Dull Knife (Gilbert Roland) split up, the latter's band surrendering to an army post commanded by a not unkindly but hidebound Captain Wessels (Karl Malden), who proposes to send them south again in the dead of winter. The Cheyenne refuse and, after being confined in appalling conditions, fight their way out and reunite with their kinsfolk. But their massacre by troops is only prevented by the personal intervention of the Secretary of the Interior, Schurz (Edward G. Robinson), and they are allowed to go to their homeland.

All this is true, with important omissions. The Cheyenne took forty white lives in raids along their march, including

Above, John Brown, and below, Raymond Massey in *Sante Fe Trail*.

eighteen in one village massacre, and Dull Knife's band were decimated by the soldiers after their escape from Wessels; the Indian losses were even worse than the film suggests, and while Schurz was a sympathetic administrator he did not, so far as I know, make any dramatic gesture on the Cheyenne's behalf. It is not a distinguished picture, but it reminds us of the fate of a brave and ultimately helpless people – there is a touching image of an old chief (Victor Jory) waiting in patient pride for government officials who never come, struggling to keep his feet after hours in the sun, and finally collapsing. That is Ford at his best; the film also shows him at his worst, with a tasteless and unnecessary interlude in which James Stewart and Arthur Kennedy appear as Wyatt Earp and Doc Holliday, playing the fool. If the purpose was comic relief, it failed, and did nothing for the production's dignity.

Ford showed the other side of the coin in *The Searchers*, the story of a Comanche raid in which a settler family is wiped out and their infant daughter carried off. The girl's uncle (John Wayne), a bitter and truculent Indian-hater, spends years in search of her, helped by an adopted part-Cherokee member of the family (Jeffrey Hunter), whom he treats with contempt. In time the uncle's obsession changes: from wanting to rescue his niece he becomes her deadly pursuer, his logic being that after such a long captivity she will have become an Indian herself – which she has, in the comely person of Natalie Wood, now one of the wives of her Comanche captor. Uncle makes

The Cheyenne trekking to their homeland in *Cheyenne Autumn*.

an attempt on her life, but in the end of course he relents and brings her back to the white community – in which, ironically, there is now no place for him after so many years, and the film ends on one of Wayne's most memorable exits, the solitary figure outside with the door closing on him.

If it sounds trite, Ford makes it credible, and so does Wayne, with one of his harshest performances. As usual, the director indulges in some horseplay and hearty comedy from time to time, but it is not overdone, and there is one of his most hair-raising scenes in the prelude to the Indian raid: the lonely farm under a beautiful twilight, the sudden sense of dread, lamps being blown out and shutters closed on an empty dusk full of menace. The raid is not shown; the climactic moment is when the little girl, sent out to hide by her desperate parents, crouches with her doll in the family cemetery, and an Indian's shadow falls across her.

Seven of the nine travellers in *Stagecoach*: from left, Andy Devine, George Bancroft, John Carradine, Donald Meek, Louise Platt, Claire Trevor, and John Wayne.

The Searchers is fiction, but it is based on true frontier experience, which is the criterion I have used in choosing my second group of films, each reflecting a different aspect of the real (and cinematic) West. *Cheyenne Autumn* and *The Searchers* are "Indian" films; there is only one that can represent all those "Journeys" which were so much a part of Western life, and that is *Stagecoach*.

This, Ford's masterpiece, need not have been a Western at all; the little group of passengers could have been anywhere, in any time, as de Maupassant has demonstrated. It is also a film without stars; each character carries almost the same weight as the others – the stout harassed driver (Andy Devine), the rugged guard (George Bancroft) and, in order of seating, the fallen woman (Claire Trevor), the absconding banker (Berton Churchill), the colonel's lady (Louise Platt), the gentleman-gambler (John Carradine), the timid whisky salesman (Donald Meek), the drunken doctor (Thomas Mitchell) and, on the floor, when he wasn't climbing over the roof, the Ringo Kid (John Wayne). They are the plot, the journey to Lordsburg through Apache country being merely the backcloth, and every note rings true. I write as one who has endured the acute discomfort of an antique Western stagecoach, driven the Lordsburg road,[6] and come unexpectedly face to face with Apaches – admittedly only in Sante Fe Public Library, but it was enough to give a vivid idea of historic reality. But the authenticity of *Stagecoach* needs no confirmation; it comes off the screen as a true picture of the West and Westerners – perhaps the best of them all.

We all know what "the Cowboy" looked like, but *Will Penny* gives him a character deeper than the usual stock figure. The saddle-tramp played by Heston is a simple, self-conscious soul quite lost outside his own rough world; he is illiterate, bathes eight or nine times a year, knows nothing but work and cattle; called on to join in a song, his embarrassment is painful, and the sight of a child reading sets him thinking hard. With a band

6 Which Ford did not use for his film, preferring to shoot in Monument Valley, Utah.

Charlton Heston as *Will Penny*.

of murderous eccentrics (led by Donald Pleasence) he knows how to deal, but not with a young woman (Joan Hacket) and her son, with whom he is snowbound in a lonely cabin. The prospect of love and family life is compelling, but he realises it is simply beyond him, and at the moment when all should be ending happily, he goes back to the only world he understands. It is a touching film, and a fine portrait of a type which must have been common enough in the cattle country, and of a cruelly hard existence.

"The Stranger", as personified in *Shane* has something in common with Will Penny, but is more worldly-wise altogether. On the dramatic level, he is the unexpected guardian angel,

Jack Palance, on verandah, confronts Elisha Cook Jr, in *Shane*.

and it may well be that he represents a frontier dream which has passed into folklore – many a lonely cabin and threatened family must have hoped for him. Here he is the quiet drifter (Alan Ladd), given a job by homesteaders (Van Heflin and Jean Arthur) oppressed by a powerful neighbour who is trying to drive out all the small farmers. Shane gradually emerges as their champion; when the hired gunman (Jack Palance) arrives, Shane kills him and, having served his purpose, rides away. It has been enacted on the screen a hundred times; *Shane* just does it extremely well, without heroics or false sentiment, convincing by the realism of its characters and setting. The oppressive neighbour (Emile Meyer) is no blustering cattle baron, but a not unreasonable man reluctant to go to extremes; the killer is not a swaggering bully, but a man who thinks and bides his time before luring his victim (the bewildered Elisha Cook, junior) into an act of folly and executing him with professional satisfaction. Shane, whose dark past we never discover, is not a conventional hero, just a rather better professional, albeit charming with it, and I imagine that Van Heflin was privately glad to see the back of him. It is one of those films which we believe could have happened.

The Cowboy and the Stranger are perhaps the most common hero figures in Western folklore and films, but they are run close by a third, "the Lawman", and for me there is one of these who stands head-and-shoulders above the rest. Having seen *True Grit* my one regret is that John Wayne never had a shot at Falstaff; Rooster Cogburn, the boozy, disreputable old rascal of a marshal hired by an adolescent girl to track down her father's murderer, is his best performance, possibly because the script is quite the most authentic ever written for a Western picture. Whether the principal credit should go to the screenwriter, Marguerite Roberts, or the original novelist, Charles Portis, I don't know, but for once the voice of the Old West is heard strong and clear; its splendid imagery cries out for quotation, but I will cite only Rooster's final raging challenge to Ned Pepper (Robert Duvall) – not "Reach!" or "Draw!" or "Go for your gun!" but: "Fill yore hands, you son-of-a-bitch!" Never mind the plot, listen to the characters – not only Rooster and Pepper, but the game little bantam of a girl (Kim Darby), the Texas Ranger (Glen Campbell), the renegade Chaney (Jeff Corey), and the superbly articulate outlaws encountered along the way; actors seldom get the chance to speak so well, and they rise to the occasion. It is a charming, happy film which must delight any lover of language; on the historical side there is a brief portrait of Fort Smith's notorious hanging Judge Parker whose summary justice was a Western byword in the 1880s. As to the authenticity of Wayne's performance, there were, by all accounts, peace officers not unlike Rooster Cogburn.

"The Showdown" is the essence of the Western, if not of the real West, and we have seen more long walks than enough along innumerable dusty streets. *High Noon* is regarded as the classic, and is notable for prolonging the process for more than an hour, as the newly wed marshal (Gary Cooper) tries to recruit help against the gang coming to kill him. His problems are his bride (Grace Kelly), an eager deputy (Lloyd Bridges), an old flame (Katy Jurado), and a circle of friends who fail him in the crisis, and it is suspenseful enough, although why he didn't leave town like a sensible man, or

dry-gulch the gang on their way from the railroad depot (as many peace officers would have done), still escapes me. However, as in "Hamlet", no delay, no play; the final battle, despite the presence of Lee Van Cleef as one of the gang, is an ordinary affair by *Shane* or *Western Union* standards, although admittedly better than the two major attempts to recreate the most famous of Western gun duels, the fight at Tombstone's OK Corral – which did not take place at the corral at all, but on Fremont Street, close by.

John Wayne as Rooster Cogburn in *True Grit*.

Wyatt Earp in real life, left and as portrayed by Burt Lancaster (*Gunfight at the OK Corral),* and right, Henry Fonda (*My Darling Clementine*).

What happened there in 1881 was that Virgil Earp, marshal, with his brothers Wyatt and Morgan, and a fourth man, Doc Holliday, confronted four cowboys, the Clanton brothers and the McLowery brothers; ill feeling had been building up between the Earps and the cattlemen, and Virgil now demanded that the four surrender their weapons; who started the shooting is still disputed, but one minute later the two McLowerys were dead, one Clanton was dying and the other in flight, and Virgil and Morgan Earp were wounded. An estimated thirty-four shots had been fired at a few yards' range, of which fourteen had taken effect. Wyatt Earp and Holliday were later arrested for murder, but were released. Some time after, Virgil was badly wounded in ambush and Morgan was shot in the back; Wyatt and Holliday took revenge on their attackers and then fled from Arizona.

The two dramatisations, *My Darling Clementine* and *Gunfight at the OK Corral* are not bad films in themselves,

but they are poor history. *Clementine* has Wyatt, Virgil, and Morgan (Henry Fonda, Tim Holt, and Ward Bond) as peaceful cattlemen out to avenge their murdered young brother, Jimmy. (In fact James Earp was the oldest Earp brother, and he was not involved in their feud in any way). They are assisted by Doc Holliday (Victor Mature), represented as a genteel but alcoholic and consumptive surgeon (the real Holliday was a dentist), and the gunfight is the usual messy business of people skulking in alleys and blazing away behind fences; Holliday is killed (which he wasn't), and at the end Wyatt is all set to marry Holliday's ex-fiancée (Cathy Downs). The other female lead, Linda Darnell, has perished earlier, either of gunshot or complications following an operation by Holliday, it is not clear which.

Fonda at least looks not unlike the real Wyatt Earp (the brothers were heavily-moustached men whose sober appearance gave them a totally spurious air of respectability), but

Mature is not in the least like Holliday. He does have an excellent scene, however, in which a travelling player (Alan Mowbray) dries up in the middle of Hamlet's soliloquy, and Mature carries on the speech, and does it very well.

Kirk Douglas is fine casting as the gun-slinging dentist in *Gunfight at the OK Corral*, wiry, vicious, and plainly dying of TB. Burt Lancaster is a massive and clean-shaven

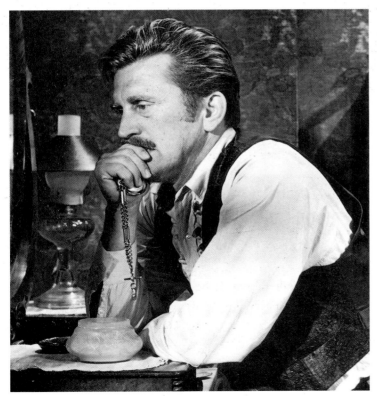

Above, J. H. Holliday, dental surgeon, and below, Kirk Douglas in *Gunfight at the OK Corral*.

Wyatt, and once again an Earp brother is murdered as a preliminary to the final shoot-out, another no-holds-barred exchange lasting five times as long as the real thing, and covering a wide area. Both films invite sympathy for the Earps which they by no means deserved, and probably the trouble in both cases is that an attempt is made to give heroic importance to what was, by any standards, a nasty little shooting-scrape. Gunmen are not, after all, heroic figures; the best films on the subject, *The Gunfighter* and *The Shootist*, show them as weary, worn-out men carrying the cross of their fearsome reputations towards an inevitable end. In *The Shootist*, Wayne is the gunfighter dying of cancer who goes out in a final blaze of violence; in *The Gunfighter* Gregory Peck, daringly concealed at the height of his matinée idol fame behind a drooping moustache, is the wanderer finding a new young challenger in every town (a phenomenon which I suspect few gunfighters really encountered) and eventually being shot from behind. That at least is true to life, if the fate of Jesse James, Hickok, Thomson, Bonney, and Morgan Earp is anything to go by. In its atmosphere and its attention to details of costume and setting *The Gunfighter* is an outstanding film which makes no concessions to romance.

Ninety per cent of lynchings in the United States took place in the South, not the West, and it is hardly common enough as a screen subject to deserve special mention, but I cannot omit one of the best Westerns, *The Ox-Bow Incident*, a harrowing little story about two cowboys (Henry Fonda and Harry Morgan) who try to prevent the hanging of three suspected rustlers (Dana Andrews, Francis Ford, and Anthony Quinn). Most of the action takes place on a lonely hillside, and consists of a debate between Fonda and the lynch posse, led by Frank Conroy, Jane Darwell, and Marc Lawrence. It is a play rather than a film, and a first-class study of violent emotion defeating reason; it is not without historic interest as an example of rough-and-ready frontier injustice.

Which brings us finally to those desperadoes who are, perversely, the heroes of the Old West; it is understandable

Jesse James, left, and as played by Tyrone Power.

that they are well remembered, but it says something discreditable about human nature, and Hollywood, that they are regarded with admiration and affection, petty and unpleasant criminals that most of them were. But they cannot be ignored, so here are a few of them, in truth and in Hollywood fancy. As with Hickok and Cody, it has to be remembered that the legends have been so inflated (and debunked) that the truth is not easy to determine.

JESSE JAMES (1847–82) and his brother Frank learned their trade in the Confederate guerrilla bands of William Quantrill and Bloody Bill Anderson during the Civil War; as irregular troops they were regarded as outlaws when the war ended, and graduated naturally to civilian crime, chiefly bank and train robbery. The patriotic aura clung to them all their lives, and they exploited it skilfully, for they were intellectually a good cut above the average road-agent; Frank was an enthu-

siastic reader of Bacon's essays and Shakespeare – no doubt it gratified him that one of their most daring robberies was at Gads Hill, Missouri. They have been variously represented as Robin Hoods and vicious thugs; Hollywood naturally chose the former, and *Jesse James*, with Tyrone Power and Henry Fonda as the brothers, is a very sympathetic treatment. The film makes the most of the true incident in which Pinkerton men bombed the James home during their absence, seriously wounding their mother and killing their stepbrother, and glosses over Jesse's cruelties. The depiction of his death, shot from behind by Robert Ford (John Carradine) while adjusting a picture, is accurate.

WILLIAM BONNEY (1860–81), better known as Billy the Kid, has never had a good film, although he is the most interesting of outlaws, because of his extreme youth and the mystery about his character – when all the inventions and

Clockwise from left: William H. Bonney ("Billy the Kid"), with Jack Beutel *(The Outlaw)*, Paul Newman *(The Left-handed Gun)*, Kris Kristofferson *(Pat Garret and Billy the Kid)*, Michael J. Pollard *(Dirty Little Billy) and* Robert Taylor *(Billy the Kid)*.

Two of the Wild Bunch: above, Butch Cassidy, and right, the Sundance Kid; below, Paul Newman and right, Robert Redford.

propaganda have been discounted, he seems to have been well-spoken and amiable in manner, in spite of his twenty-one reputed victims. There is some reason to suppose that he would not have become a notorious badman but for his involvement in a feud in which his benefactor, a British rancher named Tunstall, was murdered; the young Bonney's vengeance led on to stock-rustling, murder, and a spectacular prison break in which he killed two deputies. He was finally caught unawares and shot by Pat Garret in the dark, at the home of a friend, Peter Maxwell.

Billy the Kid was a glossy and romanticised vehicle for Robert Taylor, with Brian Donlevy as Garret, but less of a fantasy than *The Outlaw* whose chief claim to fame was the prominence of Jane Russell. Jack Beutel was a vacant Billy (in this he may have given a fair portrayal of the original, who looked like a young and half-witted Oscar Wilde), but it would not be fair to condemn either his performance or Miss Russell's, which were certainly no worse than the truly atrocious efforts of two of Hollywood's finest character actors, Thomas Mitchell and Walter Huston, as Garret and Doc Holliday respectively. I can only think that the blame lay with the eccentric millionaire, Howard Hughes, who chose to direct the film himself. At least it was a less unpleasant picture than Sam Peckinpah's *Pat Garret and Billy the Kid*, whose one virtue was the accurate reconstruction of Bonney's jail break and of his demise. James Coburn played Garret, and Kris Kristofferson was entirely miscast as the diminutive and youthful Billy.

Paul Newman did enough, in *The Left-Handed Gun*[7], to make one wish that the film had been less pretentious, and that more time had been devoted to a clear storyline than to alternating bouts of mental anguish and hysterical jollity. In the early scenes it looked as though a genuine effort was going to be made to get into the nature of the teenage desperado, but the film meandered in a confusing succession of scenes in

Like Calamity Jane, Belle Starr,
above, was highly glamourised, by
Jane Russell, top right,
in *Montana Belle*, and below,
Gene Tierney, in *Belle Starr*.

7 Whether Bonney was left- or right-handed has not been satisfactorily settled. The best-known photograph shows his gun on the left hip, but there is evidence that the negative had been reversed.

which much of the dialogue became inaudible – I still don't know what Hurd Hatfield was meant to represent. Billy's escape from jail was historically accurate; his death, with its suggestion of self-destruction, was not. John Dehner, playing Garret, was an excellent physical likeness.

Butch Cassidy and the Sundance Kid made much of the incompetence of the famous Wild Bunch, those enthusiastic dynamiters of railroad cars, and was a not inaccurate account of the careers of Cassidy (Paul Newman) and Harry Longbaugh

Judge Roy Bean's court-room saloon, with Bean seated on left, and below, Walter Brennan in *The Westerner*.

(Robert Redford), both in the United States and South America. Cassidy, whose real name was Parker, could hardly have looked less like Newman (he was a beefy bulldog of a man, descended from respectable emigrants from Accrington, Lancashire), but Redford was excellent casting as the handsome and well-dressed Sundance Kid. The film may have been a little kind to him, if not to Cassidy, who was a gentle, genial bandit by all accounts, and a fallible marksman; he was also, as in the film, a keen cyclist. How they met their ends

Tom Horn, left, and Steve McQueen.

is uncertain; the picture chose the traditional shoot-out with South American *rurales,* but it has also been stated that Cassidy committed suicide, and even that the two returned to the US and lived to a peaceful old age.

The definitive JUDGE ROY BEAN was Walter Brennan in *The Westerner,* an excellent and faithful portrayal surrounded by romanticized action. The eccentric judge, dispensing rough justice at the bar of his saloon, with pictures of his adored Lillie Langtry, the English actress, decorating the walls, is one of those improbable characters who happen to be true. He did not meet her in the dramatic fashion shown in the film (mortally wounded after a gunfight with Gary Cooper), but he did see her on stage in San Antonio in 1888, and it is said that after his death fifteen years later she was presented with her old admirer's revolver.

TOM HORN was a former soldier and Pinkerton detective who became a bounty hunter, killing cattle rustlers in Wyoming for up to $500 a head at the turn of the century; eventually he was charged with the murder of a boy of fourteen, and convicted and hanged on his own confession, which it was claimed was extracted from him while drunk, and then elaborated. The film version tells it faithfully, and leaves unsettled the question of whether Horn killed the child or not, but it is not a very good picture, probably because Steve McQueen's fatal illness is, with hindsight, already evident.

THE SEVENTH AGE
The Violent Century

The spirit of the Thirties, elegant and carefree: Ginger Rogers and Fred Astaire.
Previous page, gang warfare in the cinema, as shown in *Scarface*.

The Violent Century

If everything in the past is history, then the moment when I wrote the word "if" at the start of this paragraph is now historical, if not historic. Likewise yesterday, or last year. But these limits are obviously far too recent, and we must go farther back if we are to find the point, or area of time, at which history "begins" in the retrospective sense. We could pick on the day before the birth of the oldest person now living, but since she is a French lady of 121, that would mean settling on 1875, and plenty of history has happened since then. Or one can be subjective and take the day before one's own birth, but that won't do either – one look from my grandchildren is enough to convince me that I am not only historical but positively antediluvian. Very well, it is sometime since 1925, then. Is the Second World War history? Undoubtedly. Suez? Yes, it is. Watergate? Well . . . it will be, shortly. At this point a disc jockey's patronising chuckle is heard from the radio: ". . . and now, ha-ha, we've got a real oldie from 1981!" and I find myself muttering: "Beam me up, Scotty."

This is by way of demonstrating the difficulty, indeed the futility, of trying to choose a retrospective vantage point for this, our Seventh Age. For one thing, we are still in it, and must be conscious that the motion picture industry is in itself part of history, and all the films ever made, from *Citizen Kane* to the Three Stooges, including the "historicals", are in themselves historic artifacts of our century. That, mercifully, is no concern of mine, but even as I put it aside I am aware that there is another sense in which every film made *about* the twentieth century is historical, in that it presents a view of a time, and unless I am going to open the floodgates to every reel of celluloid since *The Jazz Singer*, a new basis of selection has to be found.

Tough, smart, stylish – and in period costume: James Cagney and Jean Harlow in *The Public Enemy*.

So far in this book, with only three exceptions, the films I have dealt with have been consciously looking back and saying, with varying degrees of sincerity: "This is how it was".

Two memorable portraits of the Depression, in the American Midwest and the Lancashire cotton towns: above, *The Grapes of Wrath*, with Henry Fonda (centre, on car), and opposite page, *Love on the Dole*, with Deborah Kerr on extreme left.

The three exceptions are *Elephant Boy, The Drum* and *Lives of a Bengal Lancer*, which were looking sideways at their own time and saying: "This is how it is", but since that time has now definitely passed into history I make no apology for having included them among the "imperial"

films, since that is where they rightly belong.

Still, having admitted those three exceptions, having called them "historical" films, on what grounds can I exclude, say, The *Grapes of Wrath, Love on the Dole* or, for that matter, *Top Hat* from a survey of historicals about the twentieth century? The periods they show are just as far back in time as my three exceptions, and just as surely gone, never to return. I think of the expressions I have used in earlier chapters – "a faithful image", "an accurate impression", "a true picture of time past". Well, *Top Hat* is all of those. What historian or lecturer could convey to a student born in 1960 a sense of what the Thirties were like, one-tenth as well as that film? Astaire springing up a flight of steps, Edward Everett Horton dithering, Ginger Rogers' poise and gestures, Eric Blore's wicked Cheshire Cat beam, the clean lines of furniture, the light, airy decor, the quick, brisk chatter, the cheery inconse-

quence and gaiety – there are the 1930s for you, or at least one aspect of them, just as *Grapes of Wrath* and *Love on the Dole* are another. All three films are accurate pictures of history, in a way which the imaginative reconstructions of our other Ages cannot possibly be; these are reality, captured at the only possible moment, for if you worked till doomsday you could not recreate them now.

It doesn't matter that they are fictions; they and all those other films of the Thirties and Forties are full of the small change of life and behaviour as it was then and will never be again, down to the tiniest details. We don't know exactly how

Dr Johnson drank his tea or Napoleon his red wine with chicken – but posterity can watch Humphrey Bogart in *Dead Reckoning*, and learn something of the character of the time from the way he smokes a cigarette – fingers on top, thumb underneath, a significant piece of body language which bespoke the tough, worldly man of the forties. Similarly, observe how he belts his raincoat in *Sirocco*, or how Alan Ladd adjusts his hat in *Lucky Jordan*, or George Sanders, in white tie and tails as the Saint, tips a taxi-driver, or those arch-tycoons Eugene Pallette and Thurston Hall comport themselves in home or office, purpling with wrath over the New Deal, or Edward G. Robinson says "Listen, you mugs", or Harry Andrews puts on his shirt in *The Hill*, with a ripping sound as his hand goes through the sleeve starched by a Middle Eastern *dhobi*. These are the merest trivia, but they are the kind of historic minutiae that were never recorded until the motion picture arrived – the commercial movie, for newsreels and documentaries record a different, less illuminating, picture of the past. The examples I have mentioned above happen to be masculine – when I think of the historic catalogue of female attitudes and behaviour in those old films the mind boggles. Some things can be described in words, and mere appearance in still pictures – but try to *explain* how the carriage, style, manner, and even state of mind of Jessie Matthews or Dorothy Lamour differed from those of today's young woman, and you may find it difficult. Show them *Gangway* or *Johnny Apollo*, and say no more.

It may be said that none of this matters – that posterity can get by without knowing how an Edwardian lady summoned a servant (Gladys Cooper can show you), or the different techniques of pipe-smoking demonstrated by Aubrey Smith, Nigel Bruce and Errol Flynn, or how Ann Dvorak used her gloves and handbag. To which I can only say that as a historical writer I wish I had such models of Elizabethan, or even Victorian behaviour, because it would tell me things about them that I cannot get from documentary or still-pictorial sources. So I don't think social historians of the future will consider our old movies beneath their notice. And if they do, and in writing their history by computer they chance to emulate Ralph Richardson in *Rollerball* and lose an entire century, they will just have to make do with *The Grapes of Wrath*, *Love on the Dole* and *Top Hat*. They will be surprised how much they learn.

They may even find information beyond the reach of more orthodox academic research. A few years ago I read an article (in a colour supplement, where else?) in which a writer stated, on apparently unimpeachable authority, that in 1946 only a minute percentage of British males wore underpants. I was twenty-one at that time, and can state with utter certainty that my generation did wear underpants – and I suggest that if the writer had viewed a selection of British movies of the period, the point would have been proved. Not

Fifty years ago it was called "glamour": Dorothy Lamour, left, and Jessie Matthews.

so, I hear the writer say – films present an idealised picture. By no means, I reply; for one thing, a sizeable proportion of young British males in 1946 had been obliged to wear drawers (woollen) and drawers (cellular) in the Forces for the previous six years, and if you think that on the day of demobilisation they tore them off with cries of "Free! Free at last!" you are mistaken. Nor were they, as the article suggested, a dirty, miserable and deprived generation; they were clean, happy and privileged in a way which, I suggest, the writer might understand better after watching, with attention, all the British movies of 1946 – followed by a week's current television and a round of modern cinemas.

I wonder what impression a viewing marathon of 1946 films would leave on the mind of someone who never knew that year. How true a picture would it give of the time? When I look back, as I frequently do, at movies of the Thirties and Forties, and compare them with the reality I knew then, as schoolboy, soldier and young newspaperman, I can say that they reflect very fairly our backgrounds, our values and some of our ideals. I insert the word "some" as one who has never been politically committed, except for brief periods after every political meeting I ever reported: if it was a Labour meeting I came out somewhere to the right of P. C. Wren; if Conservative, my feelings would have made Lenin look like a hesitant moderate. But I concede that those with strong political views might not think that old movies gave a true picture, inasmuch as they had no time for extremism either way. What does come off them, very strongly, is a remarkable innocence. No doubt the Hays Office and the British Board of Film Censors had something to do with it, but not all that much. It was, as I look back and remember, a very innocent time – even with the Depression and Hitler and the atom bomb, it was still innocent. Perhaps that was why they happened.

Before turning to actual "history" films of the century, I should make one last point. It is common to suggest that films of the Thirties, and especially of the Forties, were vehicles of propaganda. Of course they were. The cinema was the most

powerful propaganda medium in history, until John Logie Baird started playing Pandora, and during the war it was employed to the full, as television documentaries are never tired of pointing out. I have news for the documentary-makers: we *knew* it was propaganda, and we were all for it; we would have felt neglected and let down if we hadn't been given it. It didn't convince us, or give us false illusions, nor did it mislead us. I suppose a modern viewer of *The Way Ahead* might think that it imbued my generation with martial ardour. Like hell it did. Do you remember how it ended, with David Niven and Co. advancing grimly to engage the enemy? I watched it in a cinema in Assam, just before going into the line, and as the end titles came up my mate Stanley observed sourly: "And you know what happened to that bloody lot, don't you?" We knew, all right, or if we didn't we soon found out. The British public were well aware of the score. They had a fair idea of what was true and what was false and what was glamourised and what was slanted; nobody ever sold them anything, except hope. The so-called propaganda of the wartime films was the equivalent of a pat on the back, and a reminder that what they were doing was worth while, in the short term at least. Indeed, they didn't even think of it in terms of "worth while"; it was just plain stark necessity. Most important, they could see the point of the propaganda. Does it ever occur to modern cinemagoers that *Dirty Harry* and *Animal House* and *Full Metal Jacket* and *Kramer vs Kramer* may be propaganda, too, whether their makers know it or not?

Confronted by the mass of twentieth-century material, from which I must select only a score or so of pictures, I look for manageable themes and subjects. Two are obvious, the First and Second World Wars – whatever is remembered from this century, those two events are going to be high on the list. The first is genuine history to me, something before my time, learned about only from reading, from listening to parents and especially my father and uncles. The second I knew, and the best I can do is compare its films with my own experience. What else will be remembered? I can only guess – huge material and

Behind the lines in *All Quiet on the Western Front*: far left, Slim Summerville, Louis Wolheim (with cap raised) and Lew Ayres (seated centre).

scientific advance, the birth of television, space travel, atomic energy and the like? There haven't been all that many "historical" movies about them – not enough, anyway, to qualify them as cinematic themes, nor do I have the expertise necessary to comment on them. One thing there is, though, for which I *fear* the twentieth century may be remembered: it seems to me possible that it may be regarded by posterity (assuming there is one) as the time when the civilised nations of the earth began to commit suicide – and I am not thinking of atomic weapons.

Up to now, mankind has been able to cope, more or less, with itself and its planet. If we look back (and our historical movies are not irrelevant) we observe, in a pretty bizarre catalogue of wars, plagues and great race movements, one enormous hiccup in human progress which occurred after Christopher Plummer collapsed the Roman Empire, and did not really get over until the Middle Ages. It may be that we are about to enter a new Dark Age, not because we are liable to blow ourselves up but because we (by whom I mean governments and leaders of thought and education) have lost our view of right and wrong and common sense. No doubt, in a few centuries – sooner, if mankind is lucky – the Gods of the Copybook Headings will limp up to explain it again, but in the meantime things are getting just a bit out of control. I know, it has been said before, and this probably seems an unwontedly solemn departure for a book about historical movies. But it is not irrelevant, for if there is a theme which may be examined in films, it is the changing attitude to violence – and violence, in the long run, is what shapes human affairs, as Archimedes discovered to his cost. Whether we will be called The Violent Century or not we cannot tell; it may be argued that other centuries have shown just as great a will to violence, but lacked the equipment to make quite such a thorough job of it as the years 1900–97 have done. Other centuries may have enjoyed violence as much, but I question whether any century has shown quite such incompetence in dealing with it. And this is a question of state of mind and will. It is now accepted that bloody violence is a part of everyday life, and what would once have made glaring headlines now rates a paragraph at the foot of page seven.

It is possible to look at this process as it has been reflected in the cinema – the two World Wars obviously come into it, although it is the changing attitude to widespread civil violence that I am really thinking of. With that in mind, I propose to look at one aspect of it, as depicted first in the gangster movies of the Thirties and Forties, and in their successors, the violent films of the postwar years.

So, first of all to what used to be called the Great War – a neat and convenient label which I shall employ for brevity. It has received only a moderate amount of attention from Hollywood, and far, far less than its successor – war was much less fashionable in the Twenties and Thirties than it became in the Forties. But it inspired what is arguably the finest of all war pictures, *All Quiet on the Western Front*.

This has been described as the best pacifist propaganda ever created, and I am inclined to agree. By modern standards it can look makeshift and obvious, its dialogue corny and its attitudes simple to the point of banality. But truth frequently is banal, and in 1930 those lessons which Europe had known and been digesting for fifteen years were being read aloud for the first time, in a series of stark illustrations. The worthy German schoolmaster, eyes shining with patriotic zeal, exhorting his pupils to fight for the Fatherland; the boy in his uniform meeting his mother's horrified stare and his father's joyous pride; the discovery that the despised postman of yesterday is now the martinet sergeant; the confusion of training and the bewilderment of going to the front; the surprising kindliness of the old sweats to the new recruits (that is so true, and it is something that Hollywood seemed not to understand about the next war); the shock of action and of seeing the enemy for the first time – that rushing advance of the French infantry is one of the great battle scenes; the gradual acceptance of death and danger and discomfort, until the boy of 1916 has become the veteran of 1918, and like so many veterans, grows careless.

One could pick out a score of memorable things from *All Quiet*; I will settle for three which struck me as specially true. One is the capturing of that confused, time-wasting uncertainty of just-behind-the-lines, when no one seems to know quite what they are there for, or what is going on. Another is the strange near-embarrassment of homecoming, the restlessness to get back to the world of war (which is plain silly when you come to think of it). The third is the characters of the old soldiers, the groaning, permanently despondent Tjaden (Slim Summerville), and the tough, tired, patient, gentle old sweat Katczinsky (Louis Wolheim); they belong with Shakespeare's Court, Bates and Williams, and with his four captains. They are in every army. Lewis Milestone deserved his Oscar; Wolheim should have got one too, and Lew Ayres at least a nomination for the way he turned Paul Baumer from a boy into a man.

Paths of Glory is a harrowing film of the worst side of human nature, and prompts an even stronger revulsion to war than *All Quiet*: not many films can make me angry, but this one does. A French general (George Macready) is ordered to take an impossible position on the Western Front; the attack fails, and when one of his units does not leave its trenches, he orders his artillery to bombard it, an order which is rightly (and incidentally, legally) disobeyed. A court-martial is ordered, and three soldiers from the attacking units are condemned and shot for cowardice, as a token punishment, in spite of the efforts of their defending officer, who is also their CO (Kirk Douglas). The fact that the three are brave and entirely innocent men counts for nothing with Macready or his superior (Adolphe Menjou), immersed as they are in military politics.

It is superbly filmed. The infantry attack is even better than the action scenes in *All Quiet*, and I imagine it is a true picture; it may seem incredible nowadays that people could be induced to do such things, or that commanders could hold the views of Menjou and Macready, but we know that they could and did. I assume it is based on a true incident. Even better than the battle sequence are the exchanges of Douglas, Macready and Menjou, all of whom perform splendidly; Macready was one of those distinguished players who was never properly recognised. There is also excellent work by Ralph Meeker, Timothy Carey and Joseph Turkel as the three accused, by Bert Freed as a sergeant, and by Wayne Morris as a laggard lieutenant who, after choosing as one of the court-martial victims a corporal who knows him to be a coward, finds himself in charge of the firing squad. It is the more interesting that Morris had a most distinguished career in the Second World War. *Paths of Glory* is a horrible film, really, and an outstanding one.

Sorting fact from fiction is a main aim of this book, but when one turns to *Lawrence of Arabia* it becomes impossible, for the man himself was such a romancer, and his biographies are

The attack on "the Anthill" in *Paths of Glory*.

so contradictory, that there is no finding the truth. Sixty years ago he was the arch-hero, although I confess my own enthusiasm was dampened by a lecture delivered at our school by one of his old comrades soon after Lawrence's death in a motorcycle crash involving two schoolboys – one of the lecturer's points was that it seemed a damned shame that such a great soul had perished while the two boys had survived; he didn't seem to be aware that six hundred pairs of young eyes were regarding him with a stony expression which said: "Oh, yeah?" Since then Lawrence has been pilloried as a self-publicising, lying, perverted boaster, although that isn't inconsistent with being a hero, too. He was possibly all the things that have been said about him; what is sure is that there was something special in him that commanded respect, admiration, and, at least, attention.

Peter O'Toole does him very well in a film of majestic size that is splendid to look at and listen to. It follows the main facts well – the awkward young Army don going into the desert, inspiring (if that is the word) the desert tribesmen, creating a sort of Red Shadow legend by his exploits, and going home into the mystery that has surrounded him ever since. The film has been criticised for not elucidating his character, but it is hardly alone in that; the one major point in which I believe it is probably wrong is in taking Lawrence's word for the Deraa incident, where he was allegedly assaulted by a Turkish bey (Jose Ferrer); that, I understand, is now regarded as one of his fictions. It also leaves out his story that during the charge at Akaba he blew out his own camel's brains in his excitement – an odd tale for a boaster to tell, and it would have been something of an anticlimax in a most spectacular scene.

Omar Sharif became a star overnight with his portrayal of a young Arab chief, Anthony Quinn gave a full-blooded performance as the old desert warrior Audah Abu-Taiyeh, Jack Hawkins was a believable Allenby, and Alec Guinness (who

T. E. Lawrence, left, and Audah Abu-Taiyeh. Right, Peter O'Toole and Anthony Quinn in *Lawrence of Arabia*.

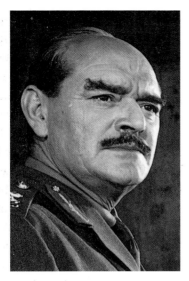

General Allenby, left, and Jack Hawkins.

always seemed to me perfect casting as Lawrence) was a dignified Feisal.

Not far away, in the same war, Victor McLaglen and his troopers were getting thoroughly lost in the Mesopotamian desert in *Patrol*. This piece stands up very well, considering its story has been used a score of times since – the little group beleaguered in an outpost, with the characters inter-reacting: the tough, tolerant sergeant (McLaglen), the religious maniac (Boris Karloff), the ex-vaudevillian (Wallace Ford), the gentleman ranker (Reginald Denny, and very good, too), the inarticulate Scottish muscleman (Alan Hale), the Jewish boxer (Sammy Stein), the public schoolboy (Douglas Walton) and so on. One by one they are whittled away by besieging Arabs, and only the sergeant survives (in Philip MacDonald's novel there were no survivors). The film's chief virtue is that the cast behave more like soldiers than actors, and there is an appalling fascination about who is going to go next.

In *The Dawn Patrol* there is never any doubt: Flynn is going to perish gloriously undertaking a hazardous bombing mission over Flanders, but not before we have seen what I take to be a reasonably faithful picture of an RFC squadron

in France, and of the intolerable strain of sending people out to die. The whole idea has suffered the fate of many stark truths – parody, with Snoopy and the Red Baron providing the final send-up. In this film the crux is that Courtney (Flynn), a daredevil pilot commanded by the long-suffering Brand (Basil Rathbone), discovers the intolerable burden of responsibility when Brand is promoted to a staff job and Courtney has to take his place. His best friend, Scott (David Niven), is shot down but survives; Scott's younger brother (Morton Lowry), sent up by Courtney, is killed, insults are traded and faces slapped, but the quarrel is eventually composed and Courtney finally sacrifices himself in place of Scott – who in turn finds himself carrying the cross of command.

It is a variation on the *All Quiet–Journey's End* theme, emphasising the endless futile circle of waste, and not badly done at all, with good aerial combats (some of them lifted from an earlier version). It is really Niven's film, but the scene

From left to right, Basil Rathbone, David Niven and Errol Flynn
in *The Dawn Patrol*.

that sticks in mind is Brand, cheerful and relaxed, revisiting the squadron and unintentionally bringing Courtney's nerves to snapping-point. I remember my parents discussing afterwards whether such films should be shown as entertainment; curiously, it is not a question that I ever heard after 1939, when war films were accepted as an essential part of war.

How well films like these five depicted the reality of the Great War it would be presumptuous of me to say, since there are thousands living who can speak with personal authority, and I cannot. I imagine they did it well; at least I don't remember them ever receiving the kind of criticism (and even abuse) which was sometimes levelled at the screen between 1939 and 1945, usually by Forces audiences. Of course, the war-film clichés – a principal target for derision – were not really established as such before 1939, but there was more to it than that.

I would guess that people, including cinema audiences, carried the Second World War more lightly at the time than it had been possible to do between 1914 and 1918; that war had become an unimaginable horror; ours was turning out better than had been expected, on the whole; we had not been gassed or obliterated by aerial bombing. And doubtless the Great War seemed all the worse for its senseless, useless waste; whatever horrors the Second War contained, no one doubted its necessity at the time, and that I should think made it easier to bear – we did not know the worst until 1945. At any rate, no one has ever been able to take Great War movies lightly; Second War movies could be treated on their merits, which were sometimes non-existent. Everyone knew they were a wartime industry, anyway. And since then, whether made during the war or after, they have become just another school of films.

Before turning to them, there is another phenomenon of the twentieth century which certainly qualifies for mention on the grounds that it is historical, important, and has had many films devoted to it, and that is the Russian Revolutionary movement. By rights its pictures deserve a chapter all to

themselves – and immediately the horizon widens to include *The Battleship Potemkin* and other Soviet productions, which cannot be overlooked if the subject is to be covered properly, and yet are outside the limits I have set for this book. I realise that this is one area in which Hollywood's historicals alone are just not enough for a film-and-history comparison, so I shall do no more than recall the splendid sets and costumes of *Nicholas and Alexandra*, in which Michael Jayston was a remarkable double for the unfortunate Tsar; Ralph Richardson's patient old aristocrat in *Dr Zhivago*, contemplating an unpeeled potato and observing complacently "Scratch a Russian and you'll find a peasant"; and the haunting suspense of that scene in *Knight Without Armour* in which Marlene Dietrich, waking to find herself alone in her beautiful mansion, runs out into the deserted garden and is confronted by a crowd

Marlene Dietrich prepares to confront the revolting peasants in *Knight Without Armour*.

of silent peasantry, the white fairytale figure alone in the presence of the Revolution.

If this were a full-length work about World War Two films, I should have to split them into categories: contemporary and otherwise, US films about Britain and about the US, British films about the home front and about the Services, war-based fictions and semi-factual pictures, comedies, musicals, shorts, and so on. As it is I must pick only a few, with first of all some random thoughts about wartime pictures in general.

The British film industry did a superlative job, with its commercial films, in mirroring the country between 1939 and 1945. It is simply all there – rationing, the Blitz, sticky brown paper on windows, gas-masks, ARP wardens, the black-out, evacuees, the Look-Duck-and-Vanish volunteers who became the Home Guard, barrack rooms, air-raid shelters, sirens, shortages, sweet coupons, Careless Talk posters, five inches of water in the bath, Spam, snoek, and Ulster Fry, queues at the butchers, "under the counter", Brylcreem, 48-hour passes, and all the rest, captured in perfect detail. And do not be misled into thinking that the "big" pictures are necessarily the greatest mines of detail; you will see just as true a picture in the Old Mother Riley productions. It may seem exaggerated, over-the-top in its characterizations and its stiff-upper-lip attitudes and solemn propaganda. Not at all; Britain was really like that, and anyone who supposes that Captain Mainwaring of *Dad's Army* is a latter-day caricature can rest assured that Mainwaring was there, in his hundreds of thousands. Arthur Lowe, brilliant actor that he was, built his writers' creation into a real person who could have been dropped straight into 1940, and no one would have known the difference.

Often it is not an entire film, but a brief excerpt, which can capture a wartime image exactly; here are just a few that I remember – the underground station jammed with sleeping families in *I Thank You*; Jimmy Hanley discussing why he wouldn't take a commission in *The Way Ahead*; the impression of blacked-out streets and curtained doorways in *Contraband*, a thriller featuring that most sophisticated of romantic teams, Conrad Veidt and Valerie Hobson; Jean Simmons singing at a concert in *The Way to the Stars*, and the silent tour of the camera over the deserted airfield in the same film; Stewart Granger's spiv in *Waterloo Road;* Margaret Rutherford organising a pageant in *The Demi-Paradise* ("Trumpeters, to your rostra!"); George Cole's evacuee in *Cottage to Let*; Noël Coward talking to his crew in *In Which We Serve*; the Blitz, and the streets and pubs and shops of *The Bells Go Down*; the true military spirit of *Private's Progress*, and Terry Thomas (a wartime type caught like a fly in amber) addressing German prisoners: "You've behaved like a shower, and you'll be treated like a shower!"; Harry Andrews' RSM in *The Red Beret*; Bonar Colleano as the eternal American in *A Matter of Life and Death* and countless other films; the snoods and handkerchiefs bound round the heads of Anne Crawford

From left, Philip Friend, James Mason and Beatrice Varley in *The Bells Go Down*.

Noël Coward, right, and behind him John Mills in *In Which We Serve*.

and Patricia Roc (to keep their hair out of the machinery) in *Millions Like Us*; the sunlit meadow in *Tawny Pipit*; Joyce Howard, Lilli Palmer, Jean Gillie and the other ATS girls in *The Gentle Sex* (a film whose commentary by Leslie Howard would send modern feminists into a frenzy, but true nonetheless); *The Way to the Stars* again, and Trevor Howard's observation as Spitfires fly over: "Fighter types . . . victory roll, top button undone . . . bad show, I think"; Beatrice Varley, Kathleen Harrison, and all the other "Mums"; Billy Hartnell coming to attention, Miles Malleson dithering with his sermon notes, Alastair Sim's bedside manner, and Stanley Holloway doing

anything in any film you care to name – yes, if truth is the criterion, they were "historical" films.

American films about Britain obviously could not capture atmosphere in the same way, but they tried, with British writers, players, and directors, and did wonders for morale – it is not often realised how much it meant to us to know that there were people across the Atlantic who cared as much as the American film industry did. Perhaps the most conscious single effort was *Forever and a Day*, which simply told the story of an English house from Trafalgar onwards; it was made by a host of contributors, mostly British (alas, there was no part for Ronald

Colman, despite his protest: "Just put me in the crowd and I'll wave my hat!"); there is no room for the list, but it is worth seeing for Claude Rains' wicked squire, Charles Laughton's tipsy butler, Victor McLaglen's commissionaire, and the unique spectacle of Cedric Hardwicke and Buster Keaton as plumbers installing a bath.

The great success was *Mrs Miniver*, an extraordinary film about a most unlikely English family in an England that existed only in romantic imagination, and yet managed to strike a true note. Its propaganda value was enormous, for it seemed real to American audiences and, in Churchill's words, was worth battleships to Britain in terms of morale. For all its melodrama and some bizarre casting, it contained one of the wartime cinema's most moving passages: the final brief sermon in the village church with the RAF planes visible overhead through the shattered roof. The vicar was Henry Wilcoxon; he and the director, William Wyler, wrote the sermon overnight, and it was filmed next morning; perhaps no British actor contributed more to his country's war effort in such short space.

It has been suggested that American film-makers were hesitant about taking too pro-British a line early in the war; if so, I for one never noticed: they seemed to be whole-hearted from the moment the cinemas reopened after the brief hiatus in that first winter. There was a natural concern in Washington that propaganda should not be too overt while America was still officially neutral, and no doubt *The Mortal Storm*, *Confessions of a Nazi Spy*, and even Betty Grable in *A Yank in the RAF* caused consternation in isolationist circles and fury in Berlin; they were meant to.[1] *Confessions* nailed Warners' colours to the mast before the war had even begun; it is an outright attack on Nazi subversion in the US, with Edward G. Robinson as the G-man exposing the plots of Paul Lukas and George Sanders, and has that convincing semi-documentary

1 One of the first anti-Nazi pictures from Hollywood, Hitchcock's *Foreign Correspondent*, received a remarkable accolade, being described as "a masterpiece of propaganda" by no less an authority than Goebbels.

Hollywood's tribute to Britain at war: the closing scene of *Mrs Miniver* with Henry Wilcoxon in the pulpit.

quality which Hollywood was so good at.[2] *The Mortal Storm*, in 1940, was equally uncompromising in depicting the effects of Nazism in a provincial German town, with Frank Morgan as the steadfast old professor and James Stewart and Robert Young the respective personifications of old-fashioned decency and the New Order. As I recall, the name "Germany" was never actually used in the film, but the casting of Ward Bond as a storm-trooper said it all, and as a result MGM productions were banned from the Third Reich.

Hollywood's most interesting war pictures, both before and after 1945, were those set in a shadowy half-world, usually in Occupied Europe, far from the actual battlefronts. It was peopled by tough American soldiers of fortune (Bogart, Raft, and others), gorgeous Continentals whose wardrobes and coiffures seldom took account of wartime austerity (Lamarr, Bergman, Hasso, Munsen, and Michele Morgan), and sinister men of mystery like Greenstreet, Lorre, Bromberg, Geray, and Lukas, who exchanged messages in sleazy cafés, dark streets and sometimes quite opulent nightclubs. There were sophisticated European resistance fighters of the Henreid-Dorn-Aumont school, and endless platoons of Gestapo thugs headed by Veidt, Massey, Preminger, and Francis L. Sullivan. They were dark, desperate pictures, full of sadness and sacrifice, but illuminated by the hope of a better world some day; to that end Monty Woolley smuggled small children out of France, Bogart gave up Bergman and escaped from Devil's Island, Cagney perished in the hands of the Nazis, and Leslie Howard disappeared into the fog at the end of the platform.[3] They were a definite school of films, certainly not historical, but

Hollywood's arch-intriguers: Sydney Greenstreet and Peter Lorre conspire in *The Mask of Dimitrios*.

interesting as romantic propaganda of the war behind the war.

American Forces films tended to be fictions firmly based on fact, but I should want to hear the views of Pacific veterans before commenting on *Wake Island, Bataan, Gung Ho!, Sands of Iwo Jima*, and the rest; they run parallel with my own part of the war, and I know what a hash the cinema made of that. So I shall pass on to a random selection of films of the 1939–45 war which can be called historical; it has to be brief and arbitrary, but I shall cast the net as wide as possible, beginning with an

2 Three years later, just after Pearl Harbor, Warners released *All Through the Night*, a comedy-thriller on the same theme as *Confessions*, with Nazi agents plotting sabotage in New York. It is remarkable not only for its prestigious cast – Bogart, Veidt, Lorre, Judith Anderson, William Demarest, Barton McLane, Phil Silvers, and Jackie Gleason – but for the success with which it gets high-spirited fun out of a subject which was no laughing matter in 1942. Historically it is fascinating evidence of the exuberance with which America met the war.

3 In *The Pied Piper, Casablanca, Passage to Marseilles, 13 Rue Madeleine* and *Pimpernel Smith* respectively.

almost forgotten picture which deals with the pre-war period, but qualifies for obvious reasons, not least its unique casting.

The Hitler Gang purports to show the rise of Nazism, starting with Hitler (Robert Watson) blind in hospital in 1918. He is subsequently employed by Röhm (Roman Bohnen) to infiltrate the German Workers' Party, and we see him recruiting and organising his infamous henchmen, Hess, Goering, Himmler, and the rest, being imprisoned in Landsberg, dictating *Mein Kampf*, conniving at the murder of his own niece, Geli Raubal, turning on Röhm and the Brownshirts, and finally coming to power. It is a reasonable dramatisation of history, and has the immense advantage over most "biopics" of performers who look like the originals. Robert Watson's appearance is uncanny, and I can only suppose that he must have spent most of the war indoors to avoid being lynched; he has the gestures and manner, too, so far as one can judge from newsreels, and it is a riveting performance. Victor Varconi is an equally remarkable look-alike for Hess, and Luis van Rooten an immediately identifiable Himmler, but the supporting honours go to Martin Kosleck as a smooth and insinuating Goebbels. *The*

The Hitler Gang was remarkable for the resemblance of many of its players to the originals, and for the performance of Robert Watson (normally a comedian) as Adolf Hitler. From left, Goebbels (Martin Kosleck), Hess (Victor Varconi), Hitler, Goering (Alexander Pope) and Himmler (Luis van Rooten).

Hitler Gang is a modest film, but it has a little niche of its own for those human images.

From the great catalogue of British Forces films I choose three, one for each service, beginning with perhaps the most important battle of the war, and possibly of the century. There may have been better pictures about the RAF, but as a piece of history *The Battle of Britain* cannot be overlooked. How accurate its technical details are I obviously cannot say, but the names of Tuck, Lacey, and Galland among the advisers should be enough to satisfy most critics.

It begins with the hasty pull-out of the RAF's last squadrons from France in May 1940, and Curt Jurgens' demand for British withdrawal from the war delivered to Ambassador Ralph Richardson, while in England Dowding (Laurence Olivier) is facing the stark fact of Germany's 4–1 superiority in the air. At a humbler level one sees the Luftwaffe itching to go, Robert Shaw putting a new pilot through his paces, Christopher Plummer and WAAF Susannah York undergoing marital difficulties, and over the southern airfields a fine summer tranquillity, broken by the shattering blitzkrieg of Eagle Day (10 August) when the German planes sought to destroy the RAF on the ground by devastating the fighter stations behind the Channel coast. Then the six-week battle, with the reserve of British pilots dwindling, Goering's decision to switch to the Blitz of London, and the hectic climax of September when the Luftwaffe's attack was finally broken.

To make sense of this confused campaign is something of a feat, and a good balance is achieved between the bewildering aerial combats and the personalities at ground level. The frantic speed of the fighting aircraft makes identification next to impossible (I still don't know what became of Michael Caine), but the overall effect is impressive, with the Spitfires swarming like gnats, planes exploding luridly and crashing into the sea, the airfields being ripped into smoking ruins by the dive-bombers – and then cutting away to the quiet order of the control room, or Goering ranting at his flyers, or the peaceful shots of young men lounging in the sun waiting to scramble.

There are some memorable shots: the pathetic line of WAAF casualties lying under a blanket, the British pilot (Edward Fox) parachuting into a suburban greenhouse and finding a small boy at his elbow offering cigarettes, and at the end the Luftwaffe mess, with the pilots sitting at dinner in total silence. I should think it is as good dramatised history as one can get.

Big novels do not always translate well to the screen, and it is to Eric Ambler's credit that so much of the best in Nicholas Monsarrat's *The Cruel Sea* finished up on the screen. There is no plot, in the usual sense, about the story of a naval corvette, simply the progress of characters and ship through the perils of Atlantic convoy, torpedo attack and submarine hunting; it is the kind of fiction-documentary at which British studios excelled, without heroics or dramatic contrivance, and with a merciful absence of "confrontation" – the nearest to this is the mild persecution of junior officers by Stanley Baker, which is not overdone. Of course it is Jack Hawkins' film; it was his special talent to personify the ideal British officer – competent, tough, not unsympathetic but by no means given to undue emotion. There is nothing "glorious" about him or about the film, which is a bleak picture of a dreadful, cruel war fought in appalling conditions; the action sequences are both spectacular and grim, including the famous harrowing sequence in which Ericson (Hawkins) steams through a group of survivors in the water in pursuit of a submarine. Personally, I think he was wrong, but that's neither here nor there. *The Cruel Sea* is mercilessly authentic, and can serve as the model for films of naval warfare.

Ambler also has the rare distinction of writing (with Peter Ustinov) the best film ever made about British conscript soldiers, *The Way Ahead*. Unlike the last two films it was contemporary, and had to stand the immediate test of exposure to relentless critics like me; we found no fault with it, and having since exchanged service reminiscences with Peter Ustinov and discovered entirely common ground, I am not surprised. It is the first film in this book of which I can say,

Air Chief Marshall Lord Dowding, who led Fighter Command in 1940, and, right, Laurence Olivier in *The Battle Of Britain*.

from the certainty of first-hand knowledge, that it is a true historical picture.

It is about a group of civilians who come together in an infantry platoon, undergo the ups and downs of training, are slowly transformed into soldiers, go overseas to the initial boredom of North Africa, and in the closing scene are shown advancing into attack for the first time. There is the department store executive (Raymond Huntley), his nervous subordinate (Hugh Burden), the farm labourer (John Laurie), the eager cockney (Leslie Dwyer), the studious debt-collector (James Donald), the brash young suburbanite (Jimmy Hanley), and the lugubrious boilerman (Stanley Holloway), all under the command of the young Territorial subaltern (David Niven) and his tough, dapper, ruthlessly efficient sergeant (Billy Hartnell). And it is just beautifully done; every character is right, and every incident rings true. Niven is the perfect subaltern, keen, energetic, not totally sure of his ability to be a mixture of fighting leader and mother hen; as for Hartnell, he doesn't play the part, he is it: the pared-to-the-bone immaculate figure, the hard eye, the cold barking voice – how you hated it, and how you missed it later on, when you realised what a good man was underneath. The others are perfect types, with the sceptical, resigned Huntley outstanding.

Niven, if I remember the script aright, had been at Dunkirk, that chronic shambles which, through the unique British mythological process, has been transformed into a heroic legend; it isn't that we actually enjoy catastrophe, but there is a national or racial knack of making the best of it, in a bellyaching sort of way. This was well caught in *Dunkirk*, in which the essence of an enormous subject was condensed by homing in on two widely separated groups – an infantry section adrift in France under the uncertain leadership of Corporal John Mills, and a party of those heroic small-boat owners who took their civilian craft across to the beaches for the evacuation; two of them are played by Bernard Lee (aggressive and smouldering with rage over government incompetence) and Richard Attenborough (a reluctant small businessman). Eventually the two groups come together on the stricken beaches, and

get back to England by the skin of their teeth, not without considerable loss.

My admiration for Mills and Attenborough increases with each new part I see them in. Attenborough is so good that one takes him for granted, and Mills catches exactly that bewildered-but-bash-on-regardless reaction so common in the ordinary man suddenly faced with responsibility. The slow, anxious build-up for the two boat-owners is balanced against the frantic scramble of Mills' section through enemy-occupied country; and the strafing of the beaches, the shots of the weary lines waiting hopelessly in the water to be rescued, and the desperate confusion of evacuation manage to look impressively large-scale.

Not, admittedly, as spectacular as the return four years

The evacuation of the beaches in *Dunkirk*.

later, when Darryl F. Zanuck assaulted the beaches in *The Longest Day* with a host of stars which looked as big as Eisenhower's invading army. This was good history both of the grand design and of the individuals involved, and it is an interesting reflection of how truth outstrips fiction, that if some of the real incidents depicted here were shown in a melodrama, they would be laughed off the screen – Red Buttons dangling by his parachute from a church clock and being deafened by the chimes is acceptable because we know it happened, but present it as fiction and it would be considered well over the top.

There are many other war films worthy of mention – *Sea of Sand*, a most believable recreation of a Long Range Desert Group raid; *A Walk in the Sun*, following an American platoon in Italy; *The Desert Fox*, a good biographical piece on Rommel's involvement in the plot against Hitler, with James Mason at his best; *Mr Winkle Goes to War*, memorable for Edward G. Robinson's portrait of a middle-aged civilian pitched into conflict; *The Twenty-fifth Hour*, possibly Anthony Quinn's finest performance, as the eternal displaced person; *Pork Chop Hill*, which is from the Korean War, and is the most truthful picture of infantry action I have ever seen – to say nothing of documentaries like *Target for Tonight* and *Miss Grant Goes to the Door*, a brilliant little propaganda short featuring Flora Robson as one of two spinsters who trap a German parachutist (Manning Whiley). But I close this short survey with two films which are not historical, but are included for personal reasons.

The Long and the Short and the Tall is about infantrymen in the jungle of South-east Asia, and as a former rifleman in Fourteenth Army I would not want anyone to think that it is an accurate representation of service in that theatre, or that its whining, hysterical, garrulous caricatures bear any resemblance to real soldiers. It is not the only film to attribute exaggerated emotions to military men in combat, but it happens to be one of which I can say that it does not, to put it mildly, tally with my own experience. It trivialises war, most of its conversation is ludicrous, the needling and hatred would not have been tolerated in a real infantry section for five minutes, and it lacks any sense of how soldiers think or behave in action. For example: they do not discuss the Geneva Convention; they do not go into pathetic heart-searchings about killing a Japanese prisoner (they either do or they don't); the notion that they would attach importance to the kind of cigarettes the prisoner was carrying is simply nonsense in a theatre where both sides commonly smoked each other's, including those looted from the Chinese; they do not have impassioned arguments about whether or not to obey orders; above all, they do not shout the odds when there are Japs about. I will say no more except (and this applies to numerous other films) that anyone who tries to pull a grenade pin with his teeth is going to find himself applying for dentures.

Having declared my interest, it might be thought that I would wax indignant about *Objective Burma*, which caused such a furore in Britain (where it was withdrawn) in 1944, because it showed Errol Flynn and an American unit "recapturing Burma single-handed", as one critic put it. The British contribution to Burma was not mentioned, and the fury this aroused in the press, and in certain public figures, knew no bounds, or so I am told. I have seen *Objective Burma* since, and it is a rather long run-of-the-mill war picture; bits of it are quite good. But I see no good reason why it should have been considered a mortal insult to us in Burma. There *were* American units fighting there, admittedly in a sideshow to the main British-Indian campaign, but if Warner Brothers wanted to make a movie about their own troops, why not? Should they have refrained just because the British film industry had shown a notable lack of interest in the Burma war? As for *Objective Burma*'s not mentioning the British contribution – did *The Way Ahead* or *The Cruel Sea* mention the Americans?

Of course the reason for the furore was obvious – Flynn himself, the screen hero who was a notable absentee from the forces (for medical reasons, I'm told), formerly a British or Australian subject, and notorious in his own right. But I suspect there was another reason, and that was a guilty feeling among the powers-that-be, and the press, and sections of the public, where Fourteenth Army was concerned – the papers had been calling us "the Forgotten Army", a phrase which we bandied about with derision, and public indignation over *Objective Burma* was a way of telling us that we were not being forgotten after all. Our families at home were certainly sensitive on our behalf, understandably, but our own reaction to the storm was that we would have quite liked to see the picture. Nor do I imagine it would have had an unfavourable reception, although technical details would certainly have been criticised. For the record, my unit saw one film during the Burma war, and that was in April 1945, when we had been "leapfrogged" by another division and were temporarily out of the line; it was a makeshift, open-air film unit, and the projector gave up half-way, to roars of rage and disappointment. The film was *Northern Pursuit*, with Errol Flynn.

Incidentally, while I cannot say with authority who were the favourite male stars with the Forces (Alan Ladd was certainly high up), my recollection of barrack-room opinion, audience reaction, and pictures pasted on canteen walls suggests that the top female attraction was not Lamour or Grable or Hayworth, or even the well-regarded Veronica Lake, but June Allyson. A psychologist would probably say she was the ideal "girl next door", and that may well be the explanation.

There is, of course, yet another war which has preoccupied Hollywood in recent years. It is difficult to think of Vietnam in historic terms, because it is still so close, and the emotional upheaval consequent upon defeat still continues, and is confused by recrimination, doubt, injured pride, guilt, and all the bitterness of moral debate about the justice of the war and the way it was waged. So far as a sympathetic outsider can see, America still does not know what to think about the Vietnam tragedy, and the uncertainty, and extremes of opinion, have been reflected in its films, from the jingoistic flag-waving of *The Green Berets* to the purported harrowing realism of *Platoon*.

It is not for a non-participant to offer opinions, much less

June Allyson.

judgement, especially when he is aware that time, and Vietnam itself, have transformed attitudes to war out of all recognition since his day. Hollywood's representations of Vietnam (it is probably Thailand or Central America, in fact) look very like Burma fifty-odd years ago; the dangers, discomforts, and technical problems of infantry fighting seem much the same; the expenditure of ammunition looks unnecessarily extravagant; and the weaponry is more elaborate. But what has altered beyond belief (and I will take the film makers' word for it, because all I read and hear bears them out) is the mind and outlook, indeed the very soul, of the soldier. I could compare notes with a Vietnam veteran, and find much superficial common ground, but I doubt if I could understand his war as he understood it. Our war was simple, in itself and its aftermath, but not his. This may be why films of the Vietnam war have tended to leave me in a state of depressed confusion, tempered only by gratitude that our war was clouded by no unanswerable questions.

Frankly, I am not convinced that some of the film-makers

know precisely what they are trying to convey beyond the fact that war in the Far East has a beastliness all of its own. *The Deer Hunter*, at interminable length, followed three comrades (Robert De Niro, Christopher Walken, and John Savage) from their rather raucous civilian life in a Pennsylvania steel town to their ordeal at the hands of the Vietcong, who made them play Russian roulette – something which, I am assured, did not happen in Vietnam, although in the film it seemed rather more credible than the mechanics of the trio's escape from their captors. Thereafter De Niro and the crippled Savage got home, while Walken remained in Saigon, apparently playing Russian roulette for a living. Why he did this, to the point where he blew his brains out, I did not understand, nor, by that time, did I greatly care. I did not feel that I had learned much about Vietnam, or the men who fought there, but possibly I am just on the wrong wavelength.

Apocalypse Now, despite its portentous title, had an eerie, believable quality in those extraordinary shots of electrically

lit outposts on the jungle river up which Martin Sheen was travelling in search of Marlon Brando. The helicopter gunship raid was convincing, and Robert Duvall's commanding officer was an excellent study. It is said that the film bears some relation to *Heart of Darkness*, which I suspect might be news to Joseph Conrad.

Rambo, First Blood, Part II was almost a relief. Here at least was pure fantasy, firmly based on that unhealthy American dream of a superman endowed with godlike invulnerability and a lust for slaughter which verges on the sacrificial. It was less gory than I had been led to believe by the storm of critical censure, well directed in its action scenes, and photographed with all Jack Cardiff's expertise. Of course it was tripe, with Sylvester Stallone pounding sweatily through the jungle, butchering everyone in sight, resisting torture by fiendish Russians, and escaping by helicopter with a ragged band of POWs. But if it was an enormous exercise in wishful thinking, that is understandable, and if the net result was on a level

Changing images, the sergeant then and now: Billy Hartnell in *The Way Ahead* . . .

. . . and Tom Berenger, in *Platoon*.

with comic books about Sergeant Fury and his Howling Commandos, it still may be that the motives which inspired Stallone to make the film (apart from the obvious commercial ones) were not entirely unworthy. Like *The Deer Hunter* and *Apocalypse Now*, Rambo's historical interest is for the future, when it may serve to show, not what Vietnam was like, but what American film-makers felt impelled to say about it afterwards. Incidentally, I would not have wanted Rambo in my rifle section; too volatile by half, and anyone who disdains a shirt in jungle country is asking for trouble.

These three films are merely interesting, but *Platoon* is terrifying. Not because of its horror and violence, but because I suspect it is a true picture, and that makes me tremble for the safety (to say nothing of the good name) of Western civilisation. I would prefer to believe it is a grotesque fiction, but good authorities have acclaimed it as an honest portrayal of the Vietnam war, and if it is, then there is no doubt why America lost. On this showing, they didn't have an army.

For the soldiers of *Platoon* are simply not fit to go into action. They are brutal, degraded, nasty, hysterical, drug-sodden slobs, without decency or discipline, apparently hating each other, despising their leaders, and generally disgracing the profession of arms. Their evil genius is bad Sergeant Barnes, who murders good Sergeant Elias, a witness to Barnes' atrocities against Vietnamese villagers. Barnes in turn is murdered by the platoon innocent, an incident which gives point to the film's closing monologue: "The enemy was in us; we fought ourselves . . ." That may well be true, like all the blood, carnage, and pretentious talk with which the film abounds; the danger is that audiences may regard it as typical of all warfare, and the conduct of the principals as acceptable, and even excusable. They may even tell themselves that Barnes, with all his beastly faults, is a darned good soldier; he isn't. He is a rotten soldier, and I wouldn't bet on his platoon to beat the Band of Hope.

As I said, I am reluctant to believe *Platoon*, because the Americans of 1942–45 were not like this; they were good soldiers. But if *Platoon* is true and the fine army of Normandy and the Pacific did indeed degenerate to this extent, *Full Metal Jacket* may help to explain why. Half of it is devoted to the training of Marine recruits, the chief aim of which seems to be to degrade and dehumanise them, consisting as it does of head-shaving, subjection to the filthiest kind of verbal abuse, physical assault from their demented instructor, the chanting of imbecilic slogans, and other ritualistic caricatures of discipline. Of real soldiering they are taught virtually nothing, except how to go over a childishly simple assault course; obscene screaming and tough talk are what pass for instruction – and I just don't believe that is all the US Marines teach their recruits, although it is all we see here. Small wonder that the platoon butt, after being beaten in cowardly fashion by his loyal comrades, goes mad, shoots the sergeant, and then commits suicide. (*Platoon* is right; this lot don't *need* an enemy.)

The second half gives an entirely believable picture of Vietnam, even if it was shot on the Isle of Dogs; it is infinitely better as a film than *Platoon*, for all the latter's awards. There is a superbly photographed patrol action which ends with the knocking-out of a Vietcong sniper, who turns out to be a teenage girl; she is badly wounded, and the patrol stand around in heavy-breathing consideration of whether to finish her off or not – none of them seems to realise that they are presenting a fine flat-footed target for any other snipers who may be about, but after the training they've had, why should they?

That is a technicality; overall the two films are deeply disturbing in their reflections of attitudes and conduct, and in their apparent assumption that a gruelling campaign entitles men to behave like brutes – indeed, that it is necessary for them so to behave. I will not believe that they are true pictures for all the Americans in Vietnam, but if they reflect any truth at all then the Pentagon, far more than bad Sergeant Barnes or the obscene and amateurish buffoon of an instructor in *Full Metal Jacket*, must take the blame. This was no way to go to war.

The Killing Fields, a harrowing recreation of civilian suffering in the Cambodian phase of the war, is splendid as a film in

Humphrey Bogart, the arch-gangster of pre-*Casablanca* days, as Duke Mantee in *The Petrified Forest*.

its own right and as a piece of history; it also turns into a first-class cliff-hanger. Dith Pran (Haing S. Ngor), assistant to an American journalist (Sam Waterson), has to be abandoned when his employer is evacuated from Phnom Penh, which is in the hands of murderous rebels; thereafter the question is how Pran, enslaved as a labourer, is going to win his way out to freedom. It is a gripping, frightening film, wholly convincing in its picture of a war-torn countryside reduced to anarchy; Waterson has never performed better, and if the late Dr Ngor was as good a medical practitioner as he was an actor, his patients are to be envied.

Finally, to the crime pictures, which in a sense are historicals so far as they mirror a phenomenon of the Thirties, although how accurately they do it is another matter. They are, at least, of interest as a contemporary view and they may eventually have a profound significance for historians as signposts to the nature of our century. For their great appeal is one of the basest imaginable, and it is their violence and cruelty. For all the lip-service paid to "social conscience" and pious talk about exposure and informing the public, the plain truth is that the gangster movie pandered shamelessly to the worst side of human nature – and still does. There is no need to dig deep about it, and theorise that the audiences of the Depression took to it all the more readily because it expressed their subconscious desire to be revenged on society; brute force fascinates, and if the gangster is given an outward attraction he becomes a hero – which he did.

Knowing that the prime interest of the commercial film is to make a profit, it is difficult to take too seriously the foreword to one of the first gangster pictures, *Public Enemy*, which states that the film does not wish "to glorify the hoodlum or criminal", since that is precisely what it goes on to do. It could hardly do anything else with James Cagney in the lead, for few film stars attracted as much affection and admiration as he did; he was a most gifted actor as well as an engaging personality, and one jaunty squaring of the shoulders with a self-deprecating grin was enough to put the audience in his pocket. He managed to look half his age, and not until *White Heat*, made in his fiftieth year, did the boyish charm finally fade. He was also small (as most of the great screen gangsters were), and a living reminder that you didn't have to be big to be tough.

Even the ugly ones were attractive. Edward G. Robinson was a spellbinder; where Cagney enlisted sympathy by his bright spirit and the suggestion that his gangster was a redeemable square-shooter, Robinson did it by exuding ruthless determination and strength of character – never mind if it was bad character, it was not going to be pushed around, and it had all the fascination of power. Again, as with Cagney, it was only with age that Robinson's attraction faded; Rico and all his other gangster impersonations had none of the soulless evil that he suggested in *Key Largo*, when he was in his fifties.

And of course both of them frequently appeared on the right side of the law, and some of the decency stuck when they stepped back behind the tommy-gun. This was also the case with George Raft of the poker face and liquid eyes; hoodlum he might be, but all the world knew he was a beautiful dancer.

Really only Bogart carried no heroic aura as a gangster of the Thirties, when he was commonly seen as the treacherous weasel whom Cagney shot in the last reel. *Casablanca* changed all that, and set him on the way to being a cult figure, and

he seldom returned to crime thereafter (*The Desperate Hours* being a notable exception). But in his day he was probably the most convincing gangster of them all, and alone in bringing no glamour to his parts: give him a two-day growth and a grubby shirt, and the manic snarl and beautiful impedimented voice did the rest.

Little Caesar and *Public Enemy*, both made in 1930, started the rot, and it is difficult to see how they can honestly be said to have anything to do with "social conscience". The belief that if you show something unpleasant you have automatically "done something about it" by bringing it to public notice, is as prevalent now as it was then – as witness the relish with which TV revels in social evils nowadays; there is almost a smug sense of virtue in the exhibitor, and an implication that it is now up to the public, the medium having already done its share.

Public Enemy, which shows the rise and fall of a young hoodlum, Tom Powers (Cagney), offers no solution beyond a closing suggestion that something will have to be done; in the meantime we have seen Cagney going wrong as a child, being beaten by his father, stealing watches, graduating to armed robbery in which a policeman is killed, carrying out a revenge killing, being badly wounded and reconciled to his family, and finally being kidnapped and executed by rival gangsters. He has, along the way, had the compensations of money to burn, Jean Harlow, and a lifestyle which must have looked attractive during the Depression. And always we understand that he is a decent lad at heart, and not truly in the same class of wickedness as Rico in *Little Caesar* or Tony Camonte in *Scarface*.

They were a repulsive pair, but for all their violence and tough talk, did they really do anything to alert the public to the menace of organised crime, of which Al Capone, on whom they were presumably based, was only the most notorious visible symbol? We know they did not, that their treatment was superficial and could give no notion of how the crime network operated, or of the extent of its corrupting influence on society. But

Al Capone, top left, and clockwise, Edward G. Robinson (*Little Caesar*), Paul Muni (*Scarface*), Robert de Niro (*The Untouchables*), Rod Steiger (*Al Capone*).

they did emphasise, if not glorify, the compelling attraction of brute force, and made it plain that crime paid, up to a point – the most vivid memory that most people carried away from *Scarface* was probably of the dying George Raft subsiding in a doorway, still spinning his coin, but I have no doubt that the scene in which Paul Muni gloats over the fine shirts he can now afford to have laundered daily was also noted at the time.

Whether gangster pictures encouraged crime or not is a fruitless debate; there is no doubt that they glamourised it.

This was already being said in the 1930s, by the US Production Code Authority and by religious groups, to which the industry deftly responded by switching Cagney and Robinson (temporarily, at any rate) to the side of law enforcement. It was a cosmetic operation, and may even have been

The Dead End Kids in uncharacteristic pose: from left, Gabriel Dell, Bernard Punsley, Huntz Hall, Bobby Jordan, Leo Gorcey and Billy Halop.

a harmful one in that the films which resulted tended to give the impression that the answer to organised crime was to go out and shoot a few gangsters. This was implicit in *I am the Law*, in which Robinson is a law professor crusading against the underworld, and in the earlier *G-Men*, in which Cagney is a young lawyer who joins the government service to avenge the murder of a friend; he does so with the blessing of another friend and former racketeer, a fact which does him no good when it comes to the notice of his hostile superior in the service (Robert Armstrong). To make matters worse, Armstrong resents Cagney's attentions to his sister (Margaret Lindsay), and there is much rugged confrontation and misunderstanding before the obligatory gun battle in a garage in which villainy in the appropriate shape of Barton McLane is duly disposed of. As a depiction of life in the field with the FBI it apparently

satisfied J. Edgar Hoover, but thoughtful members of the audience may have wondered if filling McLane with lead was really enough to bring organised crime to its knees.

For the most part the later films of the Thirties were more sophisticated, and began to concern themselves more with the causes of crime, in an extremely bland and simple way. This was when social conscience began to be talked about; films like *Dead End*, introducing the celebrated Kids, emphasise the effects of deprivation by showing the ragged urchins in poverty and squalor alongside the opulent homes which have sprung up along the waterfront. Humphrey Bogart is the gangster returning to the scenes of childhood and being rebuffed by his mother (Marjorie Main) and disillusioned by his former girl (Claire Trevor), who has become a streetwalker; in the meantime Sylvia Sidney is trying to keep her young brother (Billy

James Cagney en route to the electric chair in *Angels with Dirty Faces*, with Pat O'Brien as the priest.

Halop) on the straight and narrow, assisted by an impoverished architect (Joel Macrea). The plot thickens with Bogart trying to kidnap a rich child and being shot by Macrea, while young Halop, who has made free with a knife given him by Bogart, is last seen in the grip of the law and headed for reform school.

Dead End was of course a play, and is filmed as such; it is a good depressing piece, but the message that came across strong and clear to the youth of 1937 was what a splendid, uninhibited bunch the Dead End Kids were. They became heroes overnight, and especially the gifted young comic actor Huntz Hall and the stocky, derisively wise-cracking Leo Gorcey; I would guess that the latter was the most mimicked performer of his day, by juveniles all over the English-speaking

world. It was taken for granted that they were decent lads underneath, lovable little rascals who were the victims of their environment; when they set on a rich boy, beating him up unmercifully, stealing his watch, and tearing his clothes to shreds, it was not shown on screen, although Halop's attempt to carve up Gorcey for squealing was. In fairness I don't think the film and its successors realised how they were glamourising the juvenile delinquent, but they did.

Their second film, *Crime School*, with Bogart this time an enlightened reformatory warden, was a plea for the humane treatment of young offenders, but it did not alter the Dead End Kids' image, and what that was meant to be was made plain by the title of their third picture, *Angels with Dirty Faces*. This was a brilliant film, not least for the way it got the best of both worlds – it fairly dripped social conscience, and the murderous hoodlum was glorified as never before.

Rocky and Jerry are two likely lads disturbed by the police while robbing a box-car; they run for it, but while Jerry escapes and grows up to be a priest (Pat O'Brien), Rocky is caught and goes the way of reform school to become a full-fledged gunsel (Cagney). On his release after a prison term he is hailed as a hero by the neighbourhood boys (the Dead End Kids), who are under Father Jerry's care, but meets with a cold welcome from his partners in crime (Bogart and George Bancroft). To cut a long story short, Cagney finally murders Bogart and is sentenced to the electric chair. The hero-worshipping Kids look to him to go out with colours flying, but Father Jerry talks him into turning coward at the last minute, to the disgust of the Kids who, we are asked to believe, will be turned off lives of crime as a result of their idol's poltroonery. Well, perhaps they were; the audience, on the other hand, were left to contemplate the ultimate heroism of turning yellow in a good cause,[4] and you cannot present the gangster more sympathetically than that.

The message of the film is "There but for the grace of God go I", the assumption being that only Jerry's fleetness of foot as a boy saved him from Rocky's fate. I don't believe it, or that Rocky would have become a virtuous citizen had he been the one to escape; the little thug had the gallows mark on him from the start. But whatever one thinks of the film's morality, emotional pressure, and sociological conclusions, it is a most skilful production and well acted, most notably by Franklin Burke, whose playing of the boy Rocky is a perfect study of Cagney.

4 Cagney and O'Brien discussed the film on television a few years ago, and one of them (I forget whom) put forward the interesting thought that Rocky's cowardice might, in the end, have been genuine. Such was Cagney's persona that I doubt if any viewer of 1938 would have thought this for a moment. If Bogart had been given Cagney's part, now, it would have been another matter – and a much more interesting film.

Cagney the hero and Bogart the rat were at it again in *The Roaring Twenties*, a lively tale of ex-servicemen turned bootleggers, and in the same year, 1939, Cagney was teamed with Raft in *Each Dawn I Die*, which I mention as an example of another variant on the gangster film, the criminal-as-victim picture. At that time it had not become fashionable to show to criminals the consideration bordering on respect which they frequently receive today, and any exposé of prison conditions demanded that the principal should be an innocent man wrongly convicted; the sympathy which the film invited for him inevitably attached to the other inmates.

The first of these films, *I am a Fugitive from a Chain Gang*, had been made in 1932, with Paul Muni as the innocent sent to a horrifying penal settlement in the South, from which he escapes, later surrendering to the authorities on the understanding that he will be paroled on completing a token sentence. The promise is broken, he escapes again, and will obviously be a fugitive for life. The film is said to have had great impact in its exposure of the shocking conditions of the chain gang, but of course the issue is clouded by the use of the innocent victim; had Muni been guilty, the evils of the system could have been more fairly judged.

Each Dawn I Die has a crusading reporter, Ross (Cagney) framed by corrupt local officials and sent to a penitentiary where he meets and eventually becomes friends with Stacey (George Raft), an important mobster doing life. When Stacey makes a daring prison break Ross is implicated, with dire consequences which include solitary confinement and refusal of parole. Stacey, realising that Ross is suffering on his behalf, gives himself up out of loyalty, and in the inevitable attempted mass escape forces a confession out of one of Ross's framers (Alan Baxter) in the presence of the governor (George Bancroft).

Thus all ends happily, and a fairly silly story it is, redeemed by a performance from Cagney which is among his best, and a chilling insight into American penal conditions of the time. Loyalty and courage are the keynotes (and when were they not

Prison inmates in *Each Dawn I Die:* from left, Maxie Rosenbloom, James Cagney, Stanley Ridges, Ed Pawley and George Raft.

in a gangster picture?), but the dishonesty of this kind of film is in the one-sidedness with which it tries to enlist our emotions. Prison life is harsh, therefore we are to be sympathetic not just to Ross, but to lovable Maxie Rosenbloom and old Stanley Ridges, whose life is made unbearable by a brutal guard (John Wray). What they are inside for we don't know, but we are meant to feel for them, and give no thought to why they are there in the first place. The villains within the walls are definitely Wray, and convicts like Baxter and Limpy (Joe Downing) whose offence in the eyes of the audience is not that they are criminals, but stool-pigeons despised by the convict fraternity.

Hollywood gangsters were clearly divided between the semi-heroic (Cagney) and the rats (Bogart, McLane), and there was a large and sympathetic core of comic hoodlums (Edgar Brophy, Rosenbloom, sometimes Abner Biberman and Sheldon Leonard) who really belonged in *Guys and Dolls* rather than in crime drama. Their exploitation reached its height in pictures like *Robin and the Seven Hoods*, which may be comedies but still do not bear very close examination so far as their underlying philosophy is concerned.

This may seem unduly censorious of what are, after all, entertainments, but it is at least legitimate to question the values of an industry which has pretty consistently invited its audiences to admire and identify with selfish and unpleasant thugs. We have seen the romantic glow cast over the Butch Cassidys and the Jesse Jameses; from films of the Thirties onwards to modern television we have been treated to an endless procession of safe-crackers, conmen, thieves, murderers, gamblers, and kindred villains, and it is no defence to say that they are shown in an unsympathetic light – make them central characters and you invite the audience to their side, tying the viewer's emotions in with theirs. Glamourise them as likeable rascals, and you simply compound the felony.

Enjoyment of violence was an important element of the old gangster movies, but at least their makers did not seem to revel in it as more recent film-makers have done. The pornography of violence, the enjoyment of cruelty and destruction for its own sake, is now essential. I hope it reached a peak in the work of directors like Sam Peckinpah, which at its worst was truly disgusting, as in *The Wild Bunch*, a foul film which for some reason received enthusiastic reviews. One critic wrote of it: "The bloody deaths are voluptuous, frightening, beautiful", and described it as an "imagistic epic". I don't know if that critic has ever seen bloody death, but it is not beautiful at all, and there is nothing clever or artistic or worthy about its portrayal ad nauseam. What effect films like that have on an audience, I am not sure, beyond the obvious one of debasing and degrading taste, and dulling decent sensibility. It is all the more depressing because Peckinpah could and did make good films like *Ride the High Country*, which is an offbeat and often touching Western about two old-timers, Joel Macrea and Randolph Scott; no one denies his technical skill, but one can regret its use to such unworthy ends as *The Wild Bunch*.

I mention it as typical of an attitude to violence which is now widespread in the cinema and which I at least find extremely disturbing. It can be said that films have always been violent, and I can cite scenes from pictures dealt with earlier, which in cold print may seem as horrifying as anything in Peckinpah – a face being branded in *Captain Blood*, floggings in the *Bounty* pictures, impalement in *The Sign of the Cross*, and so on. But they weren't, and if anyone asks "What's the difference?", I can only say that there is a way of doing these things, and a good director like Curtiz or DeMille knows it, just as writers and actors know it. It's nothing that can be codified or submitted to "guidelines"; it really is a question of intent – whether you want simply to convey quickly and decently that something horrible is happening which it is necessary to show, or whether you want to rub the audience's nose in it. It's as simple as that, and all the excuses of "realism" and "integrity" are so much hypocrisy.

The violence of the gangster pictures of the Thirties was trivial in itself, and far less objectionable than its oblique glamourisation of crime and criminals; the violence of the modern cinema is pathological. It extends far outside the cops-and-robbers pictures, as we know, but they are the ones with which I am concerned, as successors to the old gangster movies and also because, while they are certainly not "historicals", they may be looked on as historic reflections one day. I mention four, three of which make up a series starring Clint Eastwood: *Dirty Harry, Magnum Force* and *The Enforcer*.

Immediately I am reminded of George Orwell's essay on James Hadley Chase and *No Orchids for Miss Blandish* – how tame its film version seems now, like *Noose* and *They Made Me a Fugitive* and those other thrillers which worried the Women's Institute in the late Forties. Orwell likened reading *No Orchids* to taking a header into a cesspool, and went on to praise, quite properly, the quality of Chase's writing. Similarly, while I think *Dirty Harry* is a beastly film, I have to concede that it is expertly made (in a way which *The Wild Bunch* is not). It is about Callaghan (Clint Eastwood), a San Francisco police officer, who turns vigilante in order to run down a maniac

Latter-day liquidators: Clint Eastwood as *Dirty Harry*, and . . .

. . . Charles Bronson in *Death Wish*.

sniper – apparently there was such a creature in San Francisco, called the Zodiac Killer, on whom the film's monster is said to be based. It is undeniably suspenseful, exciting, well photographed, and well performed by its principal; it is also shockingly brutal. In *Magnum Force* Callaghan's target is a group of police officers who are murdering criminals (though why this should worry him is not clear), and in *The Enforcer* his victims are just a gang of thugs. After which the series ended, having made astronomical profits and inspired a host of even more lurid imitations. Without Eastwood I don't suppose the films would have attracted much attention, and really he does not belong in them. Here is this pleasant looking, gently spoken man blowing people to smithereens – possibly this makes Dirty Harry all the more attractive to modern audiences, whose tastes are matter for the psychiatrist rather than the market researcher. I remember the reaction to one scene in which Callaghan has his gun trained on the face of a cornered villain, to whom he remarks that the gun may or may not be empty, and then dares his victim to reach for his fallen revolver. Nasty and sadistic, and when the villain surrendered the cinema sighed with disappointment; no doubt they felt they had been cheated out of something voluptuous, frightening, and beautiful.

The fourth film is *Death Wish*, which is unusual among the films of violence in having a discernible point to make. Its central figure is Charles Bronson, Eastwood's only serious rival in decreasing the surplus population, seen here as a family man whose wife is murdered and his daughter raped into imbecility by the spiritual descendants of the Dead End Kids. The police are helpless, so Bronson takes to the streets by night murdering muggers to such good effect that the crime rate goes down. When the police (represented by Vincent Gardenia) track him down their first concern is that he should remove his embarrassing presence, which he does, and we are led to believe (by a nice closing shot) that he will resume operations in his new surroundings.

The reactions to this picture were remarkable. In some American cities audiences applauded and cheered the vigilante, while some critics could not find words harsh enough to condemn the film and its director, Michael Winner – presumably because they thought *Death Wish* was an incitement to outraged citizens to take the law into their own hands. Both reactions were childish, perhaps, and beside the obvious point, which was that if the law and society cannot protect the citizen, it must not overlook the possibility that he may decide to protect himself. To say that, on film or in print, is not to encourage or condemn such action, but to state an obvious truth which may well be unpalatable to those whose enlightened opinions have influenced society into its present position.

And there we leave the twentieth century, having touched on only three aspects of it which are not without historical significance. It has been a critical, sombre survey of the Seventh Age, and if I could have found a legitimate excuse for attaching the label "historical picture" to *The Man Who Came To Dinner* or *The Producers* or *The Great Race* or *Blithe Spirit* or the movies of Laurel and Hardy, I would have done so gladly. It would be nice if our century were remembered for them and films like them – and for all those Biblicals and swashbucklers and Westerns and romances and epics of the past which, for some of us, are the best things the film industry ever did. I have covered them as comprehensively as I can, and apologise for any favourites omitted as well as for any factual errors I may have made along the way. If this random and no doubt erratic journey through the Seven Ages of the cinema has awakened any pleasant memories, or a wish to see again those glorious old movies, then it has been worth while, and no more than they deserve, for however flawed and occasionally inaccurate Hollywood's history of the world may have been, there is this to be said for it, that it was certainly better fun than the real thing.

Author's Acknowledgment

I am deeply grateful to Mr Robert Ferguson and Mr Percy Morrison, of the Isle of Man, who made it possible for me to view many of the rarer historical films in my own home, and to my wife for her encouragement and for compiling the index.

References

In checking historical detail I have relied mainly on the Eleventh *Britannica*, the *Cambridge Modern History*, the *Dictionary of National Biography*, the *Imperial Dictionary of Universal Biography*, the *Catalogue* of the National Portrait Gallery, and other works of general reference. Now and then I have had to go further, and the following are some of the books, both history and fiction, which I have consulted. It doesn't pretend to be a bibliography, but for those who wish to compare accepted history with costume films it may be of some interest. I should add that I have used these books to verify facts, and their authors are not to be held responsible for my opinions and conclusions.

First Age

	The Bible
Baker, G. P.	Twelve Centuries of Rome
Douglas, Lloyd	The Robe
Fast, Howard	Spartacus
Flavius Josephus	Antiquities of the Jews
Gibbon, Edward	Decline and Fall of the Roman Empire, vol. i
Grant, M.	The Army of the Caesars
Graves, Robert	I, Claudius
Homer	The Iliad
	The Odyssey
Koestler, A.	The Gladiators
Mannix, D. P.	Those About to Die
Mitchell, J. L.	Spartacus
Oman, Sir Charles	On the Writing of History
Plutarch	Lives
Scullard, H. H.	From the Gracchi to Nero
Sienkiewicz, H.	Quo Vadis?
Suetonius	Lives of the Twelve Caesars
Tacitus	Annals

Second Age

Brown, F. Hume	History of Scotland, vol. i
Duggan, Alfred	Devil's Brood: the Angevin Family
Deiss, J. J.	Captains of Fortune
Green, J. R.	History of the English People
Harris, P. V.	The Truth about Robin Hood
Haslip, J.	Lucrezia Borgia
Lamb, H.	Genghiz Khan
Lea, H. C.	History of the Inquisition, vol. iii
Oman, Sir Charles	Art of War in the Middle Ages, vol. ii
Neilson, George	"Blind Harry's Wallace" (English Association Essays and Studies)
Pernoud, R.	Joan of Arc
Ridpath, G.	Border History of England and Scotland
Runciman, Sir Steven	A History of the Crusades, vol. iii
Sabatini, R.	The Life of Cesare Borgia
Sismondi, J. C. L.	History of the Italian Republics

Tytler, P. F.	History of Scotland, vol. i
Villari, P.	The Barbarian Invasion of Italy

Also Gibbon, vol. iii (Attila).

Third Age

Ball, I. M.	Pitcairn: Children of Mutiny
Barrow, Sir John	The Mutiny of *HMS Bounty*
Cowan, I. B. (ed.)	The Enigma of Mary Stuart
Deacon, R.	A History of the British Secret Service
Defoe, D.	General History of the Pyrates
Esquemeling, A.	The Buccaneers of America
Hakluyt, R.	Principal Voyages, vols ii, iv, and vii
Hampden, J. (ed.)	Francis Drake, Privateer
Harrower, Dr Kate	"Medical History of the Tudors", presidential address to Medical Women's Federation, 1956
Jenkins, E.	Elizabeth the Great
Kennedy, G.	Bligh
Mason, A. E. W.	Fire Over England
Mattingly, G.	The Defeat of the Spanish Armada
Neale, J. E.	Queen Elizabeth I
Ritchie, R. C.	Captain Kidd and the War against the Pirates
Seth, Ronald	Encyclopedia of Espionage.

Also Notable British Trials (Kidd, Bounty Mutineers)

Fourth Age

Cronin, V.	Napoleon
Maroger, D. (ed.)	Memoirs of Catherine the Great
Macaulay, Lord	History of England
Poyntz, S.	Relation, 1624–36
Petrie, Sir Charles	Diplomatic History, 1713–1933
	The Stuarts
	Wellington
De Sandraz, C.	Memoirs of M. D'Artagnan, vol. i
De Voto, B.	Westward the Course of Empire

Sabatini, R.	Historical Nights
	Entertainment, i, ii, iii
	Scaramouche
Scott, Sir Walter	Rob Roy, introduction
Wedgwood, C. V.	The King's War
	The Thirty Years' War

Fifth Age

Douthwaite, L. C.	The Royal Canadian Mounted Police
Gross, J. (ed.)	The Age of Kipling
Haggard, Sir Rider	"Isandhlwana", written for Andrew Lang
Harris, John	The Gallant Six Hundred
Kipling, R.	Kim
	Something of Myself
Mackenzie, C.	Soldier's Life
Stanley, H. M.	How I Found Livingstone
Strachey, Lytton	Queen Victoria
Trench, C. C.	Charley Gordon
Wallace, E.	Sanders of the River
Yeats-Brown, F.	Bengal Lancer

Also C. Stein's "Isandhlwana" in Cassell's *Battles of the Nineteenth Century*, vol. i.

Sixth Age

Billington, R. A.	The Far Western Frontier
Cooper, J. F.	The Last of the Mohicans
Dillon, Richard H.	North American Indian Wars
Dunn, J. P.	Massacres of the Mountains
Graham, W. A.	The Custer Myth
Gregg, J.	The Commerce of the Prairies
Horan, J. D. and Sann, P.	Pictorial History of the Old Wild West
Hawgood, J. A.	The American West
Lord, Walter	A Time to Stand
Morison, S. E.	Oxford History of the American People, vols i and ii

Parkman, F.	Montcalm and Wolfe, vols ii and iii
	The Conspiracy of Pontiac, vol. ii
	The Oregon Trail
Roberts, K.	Northwest Passage
Wellman, P. I.	Death on the Prairie

Also the *Concise Dictionary of American History*, and *The Gunfighters, The Railroaders, The Scouts*, and *The Soldiers* from the Time-Life series *The Old West*, and *The Atlantic Crossing* from the series *The Seafarers*.

Seventh Age

For the Seventh Age I consulted no specialist works. However, in addition to the titles mentioned above, there are many publications devoted to the cinema which I have used for facts, figures, dates, cast lists, credits, and similar information about the films covered throughout the book. I am particularly indebted to Leslie Halliwell's *Filmgoer's Companion* and *Film Guide*, which have been invaluable references. Also:

Blum, D.	A Pictorial History of the Talkies
DeMille, C. B.	Autobiography
Eames, J. D.	The Paramount Story
	The M.G.M. Story
Hirschhorn, C.	The Universal Story
	The Warner Brothers Story
Jewell, R. B. and Harbin, V.	The RKO Story
Katz, Ephraim	The Macmillan International Film Encyclopaedia
Kulik, K.	Alexander Korda
Lloyd, A.	Movies of the Thirties, Forties, Fifties, and Sixties (four volumes)
Nash, J. R. and Ross, S. R.	The Motion Picture Guide, A–B
Pickard, R.	Who Played Who in the Movies
Robertson, P.	The Guinness Book of the Movies
Rozsa, Miklos	Double Life
Thomas, T. and Solomon, A.	The Films of Twentieth-Century Fox
Warner, Jack	My First Hundred Years in Hollywood
Wood, R.	Howard Hawks

Publisher's Acknowledgement

The publisher would like to thank the following for their help in the conception and preparation of this book: David Kent and Cheryl Thomas of the Kobal Collection, for helping to select all the film stills; Simon Crocker, also of the Kobal Collection, for suggesting the title; and Barbara Bagnall and Rebecca Porteous for researching the pictures of real people.

The publisher would also like to thank the following film production and distribution companies, both past and present, whose film stills and publicity portraits appear in this book: A.B.C., A.B.P.C., Anglo-Allied, Avala, Samuel Bronston, C.C.C., Columbia, Disney, Ealing, E.M.I., Famous Artists, Samuel Goldwyn, Hammer, Horizon, Imperator, Dino de Laurentiis, London Films, M.G.M., Cecil B. DeMille, Mosfilm, National General, Paramount, Rank, David O. Selznick, Twentieth-Century Fox, United Artists, Universal, Walter Wanger, Warner Bros.

Finally the publisher wishes to acknowledge the permission of the following collections to use the pictures of real people: The Bomann Museum, Celle; the British Library; the British Museum; Bulloz; the trustees of the Fitzwilliam Museum, University of Cambridge; Giraudon; Hulton Getty; the Illustrated London News Picture Library; the trustees of the Imperial War Museum, London; Richard B. Knight; Lauros-Giraudon; the Mansell Collection; the Metropolitan Museum of Art, New York; the National Gallery of Ireland; the trustees of the National Library of Scotland; the National Portrait Gallery, London; Novosti, London; Peter Newark's Pictures, Bath; Photo AKG, London; Popperfoto/Reuter; the Royal Collection, Her Majesty Queen Elizabeth II; Scala, Florence; The Scottish National Portrait Gallery; the Society for Co-operation in Russian and Soviet Studies; Satens Museum for Kunst, Copenhagen; the Swedish National Portrait Gallery, Stockholm.

Index

Titles in italics refer to motion pictures. Page numbers in italics refer to illustrations

Picture Sources

Allenby, General, *General Allenby*, by Eric Kennington

Andersen, Hans, *Hans Christian Andersen*, print by A. M. Petersen, Statens Museum for Kunst

Anthony, Mark, coin of Mark Anthony, Fitzwilliam Museum

Auda Abu Taiyeh, *Auda*, by Eric Kennington

Bean, Judge Roy, *Judge Roy Bean Holding Court at "Jersey Lilly" Saloon Courtroom, Langtry Texas*, Peter Newarks' Pictures

Bismarck, Otto, *Otto von Bismarck in Cuirassier's Uniform During the Franco Prussian War*, Loescher and Petsch, 1871, Photo AKG

Bligh, William, *Pirate Captain Bligh*, Hulton Getty

Boleyn, Anne, *Anne Boleyn*, National Portrait Gallery

Bonney, Anne, *Anne Bonney*, British Library

Bonney, William, ("Billy the Kid"), *Billy the Kidd*, c.1880, Peter Newark's Pictures

Borgia, Cesare, *Cesare Borgia*, formerly attributed to Leonardo da Vinci, Mansell Collection

Borgia, Lucrezia, *Lucrezia Borgia*, by Pinturichio, Mansell Collection

Bothwell, Earl of, *The Earl of Bothwell*, 1566, Scottish National Portrait Gallery

Bowie, James, *James Bowie*, Peter Newark's Pictures

Bromhead, Lt. G., *Lieutenant Bromhead*, Mansell Collection

Brontë sisters, *The Brontë Sisters*, by Patrick Branwell Brontë, 1834, National Portrait Gallery

Brown, John, *John Brown, American Anti-slavery Leader*, Peter Newark's Pictures

Brown, John, *Queen Victoria at Osbourne*, by Sir Edwin Landseer, The Royal Collection

Burghley, Lord, *William Cecil, 1st Baron Burghley*, by Marcus Gheeraerts, 1585, National Portrait Gallery

Caligula, Emperor, coin of Caligula

Canarray, Martha ("Calamity Jane"), *Calamity Jane*, Peter Newark's Pictures

Capone, Al, *Al Capone*, New York, 1932, Popperfoto/Reuter

Cardigan, Earl of, *7th Earl of Cardigan*, Hulton Getty

Cassidy, Butch, see Parker, Leroy

Catherine the Great, *Catherine II of Russia*, by D. G. Levitsky, Novosti

Chard Lt. J., *Lieutenant Chard*, Mansell Collection

Charles Edward, Prince, *Prince Charles Edward Stuart*, by Antonio David, 1729, National Portrait Gallery

Charles I, *Charles I in three positions*, by Sir Anthony van Dyck, The Royal Collection

Charles II, *Charles II*, 1665, National Portrait Gallery

Chopin, Frédéric, *Frédéric Chopin*, by Delacroix, 1838, Hulton Getty

Christian, Fletcher, *Fletcher Christian*, artist's impression, by Larry Learmouth

Christina, Queen, *Queen Christina of Sweden*, by J. H. Elbfas, Swedish National Portrait Gallery Archives

Claudius, Emperor, coin of Claudius and Messalina

Cleopatra VII, *Cleopatra*, Hulton Getty

Clive, Robert, *1st Baron Clive*, by Nathaniel Dance, 1773, National Portrait Gallery

Cody, W. F. ("Buffalo Bill"), *William Frederick Cody*, Peter Newark's Pictures

Columbus, Christopher, *Christopher Columbus*, Hulton Getty

Crockett, Davy, *Davy Crocket, Hero of the Alamo*, Peter Newark's Pictures

Cromwell, Oliver, *Oliver Cromwell*, by Robert Hutchinson, National Portrait Gallery

Custer, George A., *General George A. Custer*, by Matthew Brady, Peter Newark's Pictures

Disraeli, Benjamin, *Benjamin Disraeli, Earl of Beaconsfield*, by Sir John Everett Millais, 1881, National Portrait Gallery

Dowding, Lord, *Air Chief Marshal Lord Dowding*, Imperial War Museum

Earp, Wyatt, *Wyatt Earp*, Peter Newark's Pictures

Elizabeth I, *Elizabeth I*, by Nicholas Hilliard, 1575, National Portrait Gallery

Essex, 2nd Earl of, *Portrait of Robert Devereux, Earl of Essex*, by William Segar, National Gallery of Ireland

Fersen, Count Axel, *Hans Axel Fersen*, Hulton Getty

Fox, Charles James, *Charles James Fox*, by Karl Anton Hickel, 1793, National Portrait Gallery

Gandhi, Mahatma, *Mahatma Gandhi*, signed photograph, Hulton Getty

George I, *George I*, by Sir Godfrey Kneller, 1714, National Portrait Gallery

Gladstone, W. F., *William Ewart Gladstone*, by Eveleen Myers, 1899, National Portrait Gallery

Gordon, General Charles, *Charles George Gordon*, by Julia Abercromby, National Portrait Gallery

Grant, General, *General Ulysses S. Grant*, by Matthew Brady, Peter Newark's Pictures

Gwyn Nell, *Eleanor Gwyn*, Sir Peter Lely, Metropolitan Museum of Art

Hamilton, Emma, *Emma, Lady Hamilton*, by George Romney, 1785, National Portrait Gallery

Henry II, *Henry II*, National Portrait Gallery

Henry VIII, *Henry VII*, 1536, National Portrait Gallery

Hickok, J. B. ("Wild Bill"), *Wild Bill Hickok*, Peter Newark's Pictures

Holliday, "Doc", *John Henry "Doc" Holliday*, Peter Newark's Pictures

Horn, Tom, *Tom Horn Plaiting the Rope that Hanged Him*, Peter Newark's Pictues

Jackson, Andrew, *General Andrew Jackson*, from a painting by Asher B. Durand, Peter Newark's Pictures

James, Jesse, *Jesse James*, Peter Newark's Pictures

Jeffreys, Judge, *1st Baron Jeffreys of Wem*, by William Claret, 1680, National Portrait Gallery

John, Prince, *John*, National Portrait Gallery

Julius Caesar, *Bust of Julius Caesar*, Scala

Kidd, Captain, *Captain William Kidd*, Richard B. Knight

Kipling, Rudyard, *Rudyard Kipling*, by Sir Philip Burne-Jones, 1899, National Portrait Gallery

Konigsmark, Count, *Count Philip Christopher Konigsmark*, Bomann Museum

Lawrence, T. E., *T. E. Lawrence*, Damascus 1918, Imperial War Museum

Lincoln, Abraham, *Abraham Lincoln*, by Matthew Brady, 1860, Peter Newark's Pictures

Liszt, Franz, *Franz Liszt*, Hulton Getty

Longbaugh, Harry, ("The Sundance Kid"), detail of group photograph including Butch Cassidy, Peter Newarks' Pictures

Louis XI, *Recueil d'Arras*, Giraudon

Louis XVI, *Portrait of Louis XVI*, 1775, Joseph Siffrein Duplessis, Lauros-Giraudon

Mahdi, The, *The Mahdi*, by Montbard 1884, Illustrated London News

Marie Antoinette, Queen, *Portrait of Marie Antoinette*, by Louise Elizabeth Vigée-Lebrun, 1788, Giraudon

Mary Queen of Scots, *Mary, Queen of Scots*, 1560, National Portrait Gallery

Messalina, Empress, coin of Claudius and Messalina

More, Sir Thomas, *Sir Thomas More*, 1527, National Portrait Gallery

Morgan, Sir Henry, *Sir Henry Morgan*, portrait from *Buccaneers of America*, by John Esquemeling, 1684, Peter Newark's Pictures

Moses, *Moses*, by Michelangelo, Mansell Collection

Napoleon Bonaparte, *L'Empereur dans son cabinet de travail, aux Tuileries*, by Jacques-Louis David, 1812, Lauros-Giraudon

Nelson, Lord, *Horatio Nelson, Viscount Nelson*, by Lemuel Francis Abbot, 1797, National Portrait Gallery

Nero, Emperor, coin of Nero, British Museum

Octavian (Augustus), *Head of Augustus Caesar*, Mansell Collection

Parker, Leroy, ("Butch Cassidy"), detail of group photograph including "The Sundance Kid", Peter Newark's Pictures

Peter III, *Peter III, Czar of Russia*, from a painting by G. C. Grooth 1749, engraved by Anthony Walker in 1752, Hulton Getty

Pitt, William, *William Pitt*, by John Hoppner, 1805, National Portrait Gallery

Pocahontas, *Matoaka Pocahontas*, engraving by Simon de Passe, National Portrait Gallery

Pocahontas, © Disney

Richard I, *Richard I*, engraving, National Portrait Gallery

Richard III, *Richard III*, National Portrait Gallery

Richelieu, Cardinal, *Cardinal Richelieu*, by Philippe de Champaigne, Mansell Collection

Riel, Louis, *Louis Riel, Leader of Canada's Riel's Revolt*, 1885, Peter Newark's Pictures

Rimsky-Korsakov, Nikolai, *Nikolai Rimsky-Korsakov in the 1860s*, Society for Co-operation in Russian and Soviet Studies

Rob Roy, *Rob Roy and the Clan MacGregor*, National Library of Scotland

Rogers, Maj. Robert, *Major Rober Rogers, Leader of Roger's Rangers*, Peter Newark's Pictures

Selous, F. C., *Ferderick Courteney Selous*, by Olivia Mary Bryden, National Portrait Gallery

Sherman, W. T., *W. T. Sherman*, Peter Newark's Pictures

Sophia Dorothea of Zell, *Sophia Dorothea, Queen of Prussia*, 1706, National Portrait Gallery

Starr, Belle, *Belle Starr*, Peter Newark's Pictures

Teach, Edward ("Blackbeard"), *Captain Teach, commonly called Black Beard*, from *General History of the Robbberies and Murders of the most Notorious Pirates*, by Captain Charles Johnson, 1926, British Library

Thackeray, W. M., *William Makepeace Thackeray*, by Samuel Laurence, 1862, National Portrait Gallery

Victoria, Queen, *The Royal Family in 1846*, by Franz Xavier Winterhalter; *Queen Victoria*, by Heinrich von Angeli, 1875; *Queen Victoria at Osborne*, by Sir Edwin Landseer. All from The Royal Collection

Walewska, Marie, *Portrait of Marie Valeska*, after Lefevre, Bulloz

Wallace, Sir William, *Sir William Wallace*, by A. Bannerman, Scottish National Portrait Gallery

Wellington, Duke of, *Arthur Wellesley, Duke of Wellington*, by Henry Pierce Bone, 1822, National Portrait Gallery

Zola, Emile, *Emile Zola*, Hulton Getty